A CENTURY OF
DINING
IN STYLE

A CENTURY OF DINING IN STYLE

Anne Ferguson and Carol Paterson

A & C BLACK
London

This book is dedicated to all our friends and family, past and present, and to Donald, who put up with great inconvenience and bad tempers, and who was obliged to eat everything we cooked. Without his encouragement we would never have embarked on this project in the first place.

First published in Great Britain in 2006
A & C Black Publishers Limited
38 Soho Square
London W1D 3HB
www.acblack.com

ISBN-10: 07136-5683-2
ISBN-13: 978-0-7136-5683-1

Project manager: Paige Weber
Managing editor: Susan Kelly
Book design: Susan McIntyre
Cover design: James Watson
Index: Sophie Page

Printed in China by WKT

This book is produced using paper that is made from wood grown in
managed, sustainable forests. It is natural, renewable and recyclable.
The logging and manufacturing processes conform to the
environmental regulations of the country of origin.

Every effort has been made to contact copyright holders of material
reproduced in this book. The publisher will be happy to rectify any
omissions in future printings if notice is given.

CONTENTS

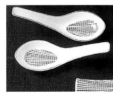

ACKNOWLEDGEMENTS

The concept for this book began, as good ideas often do, over a cup of coffee. As lecturers we had to consider research, and if we were going to do research we wanted it to be fun and to relate to all our other interests. What kind of project would involve china, glass, food and drink? The idea was born and thrashed out in a couple of hours, and no one was more surprised than we were when Linda Lambert of A & C Black agreed with us that it would make a great book.

That was several years ago, and in the meantime we have had the greatest fun acquiring, handling and borrowing so many wonderful items of 20th century design. We have filled our own houses with 'desirable' articles, turned our friends' houses upside down to recreate authentic dining situations, made friendships with experts in different fields and gained access to some of the most interesting archives in Britain. We have learned a great deal during this journey, and have certainly proved the point that research need never be boring! In an attempt to create authenticity, some interesting 'live' dinner parties became part of this book. All the food in the book has been photographed without tricks or 'make-up', and we would like to state that no morsel of food was left uneaten.

A very special thanks to the following people, whose homes we turned upside down in the making of this book and who provided us with a great many invaluable props, historical items from their collections, occasional recipes and essential moral support: Meg Ferguson, John Allen, Jon Crane, Caroline Stewart, Roger Farnham, Charles and Sally Jamieson, James Ferguson, Eleanor Mason, Joyce and Rob Hall, Patricia and Sandy Bennett, Val Hargreaves, Jane Ridder-Patrick, Janet, Peter and Anne Christie, John Barrett, David and Patricia Gordon, Anne and Jim Rafferty, David and Marie Craig, Margaret and Billy Allan, Sandi Anderson, Lea Allan, Nicholas Oddie, Liz Arthur, Mr and Mrs Thomas Joshua Cooper, Ian Morrison and his mum (who thankfully threw nothing out in her entire life). Thanks to Christopher Paterson for invaluable culinary advice.

Many thanks to Mr Charles Hajdamach, who let us loose in the Archive of Broadfield House Glass Museum and provided us with invaluable information and numerous cups of tea. Thanks also to Mr Richard Van Riel of Pontefract Museum for information on Bagley and to Nigel Benson and Jeanette Hayhurst, who inspired our initial glass collecting.

Our apologies to anyone we may have inadvertently forgotten to thank!

INTRODUCTION

This book is about eating – our most basic need. It is also about the style in which we live our lives. We have tried to document the ways in which people in Western society consumed food throughout the 20th century, and to show how social change was reflected in the manner and taste of each decade.

From the Edwardian era, with its attempt to break from Victorian ideals, to the computer-generated, gadget-filled kitchen of the 21st century, the tableware used in our illustrations is original and recipes have been adapted from contemporary sources.

Dining is not just a matter of eating. It involves all kinds of associated activities, products, goods and services. The art of bringing these elements together creates the essential image of dining in style at every period in history.

By focusing on some of the key companies and personalities which have driven the century along its path, we hope to encourage people to find out more about the wealth of designers and food experts who dominated throughout the period. We hope that this book will also inspire people to start collecting some of the gems of the 20th century before it is too late. Great objects were made throughout the century, some very humble and for everyday use. Many of these items can never be reproduced with the same quality as the originals possessed. It is still possible to find wonderful pieces of 20th century tableware for very little money, and we hope to encourage collectors to think about the name behind each object as well as its place in history.

The book is divided into nine chapters, each of which represents a decade of the 20th century (except for the first chapter, which covers the first two decades). Each section contains at least one dining situation, ranging from a society lunch through to a children's high tea to a fondue dinner party. We set out to create a real 1930s lunch or a 1960s dinner using the food that was eaten at the time, as well as contemporary tableware and presentation. Key designers and companies are discussed in more detail, as well as the social background of each period.

We have included tried and tested recipes for the food shown, and we would love to think of decade dinner parties springing up all over the country. We certainly had great fun setting up and eating at our parties. Just make sure that your guests love carrots before embarking on a 'wartime lunch'!

1900 ~ 1919
A New Century

The 20th century began with Britain at war with the Boers (1899–1902) and with a change in the monarchy. Queen Victoria died in 1901, having ruled for over 60 years, and her influence lived on in the first years of the new century. Her infamously high-living son Edward, who had enjoyed life to the full as The Prince of Wales, now came to the throne at the age of 52. Despite Edward's death in 1910, the Edwardian era continued in spirit until the outbreak of the First World War. Edward revived the pageantry of the monarchy, which had been suppressed during Victoria's long years of mourning, but his years of decadence as The Prince of Wales in the 'Naughty Nineties' were replaced by a more masculine and sober approach in the new century.

It was an age of scientific innovation and advance, particularly in physics, with the publication in 1905 of Einstein's *Relativity: The Special and General Theory*, and the publication of Sigmund Freud's *The Interpretation of Dreams* in 1900. Significant developments were being made in railway and motor travel. The first motor bus appeared in London in 1904, and by 1910 there were more motorised taxis in the city than horse-drawn cabs. Shipping was becoming bigger and faster, although the Titanic disaster of 1912 was a great setback to progress.

ABOVE Pressed glass coronation commemorative plate.

LEFT Royal Doulton coronation commemorative tobacco jars.

The first successful attempts at flight by the Wright brothers took place in 1908, and Bleriot flew across the Channel in 1909. New technology appeared in the form of the wireless, the gramophone, the telephone, the typewriter and even the electric kettle during the Edwardian era. Life was speeding up.

There was still a huge gulf between the rich and the poor, but by 1900 a large middle class had emerged which tried to emulate the style of the aristocracy. Servants were deemed a necessity in all middle-class households.

This was the era of the department store. Harrods and Debenham and Freebody were well-established. The Army & Navy Stores catered for all parts of the Empire, and their customers had to be members to maintain the perception of exclusivity, but the new middle classes could buy their furniture and household goods from the newer London department stores such as Waring & Gillow, which opened in 1905. The American Gordon Selfridge opened his Oxford Street store in 1909. Liberty sold Art Nouveau and Arts and Crafts wares, and Heal's offered a range of furniture that was affordable but still approved by the Arts and Crafts movement.

The sinuous curves of the Art Nouveau style of the 1890s evolved into a more angular version, as demonstrated in the work of Charles Rennie Mackintosh. The Arts and Crafts movement, championed by William Morris and John Ruskin, had its origins in the mid-19th century with the works of A.W.N. Pugin and Henry Cole, who created them as a reaction against the Industrial Revolution. These simpler styles were in contrast to the over-decoration of High Victorian tastes, but both were popular during this period at all levels of society.

Kitchen ranges were in use, gas ovens were becoming more common and the first electric cookers appeared. Simple refrigerators or ice-caves were available, and the ice cream maker was a popular gadget among the wealthy. Many types of tinned food were freely available and considered quite exotic.

Detail of stained glass window, Glendaruel Chapel.

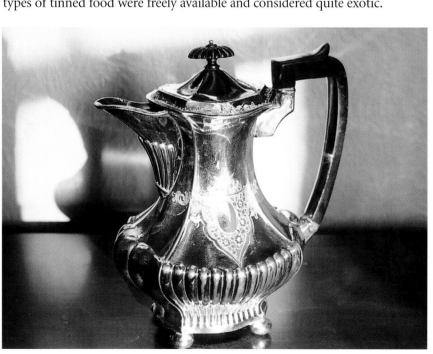

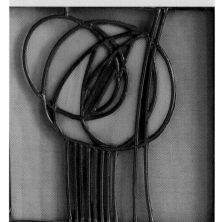

ABOVE Leaded glass detail of Mackintosh sideboard.

LEFT Silver-plated coffeepot.

In aristocratic homes dinners were still elaborate and lengthy, but with the influence of the celebrated French chef Auguste Escoffier they became lighter, as soufflés and sorbets were introduced. Eliza Acton was still of significant influence at the beginning of the century, although her book *Modern Cooking for Private Families* had been published in 1845. Mrs Isabella Beeton took over the role of guru for all things pertaining to household management. Mrs Agnes Marshall also wrote books and ran a successful cookery school in London. *Women's Weekly* magazine was launched in 1911 and included recipes and cooking advice.

George V succeeded his brother Edward in 1910 and with his wife, Queen Mary, increased the popularity of the monarchy, particularly during the war years. He relinquished all of his German titles in 1917, and the Royal Family became the House of Windsor.

During the war years food gradually became more scarce, but rationing was not imposed until 1918, when supplies of bread, meat, butter, margarine and sugar all became controlled. They remained so until 1921. In 1916, the Prime Minister Lloyd George asked the population to be economical with food and to send servants to join the Armed Forces or work in factories. This meant that even in upper-class homes women were having to cook for the first time, as there were no servants to do it for them. From 1914 onwards, many wartime cookery books appeared, introducing simpler, more basic recipes. Women were engaged in war work in the Armed Forces, on the land and in factories, taking them out of the domestic environment. By 1918, Mrs Emmeline Pankhurst's tireless campaigning for women's suffrage was finally rewarded by the granting of the vote to women over 30. In 1919, Lady Astor entered Parliament as the first woman MP. The enormous and devastating loss of life throughout the war affected people of every class, and left families without husbands, fathers and brothers. Machine guns, tanks and submarines had totally changed the nature of warfare, and the world was now irrevocably committed to the age of the machine.

Plate in the William de Morgan style.

'Tudric' pewter cruet set.

An Edwardian Picnic

Picnics were very popular and they ranged from simple, impromptu events to lavish affairs. The more elaborate picnic required armies of servants to carry all of the equipment deemed necessary for the comfort and pleasure of the guests — not to mention the vast quantities of food and drink and all of the accompanying serving dishes, cutlery and glassware.

Mrs Beeton recommended the picnic as a most enjoyable and suitable entertainment, but cautioned that it must be very well organised in order to avoid mishap and disappointment. She went on to state the importance of inviting the right people and not having too many ladies in the party. Our picnic menu is selected from popular dishes of the time.

Picnic in an Edwardian chapel garden.

POACHED TROUT

Cold poached salmon would have been a natural choice for a picnic menu at this time. We have used trout as an equally acceptable alternative. The gentlemen of the party may have provided the freshly caught fish from their day's sport.

The trout may be poached in a fish kettle or, in the modern kitchen, baked in foil in the oven. Mrs Beeton recommended 8 minutes of cooking time per pound for large, thick fish, and 6 minutes for thinner fish, when simmered in a fish kettle. She recommended that it be served with a dish of dressed cucumbers.

ABOVE Picnic detail showing a collection of Edwardian crockery and glassware.
BELOW Dressed cucumbers with fruit punch in an engraved glass jug and a printed ceramic tray.

ASPARAGUS

Asparagus was recommended at its best, used fresh, and was in season in May, June and July, although forced crops were available in certain areas in January. It would have been grown in the kitchen gardens of large estates.

The freshly cut asparagus was tied into bundles of about 20 or so stalks and cut to a uniform length, before being swiftly boiled sitting upright in a pot of salted water. We have served it dressed with a garnish of twisted lemon peel. It would have been accompanied by a pot of melted butter 'sauce', which was made by mixing 1 dessertspoonful of flour with 1/2 pint of water, mixed to a smooth paste, then warmed in a saucepan with 2 oz. of butter and salt to taste.

CHILLED PUNCH

This recipe for punch uses champagne, which was the preferred refreshment of King Edward VII.

1 bottle of rum
1 bottle of champagne
2 glasses of curaçao or other liqueur
1/2 lb. of caster sugar
2 small lemons
1 pint of water
Ice

Dissolve the sugar with the water and the sliced lemon, then add the rum and the liqueur. The champagne should be added just before serving, with a small amount of ice. Our jug of punch is garnished with cucumber slices.

DRESSED CUCUMBERS

Mrs Beeton was very particular about how the cucumber should be cut in order to ensure the best flavour, insisting that cutting should start from the thick end in order to avoid any unpleasant bitter taste. The cucumber had to be carefully peeled and cut into very thin slices. The cucumbers would then be tastefully arranged on a serving dish and dressed with oil and vinegar in equal proportion, salt and pepper to taste.

Jellies and Creams

Elaborately shaped jellies and creams were made using decorative moulds made of ceramic or a combination of tin and copper, which came in all sorts of shapes and sizes. Mrs Agnes Marshall's cookery school advertised a *Book of Moulds* which boasted 68 pages, more than 400 engravings and over a thousand kinds of mould. These would have included moulds for savouries, fish and meat as well as for desserts, tartlets and cakes. Moulds of all types were also available from the Army & Navy Stores.

For jellies and creams, moulds were used wet or slightly oiled to assist the 'turning out' process. Jellies were generally clear and flavoured with fruit, wine or liqueurs, whereas creams were made with milk, cream or custard and various flavourings. Both required gelatine or isinglass to set. Originally, cooks would have made their own gelatine from the skins and bones of animals, usually from calves' feet, but by the Edwardian era, commercially produced gelatine and isinglass were widely available for purchase. The quality and amount of gelatine used was crucial, as cheap products or large quantities could result in a rubbery texture which compared badly to the delicate outcome achieved by the traditional method. Mrs Beeton recommended Swinborne's Patent Calves' Feet Gelatine and Swinborne's Patent Refined Isinglass. The best isinglass was reputed to come from Russia and was made only from the swimming bladder of the sturgeon.

Ceramic jelly moulds on a marble-topped tiled counter.

LIQUEUR JELLY

Original recipes from Mrs Beeton emphasise the necessity of carefully removing the scum from sugar and water and gelatine mixtures as they come to the boil, and of straining the final mixture through a jelly bag. This would ensure a perfectly clear result with no unsightly patchiness in the jelly.

1 lb. lump sugar
2 oz. of gelatine
1 1/2 pints of water
Juice of two lemons
1/4 pint of liqueur (brandy, maraschino, curaçao or as desired)

Gently boil the sugar in a saucepan in 1 pint of water, and the gelatine in another pan with the 1/2 pint of water, taking care to remove any arising scum. Combine the lemon juice, the gelatine mixture and the liqueur of your choice with the sugar syrup and bring the mix to boiling point. Allow it to sit for a few minutes and then strain it through a jelly bag into a mould. Sit the mould in ice until it sets. In order to turn out the jelly, dip the mould in hot water, then make sure to dry the outside of the mould. Loosen the jelly by passing a knife round the edges, and quickly turn out onto a serving plate. (This is easier said than done, and a firm hand may be required!)

ABOVE Moulded milk and wine jellies and fruit on pressed glass dishes.

BELOW Blancmange and fruit tartlets on glass tazzahs.

LEMON CREAM

$^1/_2$ pint milk
$^1/_2$ pint cream
2 egg yolks
$^1/_4$ lb. white sugar
1 large lemon
1 oz. gelatine or isinglass

Put the cream in a saucepan with the sugar, lemon peel and gelatine and simmer over a low heat for 10 minutes, stirring constantly. Put the milk into a heatproof bowl, and add the well-beaten egg yolks. Place the bowl over a pan of boiling water and stir until the custard thickens, but do not allow it to boil. Remove from the heat and stir until almost cold. Add the lemon juice to the lightly whipped cream mixture. Gradually add the custard, and stir well until all of the ingredients are combined. Pour the mixture into a well-oiled $1^1/_2$-pint mould and leave to set.

Mrs Beeton

Mrs Beeton's Book of Household Management, which was first published as a magazine part-work in 1859, is probably the most famous cookery book of all time. It contained not only simple instructions for recipes – from breakfasts to elaborate dinners, and every conceivable occasion in between – but also advice on every aspect of running a house and managing servants. Prices of foods were included, and details of when each food was in season. Mrs Beeton's list of 'Kitchen Maxims' advocated economy in all things, careful use of ingredients and the importance of good management and tidiness in the kitchen. Clearing up behind yourself as you worked was considered essential to the smooth operation of the kitchen. The illustrations were particularly important in showing how to present individual dishes as well as various layouts of complete dinner table settings. The new 'service a la Russe' was shown, in which food is placed on the sideboard and servants serve guests individually from serving dishes. The previous fashion was for all dishes to be placed on the dining table and for guests to serve themselves. The book was produced in several different volumes and versions. The *One Shilling* edition was basically just recipes, but the preface calls it 'the one oracle in the kitchen'. Subsequent editions added recipes from 'Australia, America, France and all parts of the world', and adverts for various foodstuffs and kitchen gadgets.

Isabella Mary Mayson married Samuel Orchart Beeton in 1856. Her husband had already launched his own successful publishing company, catering for the new niche markets of women and children readers. His publication *The Englishwoman's Domestic Magazine* was the prototype of today's women's magazines, containing fiction, recipes, puzzles, competitions, agony columns and dressmaking patterns. He was the initiator of the now famous Mrs Beeton book, which took Isabella four years to research and write. Apparently, until embarking on this project at her husband's suggestion at the age of 21, she had no great love of cooking or interest in the kitchen. The book was a huge success, but tragically Isabella died from puerperal fever following childbirth at the age of 28.

Auguste Escoffier

Auguste Escoffier, one of the greatest chefs in the world and named 'the king of chefs and the chef of kings', came to England with Cesar Ritz in 1890 to take charge of the kitchens at the Savoy Hotel in London. Born in 1847 in the Alpes Maritime, he started to work in a kitchen at the age of 12, continuing to do so until his resignation from the London Carlton in 1921. He was awarded the French *Croix de la Legion d'Honeur* in 1920 and was raised to *Officier de la Legion d'Honeur* in 1928. Escoffier immortalised great artistes of his time by naming his culinary creations after them: Peches Melba, Fraises Sarah Bernhardt and Poires Mary Garden. His book *200 Favourite French Recipes* was first published in 1934, and is described as 'everyday' cooking but is also aimed at restaurateurs and chefs.

> '*One must not forget that sound cooking, even the very simplest, makes a contented house.*'
> – *Auguste Escoffier*

THE ARMY & NAVY STORES

The Army & Navy Stores began in 1871, when a group of army and naval officers clubbed together to buy a case of wine, just as the Civil Service Stores had begun in 1866 when a group of GPO clerks banded together to purchase a chest of tea. The Army & Navy Co-operative Society was available to officers, non-commissioned officers, their family and friends and officials of some service clubs and organisations. It cost five shillings for the first year, with a subsequent annual fee of two shillings and sixpence. Premises were acquired in Victoria Street, near Victoria Station, and deliveries were made in London and the suburbs free of charge, from 8.30 am until 6 pm.

The store was more like a club than a shop. It had reading rooms, writing rooms, cloak rooms and refreshment rooms, where friends could meet for breakfast or luncheon. The table d'hôte menu was two shillings and included soup or fish, entrée or joint, vegetables, a choice of sweet or cheese and butter and coffee. Gratuities were strictly forbidden, but if ordering from the main menu, when the bill was under one shilling, one penny was charged for the use of a serviette.

The extensive mail-order catalogue was available to all customers, including overseas members, and several branch stores were opened in India in 1901. Wine was a very important part of the business, but the catalogue contained everything from wardrobes to wastepaper bins, tins of custard powder to elephant's feet modelled into liqueur sets, and from hat pins to surgical trusses. All kinds of services were on offer, such as house removals, warehousing, auction rooms, estate agency, house repairs, home decorating and catering with entertainment on hire for parties. The Society even offered a big game trophy stuffing service, and sold artificial limbs for the less successful hunter. Wine remained a very important part of the business, which was appropriate to the Society's founding, but the Stores provided everything its members might require.

These glass knife rests were amongst the many tableware products featured in the Army & Navy Stores catalogue of 1907.

LEFT These silver-plated, ivory-handled fish servers in a Morocco leather case were available from the Army & Navy Stores catalogue in 1907 at a price of 27 shillings and sixpence.

Pewter Liberty tea service.

Afternoon Tea

The custom of formal 'at home' teas provided an occasion for the hostess to receive a large number of guests in one afternoon, and some kind of musical entertainment was often provided. These more elaborate events were distinct from weekly 'at home' teas, which were simpler affairs at which the mistress of the house dispensed the tea herself. The tea 'equipage' would be placed next to the mistress, with hot water in a china or silver kettle on a heated stand. The gentlemen of the party would do the necessary serving. According to Mrs Beeton, the only fare offered on these occasions consisted of bread and butter, cake and sometimes fresh fruits. We have included a Victoria Sandwich cake in our setting.

VICTORIA SANDWICH

This ever-popular light sponge cake was named after Queen Victoria, and it is the one which continues to inspire fierce competition amongst bakers, who endeavour to produce the perfect result.

The recipe here is adapted from Mrs Beeton's original. The ingredients are: 2 eggs, 4 oz. each of caster sugar, butter and self-raising flour, and a layer of any kind of jam or marmalade.

The method is to beat the butter to a smooth consistency, 'dredge' in the flour and sugar, mixing well, add the whisked eggs and beat for 10 minutes. Pour the mixture into a round buttered tin and bake in a moderate oven for 20 minutes. When cool, split and fill with jam.

Afternoon tea table with spirit kettle and gold patterned tea china from the Army & Navy Stores.

An Edwardian Dinner

In the view of Mrs Beeton, dining was a privilege of civilised people, and knowing how to dine well indicated an awareness of progress in a nation. In her opinion, dinner was the main meal of the day and therefore had to be given due consideration and treated with reverence. Our Edwardian Dinner is a simple menu, including dishes based on those which were popular at the time.

Edwardian 'at home' dinner for two.

Detail of table set with Royal Worcester porcelain and glassware by James Powell & Sons, Waterford and Stuart.

Royal Worcester

In the 1880s, Worcester was one of the greatest pioneers of English porcelain, developing new techniques such as transfer printing. In the 19th century, it fragmented into a number of different companies – Flight, Barr and Barr, Chamberlain, Kerr and Binns and Grainger and Co. – and re-emerged as the Royal Worcester Porcelain Company. A great deal of emphasis was placed on figure making and use of colour, but tableware was an important part of its production throughout the 20th century. This emphasis continues today with its kitchen and oven-to-table ware. It became a public company in 1954 and took over several Staffordshire brand names, including Palissy. The company merged with Spode in 1978.

An Edwardian Menu

Family dinners were always to be at a certain hour, and the lady of the house should always have planned the menu in advance and instructed the cook accordingly. Various rules had to be followed. Plates had to be hot, and courses had to be ready in the correct order so that they did not spoil or lose appearance. Vegetables had to be properly drained.

Menus for dinner parties were to be matched to the abilities of the cook in order to avoid stress and potential disaster, and advice was even given regarding the temperature of the dining room.

RIGHT Detail of champagne sorbet with glassware by James Powell & Sons.

SOLE WITH 'ITALIAN' SAUCE

2 soles
Salt, pepper and grated nutmeg
* to taste*
1 egg
Breadcrumbs
Butter
Juice of 1 lemon

Skin and wash the soles and remove the bones. Roll each fillet in to form a tower. Brush them with egg, cover with breadcrumbs, seasoning and small pieces of butter and place in a baking dish. Bake for half an hour in a moderate oven. Sprinkle with lemon juice and serve on a dish with 'Italian' Sauce.

'ITALIAN' (MUSHROOM) SAUCE

150 grams chopped mushrooms (for extra flavour, include a few dried porcini mushrooms which have soaked in water for about 20 minutes and use the soaking water as part of the stock)
2 shallots
1 pint of stock
1 glass of Madeira (or sherry)
Juice of 1 lemon
1 teaspoonful sugar
1 teaspoonful chopped parsley

Put the stock into a pan with the mushrooms, shallots and Madeira, and cook gently for 15 minutes, then add the remaining ingredients, and bring to the boil. Serve at once over sole.

CHAMPAGNE SORBET

Sorbets were served halfway through elaborate Edwardian meals in order to refresh the appetite for the rest of the feast. Modern ice cream makers and freezers make the preparation quick and easy. In Edwardian times, they also had ice cream freezers, but these were hand-turned and therefore more time-consuming and labour-intensive. Wealthier households would also have had an ice cave or cabinet refrigerator. Mrs Beeton offered her advice on the comparative merits of several makes in her *Book of Household Management*. The recipe here is based on one of the period.

Put the zest of 2 lemons in a saucepan with 112 ml of water and 80 grams of caster sugar, stir well and simmer until the sugar has dissolved. Strain the mixture and add 75 cl of pink champagne and the juice of 2 lemons. Pour into an ice cream maker and turn the handle until frozen. Spoon into serving glasses and store in a freezer until ready to serve.

Our version was made without the aid of an ice cream maker and was placed in the freezer for two hours, beaten hard to smooth out any ice crystals and replaced in the freezer for a further two hours, when the beating process was repeated. It was then replaced in the freezer until required.

CHARLES RENNIE MACKINTOSH

Charles Rennie Mackintosh was born in 1868, the son of a policeman. He began studying architecture at the age of 16, and in 1889 he joined the practice of Honeyman & Keppie. He attended evening classes at the Glasgow School of Art, where his outstanding drawing ability was recognised by Francis Newbery, then head of the school.

Mackintosh and his colleague and friend Herbert McNair socialised with a group of young lady students who called themselves 'The Immortals', which included sisters Margaret and Frances MacDonald. They became closer and were known as 'The Group of Four', part of the Glasgow School and the essence of the Scottish Art Nouveau movement. They worked in collaboration and designed graphics and metal-work in the Art Nouveau style. Some inspiration came from illustrations and photographs of European Art Nouveau styles published in *The Studio* magazine in London from 1893 onward, although Mackintosh was already designing his own furniture by 1890. McNair married Frances in 1899 and Mackintosh married Margaret in 1900.

Mackintosh's design work was more successful on the Continent than in the UK. He exhibited in Venice, Vienna and Turin at the turn of the century, and won second prize in a German publisher's competition to design a 'House for an Art Lover'. These designs became reality almost 100 years later when the building was constructed in Bellahouston Park in Glasgow. Mackintosh designed several churches, schools and private houses in and around Glasgow, but the Glasgow School of Art is considered his master work, built in two phases: 1897–1899 and 1907–1909. The association with Miss Cranston (see page 24) spanned twenty years, throughout which time Mackintosh created several tea rooms, most notably the Willow Tea Room in Sauchiehall Street. The Willow Tea Room opened in 1903, became part of Daly's department store in 1927 and was restored in 1980, with the Salon de Luxe and the Gallery still in use today.

TEA IN THE MACKINTOSH ROOM

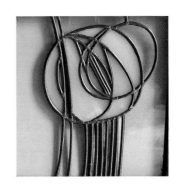

This room in the Glasgow School of Art is now known as the Mackintosh Room, but it was originally designed as the Board Room. The Board members were reportedly uncomfortable with the lightness and brightness of this predominantly white room, and they declined to use it. Mackintosh was obliged to design another room, still known as the Board Room, which has wood panelling, apparently felt to be more appropriate for the seriousness of Board meetings. We have set afternoon tea in the Mackintosh Room.

MISS CRANSTON'S TEA ROOMS

Kate Cranston was an eccentric Glasgow businesswoman who pioneered Glasgow tea rooms in the late 19th century. The Industrial Revolution and the emergence of a new, business-based middle class encouraged the conception of a new kind of refreshment establishment, and Glasgow, the 'second city of the Empire', was the setting for it. Lang's self-service sandwich bar opened in Glasgow in the mid-19th century with payment on an honour system, which survived until the Second World War.

The 'tea room' was reputedly invented in 1875 by Kate's brother Stuart, an entrepreneur in the tea trade, who came up with the idea of charging customers to taste his teas, providing bread and cakes as optional extras. In their initial conception, tea rooms were aimed at a predominantly male business clientele, in a social climate influenced by the temperance movement, with which the Cranston family was closely connected. Kate Cranston developed the idea, and by 1897 she had opened her third establishment, in Buchanan Street. It was designed by George Walton, with murals by Charles Rennie Mackintosh. The tea rooms were not actively advertised as 'temperance' establishments, and so they became popular even with those who opposed the movement, as well as the respectable middle-class ladies who

ABOVE Miss Cranston's Tea Room. BELOW Interior of one of Kate Cranston's tea rooms, the Room de Luxe in the Willow Tea Room.

formed a large part of the clientele. Ladies could visit tea rooms unescorted, as a welcome break during shopping trips. In the provision of this 'safe haven', both men and women were catered for. The dark décor of the men's areas and the lighter décor of the women's were a deliberate decision, designed to make people feel comfortable within the conventions of the age. The smoking rooms were important meeting places for businessmen, who came to them for morning coffee. In 1899 the Argyle Street tea rooms were expanded. George Walton designed the decoration and Mackintosh designed the furniture.

By 1901 and the second Glasgow International Exhibition, tea rooms were central to Glasgow life, and foreign visitors were extremely impressed with the innovative style of Miss Cranston's. The tea rooms continued to expand and develop until 1918, when Kate Cranston sold them and retired following the death of her husband, John Cochrane, in the previous year.

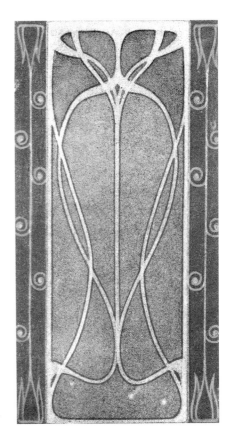

THE 'SIMPLE YET PERFECT' WEDGWOOD TEAPOT

The Wedgwood 'Simple Yet Perfect' (or 'SYP') Teapot was designed by Lord Dundonald and made from about 1907 to 1921. Its main feature is a perforated shelf on which the tea is placed. To infuse the tea, the teapot is tilted backwards onto the two rests, and the water is then added. After infusing, the teapot is returned to its normal position, thus separating the leaves from the tea. It was made in several patterns. 'Oaklands' is featured here.

LEFT Original photograph of the 'Simple Yet Perfect' Teapot, from the Wedgwood Archive.

A Mackintosh sideboard and a tea table with willow pattern china.

EMPIRE BISCUITS

Previously known as German Biscuits, these were renamed Empire Biscuits at the onset of the First World War.

They can easily be made with purchased biscuits, and are often the first 'cakes' that children make – they have always been a favourite. To make your own:

4 oz. butter
4 oz. caster sugar
6 oz. self-raising flour
1 egg, well beaten
About 3 tablespoons of jam – usually raspberry or strawberry, but suit to taste
6 oz. icing sugar
A little hot water
Glacé cheries or jelly sweets for decoration

Preheat the oven to 180°C and grease a baking sheet. Cream the butter and sugar, then gradually add the flour alternately with the egg. Blend to a smooth dough mixture and turn out onto a floured board. Roll out the dough to about ¼-inch thickness. Cut rounds with a 3-inch-diameter cutter and place on baking sheet. Bake for about 15 minutes or until pale golden. Cool on a wire rack. Sandwich together using the jam.

Mix up icing sugar with a little hot water until it is spreadable but not too runny. Ice the top of the biscuits and decorate with cherry halves or the topping of your choice.

Empire Biscuit and Charles Rennie Mackintosh fork.

GEORGE WALTON

George Walton, born in 1867, abandoned his job as a bank clerk in 1888 to set up his own design and decorating business in Glasgow, where he designed many private houses and interiors, including tea rooms for Miss Cranston. He was an important figure and had some influence on Charles Rennie Mackintosh, particularly in the idea of one designer controlling the complete look and every detail of an interior, from fixtures, fittings and furniture to the stained glass inserts in a cupboard door. Walton designed interiors in this manner for Liberty, including everything from fabrics to furniture. He also designed new shapes for Clutha Glass, previously designed by Christopher Dresser and manufactured by James Coupar and Sons of Glasgow. These ranges sold through Liberty and some had silver casings designed by Archibald Knox.

An original George Walton interior with table setting.

LIBERTY

Arthur Lasenby Liberty opened his first shop in Regent Street in 1875, believing that he could offer the public something new in fashion and homewares. He initially sold ornaments, fabric and objets d'art from Japan and the East. Within ten years, the business had expanded enormously and also sold carpets and furniture. Goods were sourced from Java, India, Indochina, Persia and the UK. Liberty wished to give the ordinary person the chance to buy beautiful things. His store became the most fashionable place to shop in London, and catalogues allowed those customers further afield to enjoy the Liberty experience. 'Maison Liberty' opened in Paris in 1890, and it survived there until 1932.

In the 1890s, many of the designers employed by Arthur Lasenby Liberty were major figures in the Arts and Crafts and Art Nouveau movements. This no doubt helped to increase the popularity of these styles although, according to Liberty's policy, the designers' identities were concealed and only the Liberty name was promoted. Through the Silver Studio, Archibald Knox was commissioned to design the silver 'Cymric' range in 1899 and the pewter 'Tudric' range in 1902. Arthur Lasenby Liberty died in 1917, but his legacy continues into the 21st century and the name Liberty, whilst carrying its own tradition, is still synonymous with excellent quality and contemporary design.

WEDGWOOD

European links were developed by several leading companies during this period, and in 1901 Wedgwood opened a showroom in Paris in order to expand into new markets. An agency was established with Georges Rouard, a leading French retailer who worked closely with the factory, and John Goodwin was appointed Art Director in 1904. Rouard also commissioned leading French artists Marcel Goupy and Paul Follet to design for Wedgwood. Follet began to work for Wedgwood in 1911. One of his designs was the twenty-piece 'Pomona' range of ornamental tableware pieces featuring apples and pears in high relief. The First World War interrupted production of his designs and they did not actually appear until 1922. Follet later ran the Pomone design studio attached to the Parisian store Le Bon Marché. Some of the 'Pomona' wares were shown at the 1925 Paris Exhibition.

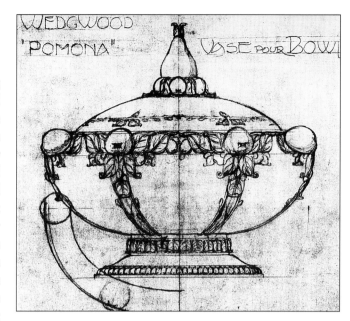

ABOVE A sketch design for Wedgwood 'Pomona'.

BELOW George Logan dinnerware in 'Pemrose' pattern, made by Keeling and Company Ltd, circa 1907.

EDWARDIAN GLASSWARE

In the late 19th and early 20th centuries, James Powell & Sons, later known as Whitefriars, was well-known for its production of high-quality glassware. The company produced a range of reproduction medieval decorative glassware, derived from European styles of the 1400s to 1700s. It had a strong association with the Arts and Crafts movement, and produced many of its own designs.

The 'Dewdrop' range of decanters, glasses, jugs and vases featured in the Liberty catalogue of 1902 has been attributed to James Powell & Sons, but it may have been made by another company such as Richardsons. Decorative tableware was produced by several factories in Stourbridge and Birmingham, and it is often difficult to accurately attribute table glass of this period, as early pattern books and catalogues are not always comprehensive and many companies produced wares of a similar style.

The style known as 'Peacock' glass, which had two-tone, green, feather-like shapes elegantly incorporated into wavy, rimmed flint glass vases, was produced by Stuart & Son. Wine glasses and decanters with spiral ribbed and indented patterns were also made by several other firms, including Thomas Webb & Sons and John Walsh Walsh. Liberty also sold Clutha Glass, which was designed by Christopher Dresser and produced at the James Coupar Glassworks in Glasgow. The most common colour was a bubbly green, and vases were made in asymmetrical organic shapes. The factory also commissioned designs from George Walton, who added patches of gold aventurine to the glass.

Edwardian drinking glasses, jug and vase.

OMEGA WORKSHOPS

The Omega Workshops were founded in 1913 by art critic and painter Roger Fry with artists Duncan Grant and Vanessa Bell. They were all members of the Bloomsbury Group, which also included Virginia Woolf, Clive Bell, Dora Carrington, Leonard Woolf and Adrian and Toby Stephen, brothers of Vanessa and Virginia. Bloomsbury meetings were often attended by other notable members of the literary and artistic world, such as Bernard Shaw, William Butler Yeats, Arnold Bennett and Lytton Strachey. The Omega Workshops were set up with the intention of encouraging young artists and designers. It was seen as an opportunity to venture into a world where money could be made but should not be allowed to compromise artistic sensibilities.

The group created interiors, furniture, stained glass, carpets, textiles and pottery. Vanessa Bell designed decorative, figurative and abstract patterns, which she hand-painted onto pottery, mostly thrown by Roger Fry. Poole Pottery offered them throwing and firing facilities, and from 1914 to 1917 pottery produced from their prototypes was sold at the Workshops. The Omega Workshops was seen by many as having indulgent Bohemian ideals which could never engender commercial success. Although their ideas were grounded in the spirit of William Morris, they did not have the same social purpose, and their style and effect were valued more than their workmanship or technique. Restrictions imposed by the First World War that affected pottery production, combined with disagreements amongst the artists, led to the voluntary liquidation of the Omega Workshops in 1920.

Vases by Stuart & Son.

THE FIRST IDEAL HOME EXHIBITION

The first Ideal Home Exhibition sponsored by the *Daily Mail* opened in London at Olympia on 9 October 1908. The Lord Mayor of London, Sir John Bell, performed the opening ceremony to the accompaniment of the band of the First Life Guards playing the opening bars of the popular American song 'Home Sweet Home'. This was the first major exhibition to concentrate entirely on the home. It was founded by Wareham Smith, Advertising Manager of the *Daily Mail*, who saw it as a publicity opportunity and a way of gaining advertising revenue from the manufacturers and exhibitors he hoped to attract. The principal target audience was the paper's readership, mainly the growing urban working population, which now had a little more money and time on its hands. The advert on the front page of the *Daily Mail* dated 26 March 1908 stated that the aim of the exhibition was to 'diffuse a knowledge of the most improved implements and contrivances of inventive science and all else that will tend to the enrichment and easing of life, or the beauty and charm of home.'

The exhibition was laid out as a series of stalls and houses, some of which were two stories high, forming streets and giving the impression of a small town. The main participants were manufacturers and retailers involved in mass-produced goods, but the exhibition also had royal support. The Queen exhibited work from The Royal Technical Schools at Sandringham. Hygiene and Cleaning was a main section, displaying new technology to aid in the eradication of germs and grime. Advice was also offered on child care, in an effort to address the huge problem of infant mortality and the falling birth rate amongst the middle classes. In a statement about the organisation of the 1910 exhibition, the *Daily Mail* said, 'It has been felt that no home can really be ideal unless it contains at least one man, one woman and, if possible, one baby, or else a good substitute.' Presumably this criterion was only for the actual stands participating in the exhibition and not for reality, but what the paper imagined as a good substitute is anybody's guess!

The 1913 exhibition included an Art Furniture section that showed designs ranging from escapist fantasy to modernist simplicity. Some settings featured influences from the romanticised historic past, whilst others showed Art and Crafts-influenced furnishings and wallpapers. The Omega Workshops designed what was described in the *Daily Mail* as a post-impressionist sitting room, which featured painted designs on the walls and furniture. Great controversy surrounded the exhibit, which was what the paper had hoped for.

The exhibition aimed to be entertaining as well as educational, and of course a major commercial opportunity for its exhibitors. Attendance at the first exhibition is estimated at somewhere between 160,000 and 200,000 during the two weeks of its run. The exhibition did not take place during the war years, but was revived in 1920, and by the 1950s audiences were numbering over a million people. It continues to be a showcase for futurist fantasies and everyday practicality.

OPPOSITE Detail of George Walton mantelpiece with Liberty tea set.

EFFECTS OF THE GREAT WAR ON DOMESTIC LIFE

The King's chef explaining how to cook 'patriotic' dishes for Christmas.

Before the Great War, the running of an average middle-class home was a very labour-intensive operation. Servants were employed to do the housework, cooking, cleaning and laundry while the lady of the house organised her staff and planned her menus. The advent of war meant that young working-class girls who would previously have 'gone into service' in a house were now employed in factories, shops, offices, on the land and even in the Armed Forces. This new independence broke the mould of the servant and master system, and housewives were forced to become increasingly self-sufficient. Economies had to be made in all areas, and this was encouraged by the government as part of the duty of every individual to aid the War Effort.

The *Illustrated War News* was published weekly by the *Illustrated London News*, and it contained articles and photographs about the latest events of the war. The items featured tended to be patriotic and uplifting rather than sensational. A regular section entitled 'Women and the War' featured articles praising the efforts of women in wartime, and listed all of the new occupations being taken up in the Women's Army Auxiliary Corps.

An edition from 14 November 1917 contains a photograph taken at the Ministry of Food, showing the King's Chef explaining how to cook 'patriotic dishes' for Christmas. It does not, however, detail what these 'patriotic dishes' actually are! Another picture shows people queuing up to sign the new Food Economy Pledge. This stated, 'I realise that economy in the use of all food and the checking of all waste helps my country to complete victory and I promise to do all in my power to assist this campaign for National Safety.' Rationing was not actually introduced until 1918, only a few months before the war ended, but it continued until 1921.

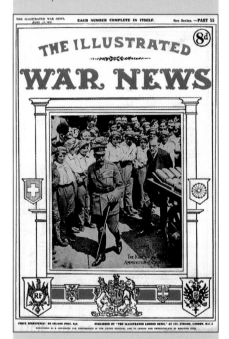

A detachment of the Women's Auxiliary Force heading for France.

1920 ~ 1929
The Jazz Age

The 1920s arrived full of hope and enthusiasm. The Western world had experienced the worst war in memory and was eager to start afresh. In many ways, the new century started in 1920. Art Nouveau, which had been the dominant influence in the decorative arts since the end of the 19th century, had become a fashionable style by 1914 and the masters of that style had now gone. Ideas which had come in with the new century had either fizzled out or become more focused. Style was now moving in two directions, and the common factor in both was an attempt to find a direction that belonged to the modern world rather than the past. In Russia the Communist Revolution was reflected in the arts, with modern ideals dominating the education of the designers and the production of goods. In Germany a similar force was rising in the work of the Bauhaus, sending shock waves throughout Europe and the USA, which were eventually to influence every aspect of people's lives.

In France a different style of 'modern' was emerging which, unlike in Russia and Germany, was not 'art for all', but a joyous outbreak of the best craftsmen working with the most expensive materials to produce a wonderful, 'elitist notion of luxury' in the applied arts. The Decorative Arts movement, which came to be known as Art Deco, had its showcase in Paris in 1925, and the influence of this exhibition was felt throughout the world for the next decade. America embraced it in the form of architecture, and it influenced everything from the Chrysler Building in New York City to the local cinemas and factory buildings in small towns. The Jazz Age included cocktails in Art Deco bars, colourful, hand-painted, geometric pottery in brightly decorated dining rooms and flowing glass figures draped around vases and lights. Plastic was used to make all kinds of decorative items for the home, from dressing table sets to picnic boxes. Art Deco was the first worldwide movement in design.

In Britain the notion of luxury was more difficult to accept in the immediate aftermath of the war. Instead of looking to France, many companies first looked back to the ideals of the Arts and Crafts movement led by William Morris at the end of the 19th century. This movement also allowed full reign to the artist or craftsman, but stated that although the designer should create work which reflected the present day, he should not ignore the best of the past.

In ceramic tableware, even the biggest manufacturers were making an attempt to break from transfer-printed lithographic designs, which had reached a rather low level by the end of the 19th century. Studios were set up within the factories for hand painting pottery and training young women to work there. At first the painting was merely filling in a single-colour transfer linear base with coloured glaze, but eventually freehand

Textile by the designer Seguy at the Calavas Studio, c. 1920.

painting became fashionable and brought a freshness and individuality to the ceramics. Daisy Makeig Jones at Wedgwood, Susie Cooper at Gray's and Clarice Cliff were the best-known exponents of this style. In the early 1920s, women were feeling a new sense of freedom, after being involved in previously unheard-of war work as well as getting the vote, and they were only too eager to be employed as ceramic paintresses.

An important new development for the new working woman was the rise of women's magazines, which brought the world of fashion and home-making into her life every week. Magazines like *Good Housekeeping*, which started in 1922, advised women on all aspects of the home, and for many women who had never needed to learn how to cook or keep house, the advice was invaluable. Other magazines addressed international style. *Domus*, the magazine of interior and architectural spaces, started in 1928. Both of these periodicals survived the whole of the 20th century.

Gas cookers were introduced, giving much more flexibility to home cooking. Recipe books were available with the cookers, and supplied new ideas for the housewife, tried and tested to suit the new equipment. In 1927, a new heatproof glass was marketed – the first Pyrex®, an invention which has changed little and is still being manufactured today. Purpose-built kitchen cabinets appeared for the first time, with internal sections for everything from crockery to mixed spices. *Modern Housecraft Vol.1* had a detailed article about the Bane of the Basement – a lift that moved food and other items from the basement kitchen up to the dining room, and disguised itself as a neat little shelving unit when not in use. Ideas like this – both good and bad – were being aired everywhere, and people were quick to respond to the beginnings of the modern world. In 1929 the BBC started the first experiments with TV, but everybody wanted a radio – by 1927 there were 3 million of them around!

Food was also enjoying some new directions. In 1889 Auguste Escoffier and Cesar Ritz had opened the Savoy Hotel in London, and this influence of French *haute cuisine* had dominated the style of restaurant dining until the war. After the war, the class barriers were beginning to break down, and more people wanted to eat out. In 1925 Marcel Boulestin opened his London restaurant, serving traditional French food and advocating a return to the best of simple, well-prepared cooking, whatever the nationality.

Entertainment of all kinds was evident in a decade of wanting to catch up on having fun, and cocktails, music and dancing were a popular way of spending a night out. In 1927 the first talking picture was released: 'The Jazz Singer'. This was the start of the most popular form of entertainment yet seen, with everyone going to the cinema by the end of the decade.

There was another side to the 'Roaring Twenties', however. Across the world there was a shortage of paid work, and as the decade progressed, the jobs became fewer. There was a General Strike in Britain in 1926, and in 1929 the stock market in New York suffered the Wall Street Crash, the effects of which reverberated throughout the world. Many large businesses went bankrupt, and fortunes were lost in companies previously considered invulnerable. The decade which had started with such hope for the future ended with the Great Depression.

COTELETTES D'AGNEAU

Take some lamb cutlets, 2 for each person, well trimmed. Brown them in butter on both sides, season them and finish them in the oven on a bed of carrots, onions and bits of bacon.

CAROTTES VICHY

Take some young carrots, scrape and wash them and cut them in very thin slices. Put a good piece of butter in a saucepan, then the carrots, sprinkle with salt and a little sugar. Cook on a medium fire until the carrots are nicely browned. The mixture of the salt, the sugar, the butter and the little water left in the carrots combines in the process of cooking to give a really delicious dish, but you must use new carrots.

POMMES DE TERRE LYONNAISE

Boil some waxy potatoes in their skins. Peel them and let them get very cold. Cut them in thin slices and toss them in a pan with very hot butter, then add salt and pepper. When they are beginning to colour, add 1 or 2 finely cut onions and finish the cooking. There should be 3 parts potato to 1 part onion. The pieces of potato and onion should have the same golden brown colour.

A Country Lunch

After the Great War, people began to return to normal life, and to feel that a new century could begin at last. This lunch served on the new 'Titian' tableware would have been served in a genteel country household for a relaxed group of friends or family. The menu is inspired by the provincial French cooking of the chef Marcel Boulestin, who had just opened his restaurant Bourgeois in London. It consists of a cream of leek soup, a baked fillet of fish with tomato crumb topping, lamb cutlets, carrots, potatoes and a crème caramel for dessert. It should possibly be followed by a rather long nap!

POTAGE AUX POIREAUX

Cut 2 or 3 leeks in small pieces and brown them in butter. Then add a few potatoes and toss them for 1 or 2 minutes. Add hot water, salt and pepper and bring to the boil. Cook for about 1 hour, and after this add a table-spoonful of cream or a small glass of milk. Squash the potatoes coarsely with a fork and stir well before serving. You can also squash the potatoes through a sieve and bind with the yolk of an egg if you want the soup to be more elaborate. Throw in a little plucked chervil before serving. In the modern world, liquidise the soup before serving!

'Titian' ware with Potage Aux Poireaux.

MARCEL BOULESTIN

Marcel Boulestin opened his restaurant in London in 1925. It was a completely new kind of restaurant for Britain. He tried to bring the best of ordinary French cooking – the *cuisine bourgeoisie* – to the British public, which had until then been used only to a rather watered-down version of Escoffier's *haute cuisine*.

The restaurant appealed to the avant garde society which emerged after the war and was very successful until it closed at the start of the Second World War. The food was beautifully cooked, unpretentious and authentic, using recipes which had been passed on from generation to generation. Boulestin was a big influence on Elizabeth David, who was to write in a similar way during the 1950s about the cooking of France and her experiences there. Boulestin encouraged the enjoyment of food. He maintained that a meal which was worth eating must take at least one and a half hours to consume.

Place setting with casserole featuring Carottes Vichy.

'The pleasure of eating is common to us with the animals; it merely supposes hunger and that which is necessary to satisfy it. The pleasure of the table is peculiar to the human species; it supposes antecedent attention to the preparation of the repast, to the choice of the place, to the assembling of guests. The pleasure of eating requires, if not hunger, at least appetite; the pleasure of the table is most frequently independent of both.' – BRILLAT SAVARIN

Marcel Boulestin wrote several books about cooking. The recipes were written in the manner of short essays, as he did not believe in exact measurements or instructions. He wrote, 'The truth is that one cannot possibly give an exact recipe: it is the part of the cook to take it and work on it in an intelligent way.' His view was that as no two apples were of the same ripeness, how could one add the same amount of sugar every time! He believed that a great cook could only work by experience, using simple, basic recipes and perfecting them with time rather than by adding new ingredients just for the sake of it.

Fish in breadcrumbs and lemon.

'Recipes, particularly French ones, are often distorted, made complicated and altogether wrong by people who think they are doing the right thing – the most dangerous people of all when cooking is concerned. So that when the usual discussion takes place about the respective merits of English or French cooking, somebody is certain to complain bitterly that French cooking is very complicated. Which is of course, a legend – most dishes belonging to the *cuisine bourgeoisie*, the only kind one does not tire of, are extremely simple – to which unfortunately recipes so-called French published in England contribute a great deal.' – MARCEL BOULESTIN

He did not disapprove of English cooking, and sung the praises of traditional recipes such as steak and kidney pudding, Lancashire hotpot and roast lamb with mint sauce. But he had no time for the attempts of English restaurants of the time to produce what was supposed to be fashionable French cooking. He wrote that they made 'strange concoctions and alarming sauces, either simplified or elaborated with names equally vaguely French.' One of his comments about English cookery concerned its absence of traditional soups; the common soup of the time was a watery offering which usually went under the name of 'consommé'. 'Italy has the Minestrone, France the Pot-au-Feu, Russia the Bortsch, Spain the Puchero and Holland the Erwensoep. All these are traditional soups eaten in many cases as much as twice a day by the people of the country. But there does not seem in England a national soup – a meal in itself for weekdays,' he wrote. It was this lack of confidence in traditional regional cooking that Boulestin tried to discourage by presenting French food at its most uncomplicated level. British food could have been treated in the same way by looking at old recipes and cooking methods and adapting them to the modern style. Later in the 20th century, Keith Floyd in the 1980s and Gary Rhodes in the 1990s approached traditional cooking in the same manner that Boulestin had advocated in the 1920s.

Boulestin brought a simple, down-to-earth approach to cooking which was way ahead of its time. By way of his books and an uncomplicated restaurant style, he allowed food to be enjoyed without the attendant trappings which were fashionable at the time. He stuck to simple, well-tried cooking which is unbeatable when food is perfectly prepared and served. He was a forerunner of the chefs and restaurant owners who were to appear thirty years later in the bistros of the 1960s. His writing has a freshness and enthusiasm for food which is still relevant in the 21st century.

CRÈME CARAMEL

For the caramel:
4 oz. sugar
1 tablespoon cold water

Melt the sugar gently over a low heat, add the water and bring to the boil. Swirl a little around the bottom of a medium-sized mould.

For the cream:
1 pint whole or evaporated milk
4 oz. sugar
4 eggs
Orange flower water or vanilla essence

Heat the milk in a pan with the sugar until the sugar is completely melted. Beat the eggs and add 2 teaspoons of orange flower water or vanilla essence. Strain into the cold cream. Pour into moulds and bake in a bain-marie half-full of water for 40 minutes or until firm. Leave in moulds to cool completely and turn out onto a small plate. Serve with whole fresh plums, or gently stew the plums with a little sugar and butter. Victoria Plums are, of course, the best!

Crème Caramel with fresh plums.

'TITIAN' WARE – THE POTTERY OF WILLIAM ADAMS AND SONS

The pottery company of William Adams was originally founded in Burslem in 1657, and it produced tableware continuously throughout the 19th century. As an old and well-established company, it was reluctant to break entirely with tradition at the beginning of the 20th century. Instead of taking a new design direction in 1920, the company decided rather to relaunch a simple pattern which had been popular in the 19th century. A new glaze was added, and this ivory base colour gave the name of 'Titian' to the range. The simplicity of the design, the hand-painted quality of the fruit and flower decoration and the rustic colours gave the range a very popular appeal. The original patterns were redrawn and recoloured to bring them into line with the rustic designs which were popular immediately after the Great War. New shapes were added to the originals until a full range of dinner and tea ware had been established. There were also fancy shapes such as candlesticks and decorative pin dishes.

The fashionable, hand-painted designs of 'Titian' ware were an important link between the Arts and Crafts movement of the end of the 19th century and the Art Deco style which was to follow during the 1920s. Many of the Staffordshire companies had replaced some of their lithographic patterns of the previous century with the more modern, painterly style. They realised that paintresses could be hired at a cheap enough rate to make hand-decorated pottery economically viable. In fact, 'Titian' was relatively cheap to buy.

'Titian' ware was advertised in *Homes and Gardens* magazine in the early 1920s, and was shown at the 1925 Paris Exhibition of Decorative Arts, where it was described by Gordon Forsyth, the critic and designer, as a 'modest country house design.' In 1930 it was advertised against a painting by Titian and described as a 'Modern Old Master'. Throughout the decade, it was subjected to this rather dubious form of advertising, which was also used to market the hand-painted pottery of Clarice Cliff and Susie Cooper.

The 'Titian' range was launched in 1920 and remained in continuous production until the 1950s. Throughout its long years of production, it was resolutely produced to the original shapes with only small changes in colour which met with the changing styles of the period. The design was finally discontinued in the mid-1950s but it remains one of the most enduring and popular designs of the first part of the 20th century.

> *'It Atones In Beauty, What It Lacks In Expensiveness.'*
> – a contemporary advertisement

Cotelettes D'Agneau on a 'Titian' ware dinner plate.

Collection of storage jars designed in the 1920s by Susie Cooper for Grays.

SUSIE COOPER

Susie Cooper was born in the Stansfield area of Burslem in 1902. Her first interest was a career in fashion design, but her application to the Design School of the Royal College of Art was rejected as she was not working in a related industry at the time. Gordon Forsyth at the Burslem School of Art suggested that she should train as a paintress in the pottery industry in order to meet the college requirements. In 1922 she joined the ceramics decorating company of A. E. Grays, where her natural skills as a painter were soon recognised and she quickly rose to the position of Resident Designer.

In 1923 the collaboration between Susie Cooper and Gordon Forsyth resulted in the production of the popular 'Gloria Lustre' range of ceramics. Although not all of the patterns were designed by Susie Cooper, this range remained in production until 1961. In the 1920s, she started to use the leaping deer motif in some of her designs as well as using it as one of her factory backstamps. The leaping deer was later developed into the sgraffito designs used on plates, platters and jugs during the 1930s.

Susie Cooper designed many items of tea ware and art pottery, which resulted in a new backstamp being produced for her output from Grays, replacing the original galleon mark. The new mark showed a steamship at full speed and incorporated the words 'Designed by Susie Cooper'. The naming of a designer on the backstamp of ceramics was a particular characteristic of the 1920–1930 period. Clarice Cliff and Keith Murray were also named on all of their works as a recognition of their skill. This device was not used again as a feature on ceramics until the end of the century, when there was a fanatical trend for everything to have a designer label.

In 1929 she left Grays to start her own company – The Susie Cooper Company. Here she started to design the shapes of the pots as well as the patterns. It was not until 1931 that she finally established herself in the Crown Works as an independent company close to the factory of Woods and Co, where most of the white blank shapes for her pots were made. During this period she designed the bright, bold, Art Deco-inspired patterns and shapes which were so popular at the time and are highly prized by collectors today. She also started to design the multicoloured, banded and polka-dotted ceramics which also became part of her trademark. Throughout the 1930s, she introduced more modern lithographic patterns to her ranges to expand the business, which could then appeal to a larger mass production market. Her most famous lithographic pattern, 'Dresden Spray', was first produced in 1935.

The Second World War effectively brought an end to decorated pottery production in 1939, and after a damaging fire in 1942, the Crown factory closed and did not reopen until 1945. Fire damage to the lithographic patterns, and also postwar restrictions on materials, forced Susie Cooper to revert to hand painting for the first few postwar years. Although the patterns were mainly prewar, the colours and new patterns were more subdued and organic in form. Some of these designs were shown in the 'Britain Can Make It' Exhibition in 1946. Some lustreware patterns were also reintroduced, but on new postwar shapes. By June 1950, she had started to produce designs in bone china rather than earthenware. Various new, elegant tea and coffee wares were introduced, including the colourful 'Lion and Unicorn' patterns used in the Royal Pavilion at the Festival of Britain in 1951.

At this time Susie Cooper was keen to start production of dinnerware in bone china, and in 1958 her company merged with the Plant China Company to allow her to design a range of flatware for the mass production market. All bone china production was moved to the Plant Works, while she still held the heart of her company at the Crown Works. In 1966 the Plant factory was taken over by Wedgwood, and The Susie Cooper Company became part of the Wedgwood Group. Many Susie Cooper patterns were continued under Wedgwood, including 'Black Fruits' and 'Glen Mist'. Designs for the famous 'can' shape which she had started to produce in 1958 were now expanded.

During the 1960s and 1970s, the name of Susie Cooper sat proudly beside the 'Portland' vase in a new Wedgwood backstamp on a stream of successful coffee wares and dinnerwares. Once again she proved her ability to design for a contemporary style by producing a range of very successful designs for Wedgwood. This was a very creative period of mass production, and patterns such as 'Carnaby' and 'Daisy' were synonymous with their times and are now considered design classics.

Eventually her ability to cope with the corporate side of the Wedgwood business became strained. With the death of her husband in 1972, Cooper resigned as a director of Wedgwood, although she still operated with them on a freelance basis. When recession brought about the closure of the

A cup and saucer for tea time designed by Susie Cooper.

Crown Works in 1980, she still continued to work from her design studio in Adams and Sons. In 1986, she finally moved to the Isle of Man, where she continued to work as a consultant and freelance designer until her death in 1995 at the age of 93.

The New World Gas Cooker cookery book *Tea-time favourites*.

Cooper was one of the few designers whose work genuinely spanned the 20th century. She consistently produced work that was at the forefront of popular taste, proving that she fully understood the market she was designing for. Without appearing to compromise her ideas, she worked successfully under her own name at the same time as working as part of some of the most important ceramic companies in Britain. This ability to be always at the cutting edge of contemporary design has made her one of, if not the, leading tableware designer of the 20th century.

THE NATIONAL MARK

The National Mark was introduced by the Ministry of Agriculture and Fisheries as a trademark and sign of government-controlled quality, to promote the consumption of home-produced goods. The mark itself was a small map of England and Wales on which appeared the Union Jack, and around it the words 'Produce of England and Wales'. When the housewife saw the mark on any goods, she was assured of a standard of quality that had the force of law behind it. Special authorisation had to be granted by government officials to any company using the National Mark on its produce. The Ministry of Agriculture supervised the packaging of foodstuffs and regularly tested samples to ensure that quality and freshness were maintained. It was an attempt by the government to reduce the import of foodstuffs, and to encourage jobs in a period of hardship by the production and sale of home-grown produce.

The National Mark logo.

'We may live without poetry or Art
We may live without conscience and live without heart
We may live without friends; we may live without books
But civilised man cannot live without cooks.' – THE EARL OF LYTTON

Cover page from the National Mark recipe booklet.

There were four points to the promotion of the National Mark:

1 A Safeguard: quality and purity were guaranteed;
2 A Timesaver: eggs were fresh and of equal weight, beef was what your butcher said it was; there should have been no questions to ask if you bought National Mark products – the contents were always fresh and good;
3 A Moneysaver: 'She knows she is getting the best and therefore it is value for money – every shopper knows that quality wins in the long run'; and
4 The goods stamped with the National Mark were British goods, made in England and Wales by British people. 'To buy National Mark products means that not only are you benefiting by its guarantee, but you are helping your own farmers and growers.'

Food produced and promoted under the National Mark included:

Beef Three grades: Select, Prime and Good – all home-killed and good quality.
Dressed Poultry Marked disc on bird.
Eggs All first-quality but graded in four sizes – every egg had to be 'candled' or x-rayed for quality and mechanically graded for weight.
Dairy Products Butter was made from pure English cream. Cheeses were Cheshire, Caerphilly and Stilton.
Canned and Bottled Fruit and Vegetables Popular brands were sold under the National Mark, but the public was encouraged to check that the mark was on the can in every case.
Jam and Honey Preserves were made from home-grown fruit and pure sugar only, and honey had no added ingredients.
Cider and Perry From home-grown fruit only.
Flour From home-grown wheat, unbleached with no additives except for a raising agent in the case of self-raising flour. There were different types and grades of flour for different purposes, and also malt flour in brown or white form with malt extract.
Wheatflakes Breakfast cereal.

Various recipe books were produced to encourage and promote the use of National Mark products, all written by leading food writers of the time. Ambrose Heath also wrote for the *Morning* and later the *Observer*, and Mrs D. D. Cottington-Taylor was the Director of the Good Housekeeping Institute.

This scrambled eggs recipe comes from the *National Mark Calendar of Cooking*, which was a small volume produced by the Ministry of Agriculture to encourage the use of the National Mark. The authors were Cottington-Taylor and Heath, and it was written in an easy, informal style. 'Evenings out, friends to dine on a snack after the theatre or the pictures: these arouse the housewife's interest in good food again. Something very attractive, something unusual, something savoury, something deliciously appetising! The gurgling stew which helped so much in the summertime is needed now in earnest and cold feet require hot soup to enliven them! She knows by now that her National Mark book can be relied upon.'

*NATIONAL MARK
SCRAMBLED EGGS
PORTUGAISE*

This makes a favourite luncheon dish!

*National Mark eggs
National Mark tomatoes
National Mark parsley
Butter*

Peel the tomatoes after plunging them into boiling water. Remove the pith, pips and juice and chop the red flesh up roughly. Season this and toss in butter until heated through. Scramble your eggs, put them in a dish in a circle and pour the tomatoes in the middle. See that the tomatoes are not wet, or the eggs will be spoiled. Sprinkle the chopped parsley over the top at the last minute.

THE GOOD HOUSEKEEPING INSTITUTE

The Good Housekeeping Institute was started in 1922 with the publication of the *Good Housekeeping* magazine, which was designed to meet the needs of a new generation of women who were facing what was realistically the start of the 20th century. The First World War had destroyed many things in British society, not least an enormous part of the male population. The necessities of the war had put new demands on women, who were involved to a previously unheard-of extent as nurses, land girls and munition workers – all jobs that women had never been asked to do before.

The suffragettes had gained the right for women to vote in 1922, and at last the voice of women was being heard as a movement in society. For many, this time meant a release from a system of repression, but for some the absence of servants in the house presented a problem. At the other end of the class scale, the servant of yesterday also had limited experience in presenting herself for a different role, and advice and sometimes lighthearted information was required. This need was filled by the Good Housekeeping Institute. It not only produced a monthly magazine to give information on all aspects of housekeeping, but also other, more specialised publications, cookery courses and a problem-solving service.

The magazine was listed as covering 'all the needs of the woman of the day', including:

> *Household Engineering and Housecraft • Cookery • Fashions • Furnishings and Decoration • Needlecraft • Health and Beauty • Child Rearing • For the Business and Professional Woman • Fiction*

CHICKEN FRICASSEE

Cooked chicken
¼ oz. butter
½ teacupful chicken stock
1 egg yolk
Pinch of nutmeg
Seasoning

Cut the chicken into small pieces free from skin and bone, and sauté them lightly in butter for a few minutes. Beat up the yolk of an egg with the stock, pour into the saucepan and stir carefully until the sauce thickens but without boiling. Season to taste and serve garnished with small pieces of toast.

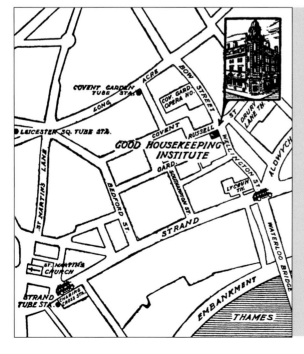

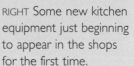

LEFT The location of the Good Housekeeping Institute.

RIGHT Some new kitchen equipment just beginning to appear in the shops for the first time.

One of the departments maintained by *Good Housekeeping* magazine was a highly organised laboratory for testing every kind of domestic appliance, method and recipe. Readers were invited to write or call, and advice and help were given free.

Courses of instruction in all branches of cookery were held in the Good Housekeeping Institute from one week to one year's duration, and included Sweet Making, Cake Making and 'High Class Cookery'. Certificates were awarded in all courses successfully completed of six months or more in length. There were also courses on all aspects of housecraft, from laundry to maintenance, which lasted from a year to a half day. The cost of the courses ranged from £50 for a full year and £7 7/- for one month in Housecraft, £60 for one year, £2 12s 6d for one week and 11s 6d for three hours in Cookery. The fees were payable in advance and included all materials. The hours of attendance were from 10 am to 1 pm and 2:30 pm to 5 pm. Students were required to have lunch and tea at the Institute at a charge of 1/6d for lunch and 6d for tea. Special overalls were required and were available to hire or buy at the Institute.

Books were also published by the Institute, covering all of the course and magazine topics. There was a major volume called *Good Housekeeping with Modern Methods –Including Catering* by D.D. Doderington, who was the director of the Good Housekeeping Institute. She also wrote the *ABC of Cookery* in 1929 which, she stated, was requested by the public to fulfil a need. 'I make no apology which would otherwise be due for the "minutiae" of the directions given,' she wrote.

In 1926 Florence B. Jack, a cookery writer for the magazine, published another Good Housekeeping book called *Invalid Cookery Book*, designed to help those looking after sick or infirm relatives.

Also in 1926, the *Good Housekeeping Dictionary of Facts* was published, which was a treasury of previously published household hints, reclassified for easy access. The volume even had a hole punched through the left-hand corner of the book to allow it to be hung in a convenient part of the kitchen, and it had an 'everclean' American cloth cover from which stains could easily be removed. It gave advice on laundry, stain removal, repairs, cleaning, home medicine and nursery as well as effective methods for waging war on various household pests. The Institute also produced service folios for those working in the service of large houses, and a sixpenny series which covered most aspects of household cookery.

The popularity of *Good Housekeeping* is clearly evident, as the magazine is still in existence today. The format has changed throughout the century, but its range of advice and information given are still true to the original ideals of the founders.

The cover of a Good Housekeeping volume by Florence B. Jack.

BAKED BANANA STEAK

Some of the early Good Housekeeping *recipes were a little outlandish!*

¹/₂ to ³/₄ lb. beef steak
2 bananas
2 or 3 slices of bacon
1 teaspoonful of sugar
Seasoning
A little water

Choose a tender piece of steak one inch in thickness. Wipe it and split it open, leaving one end open like a book. Season with salt, pepper and a little nutmeg. Cut the bananas in pieces; lay them on one side of the steak, sprinkle with the sugar and cover with the other. Place thin slices of bacon over the top and fasten together with a small skewer. Place in a baking dish with a little water and bake in the oven for about ¹/₂ hour, basting occasionally. Serve garnished with parsley or watercress.

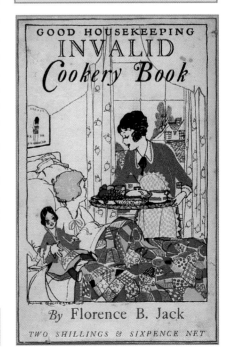

GOOD HOUSEKEEPING
INVALID
Cookery Book

By Florence B. Jack

TWO SHILLINGS & SIXPENCE NET

WOMAN'S JOURNAL

The most sumptuously produced Shilling Magazine published in this country.

Published by The Amalgamated Press Ltd., and on Sale at all Newsagents and Bookstalls. BUY THE FIRST NUMBER TO-DAY 1/-

A selection of images from the *Woman's Journal*.

WOMEN'S MAGAZINES

The first women's magazines appeared with the start of the 20th century. The late Victorians had produced periodicals which contained serialised stories usually of the romantic variety. *Woman* magazine was started in 1902, and it was the first to give articles and recipes which related to women's lives. From then onward, the rise of the periodical has been steady, reaching an almost inconceivable level of hundreds published per week by the end of the 20th century.

The first magazines seem to our eyes to be generally uninspired. The contents featured magical cures in advert form, a few fashion tips and some fiction. The 1920s saw a change when *Good Housekeeping* was published in 1922, dealing with women's issues of every kind. It was followed by *Vogue* in 1926, which dealt mainly with fashion. The *Woman's Journal* in 1927 aimed at a rather upper-class market, and *House and Garden* dealt with style in the home. All of these magazines have now entered the 21st century!

By the 1930s, the government was using periodicals and pamphlets in the form of small magazines to distribute information to the people. During the war, magazines and booklets were the perfect way to distribute advice and help with wartime restrictions. During the 1950s and 1960s, magazines became much glossier and started to break away into specialist areas. The 1960s saw the first of many weeklies designed to be collected and bound into large volumes. *Cordon Bleu Cookery Course* was the first of these, followed by many others covering DIY, painting and aspects of history. By the 1980s and 1990s, the magazine market was flooded with hundreds of weekly and monthly editions on every conceivable subject. They were often related to the media, from the 1930s booklets covering recipes and home advice on the radio, to the *Good Food Magazine*, which has covered the rise of televised cookery programs for the last 20 years.

A lacework runner from the Wiener Werkstatte in Austria.

DAISY MAKEIG JONES

Daisy Makeig Jones was born in 1881, the daughter of a doctor and the eldest of seven children, in a village near Rotherham in South Yorkshire. She was privately educated and showed an early interest in and talent for art. In 1909 she approached Cecil Wedgwood at the Etruria factory and asked if she could join the paintresses workshop. Despite some doubts about her age and class, he accepted her into the factory as a designer. She moved quickly through the factory training and showed such original skill that by 1914 she had her own studio within the factory, adjacent to the head designer James Hodgkiss.

Makeig Jones was keen to use the new lustre glazes being developed by the Wedgwood technicians at this time, which tried to emulate ancient Chinese glazes. However, she wanted to experiment with techniques such as sponging and stippling onto the clay, and painting the lustre glazes on top.

Her first designs for tableware used traditional motifs, and when these sold well she was encouraged to work on much larger items such as decorative vases and bowls. The inspiration for these pieces came from the literature of her childhood. She had loved to read books about fairies and elves and the magical countries they lived in. The range was called 'Fairyland Lustre' and it was first shown to the public in 1916 at the British Industries Fair. The pots were well-received by the general public, but they were too expensive to produce and buy for anyone but the better-off in fashionable, upper-class society to afford. The ideas were so popular, however, that several of the cheaper manufacturers, Carlton and Crown Devon, tried to copy them. The copies sold well, but were unable to achieve the richness of colour and texture that Makeig Jones had developed at Wedgwood. By 1920, Makeig Jones was well-established as a British

'In Fairyland All Things Are Possible'

TOP Nursery plate.

ABOVE Drawing of plate with a kangaroo.

LEFT Daisy Makeig Jones with ladies dressed as teacups.

ceramic designer, and was now looking farther afield for her inspiration. She studied the mythology of Europe, India and Japan, and some of her designs included much more frightening concepts. Clever marketing devices and slogans were used to advertise her work – 'Some Glimpses of Fairyland' was a title from 1920.

Wedgwood exhibited her work at the British Empire Exhibition of 1924, where a lot of interest was raised. She went on to design a large number of high-quality exhibition pieces, as well as her more commercial ranges, until the end of the 1920s.

The Wall Street Crash had a huge effect on production in the potteries, and many patterns were cancelled as Wedgwood tried to hold onto its position in the market. With the death of Frank Wedgwood in 1931, the era of the time-consuming, hand-painted pot had all but come to an end. A mass-produced article at an affordable price was demanded by the market, and in 1931 Makeig Jones was asked to leave Wedgwood. Reluctantly she left, trying unsuccessfully to destroy all of her notes and experiments in her disappointment over the dismissal. She returned to live with her family in Seaton, where she remained until she died at the age of 63 in 1945. Collectors of her work now pay huge sums of money for the pots and bowls she designed with fairies playing round them in the 1920s.

ABOVE LEFT Group of lustre vases.

ABOVE Blue lustre vase.

BELOW Red lustre vase.

ALFRED AND LOUISE POWELL

Alfred Powell was born in 1865 and educated in Uppingham. He attended the Slade School of Art, where he trained as an architect. He gained employment in the offices of J.D. Sedding, where he was able to work on concepts of design and decoration in architecture which followed the ideals of the Arts and Crafts movement. He left Sedding in 1892, and after a move to Sapperton in Gloucestershire in 1901, he continued to work as an architect while he began to dabble in craft workshops, such as chair making and china painting. When he approached the giant ceramics company Wedgwood, his first hope was to ensure some kind of survival for the Arts and Crafts trades, which he could see were in danger of being overtaken by the mechanisation in industry.

Powell's first designs for hand-painted jugs and bowls were accepted in 1903. He went to Etruria, the Wedgwood factory, himself to see them being put into production. In 1906 Powell met and married Ada Louise Lessore. Lessore's father had been a renowned French painter who had exhibited in the Paris Salon and the Royal Academy, and she was also a talented painter. The Powells often worked together on ceramic designs, particularly large-scale commissions. She had trained in calligraphy and illumination at the Central School of Art, and this high level of detailed training was to prove significant in their later work.

At the Wedgwood factory in the early 1920s, a studio was set up for quantity production of hand-painted tableware. The Powells were keen to be involved in this development of the Arts and Crafts principle of

Alfred Powell.

Louise Powell.

Powell fruit bowl made by Wedgwood.

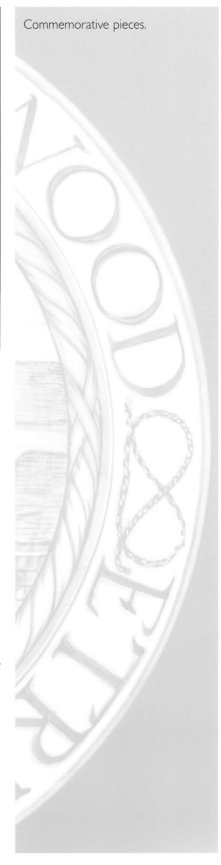

production. Many of the ceramic producers were setting up such workshops as a move against the 19th century transfer-print and hand-fill method of quantity production. The new department was started under the direction of Millicent Taplin – a notable paintress in her own right. The Powells designed the patterns and at their suggestion the paintresses were encouraged to apply the designs freehand from the original drawings. This required a high level of skill in the paintress, as some of the pieces, particularly the 'Persian' and 'Rhodian' patterns, were very large and complicated, flowing, Islamic-inspired designs. By the mid-1920s, over 50 designs by the Powells were in production from the handcraft workshop – they ranged from dinnerware to large lamp bases and vases, and often used lustre to enhance the rich patterns and colour.

Their close relationship with Wedgwood came to an end with the death in 1931 of Frank Wedgwood, who had been instrumental in introducing and working with the Powells from the outset. They had worked with one of the biggest manufacturers of pottery in the country for 30 years, successfully bringing the freedom and tradition of hand painting to the rigours of industrial production. The Powells retained some links with Wedgwood, returning to use kilns and blank shapes until their deaths in 1956 and 1960.

The Powells may have been responsible for the introduction of the painters Vanessa Bell, Roger Fry and Duncan Grant of the Bloomsbury Group to Wedgwood. Therese, Louise's sister, was married to the painter Walter Sickert, and they had lived close to the group in Bloomsbury. In 1932, Grant and Bell were commissioned by Kenneth Clark to hand-paint a dinner service for him on Wedgwood blanks, which they completed in Etruria while staying with the Wedgwood family. They made several trial designs during this period, but there was no lasting association.

DAVIDSON'S GLASS

George Davidson's glass factory was founded at Gateshead in the North-East of England during the mid-1850s. Davidson was a butcher who decided to build a glass factory to meet the needs of the local area in pressed glass lamp chimneys. The company was successful from the outset, making the lamps as imitation cut crystal in pressed glass. In the 1880s, it made look-alike porcelain, called vitro porcelain, mainly in white or opaque blue. They also made fake marble – or malachite glass, as it was known – in 'marbled' black, purple, green and blue. By the end of the 19th century, the company was producing 'Pearline', a popular range of tableware and fancies in two colours: blue and yellow.

In 1922, Davidson's produced an amber-coloured glass which had a streaky, cloudy appearance. It was a range which was to develop into one of the company's most successful lines, and was appropriately called 'Cloud Glass'. The glassmaker held a small pot of the contrast colour over the main colour. As each pressing was completed, he would dribble a small amount of the contrast colour across the main colour surface, which would start to mix in with the molten glass by the next gather and hopefully give the desired effect. The method of production was costly, in terms of time and manpower, but the glass had a modern, stylish look. It related to some of the Art Deco work being made in Eastern Europe at the time. The shapes were mainly classic Davidson's – three-piece flower bowls in various sizes and shapes, vases and dishes and trinket trays. The bowls were made around one shape, which was drawn up or flattened out in the making to change its form.

A posy in Davidson's 'Black Slate' glass.

After the colour amber, amethyst was introduced in 1923, blue in 1925, and in 1928, tortoiseshell. In 1928, Davidson's introduced red, which was a sprayed-on colour, and in 1931 it produced orange, the rarest and most prized blown colour. Green followed in 1932, and finally another version of orange in 1934. Production of 'Cloud Glass' was suspended during the war, but there was limited production of a green glass streaked with purple, called 'Briar', which was marketed during the 1950s.

Today 'Cloud Glass' has a unique place in British glass, as nothing quite like it was ever produced again. The product depended only on the skill of the factory glassmaker, and every piece was unique. As such, 'Cloud Glass' is widely collected all over the world in the 21st century.

A collection of different colours and shapes of Davidson's 'Cloud Glass'.

THE BRITANNIA POTTERY COMPANY

The Britannia Pottery Company was started in 1920 and was situated in St Rollux in Glasgow, on the site originally used by Cochran and Fleming, the 19th century tableware producer. Originally Britannia made earthenware dinnerware, using rather traditional, transfer-printed designs. These designs had their roots in the 19th century, when the Scottish potteries had played a dominant role in trade. By 1923, the company had started to produce some more contemporary designs in brighter colours which became fashionable at the time. By the mid-1920s, it was also involved in the production of hand-painted china, with patterns that rivalled some of the work of the Staffordshire and Tunstall potteries. One of its standard designs was a version of the traditional 'Willow Pattern', which it offered in both light and dark blue, and another design depicted colourful oriental scenes. Britannia also produced vividly-coloured fancy wares such as jugs, toilet and children's wares in a combination of bright-banded colour and transfer-printed designs. The company was active throughout the 1920s, closing due to financial pressures after the Depression in 1935.

ABOVE Britannia Pottery tureen.
BELOW Table set for lunch with Britannia china.

A Lobster Lunch

LOBSTER A LA RISEHOLME – with apologies to Benson!

With deep respect for Benson's *Mapp and Lucia*, we acknowledge the fact that the true recipe for Lobster A La Riseholme was lost at sea on a kitchen table, and so we give you a simple recipe for preparing lobster! (For those who have no idea what we are talking about, please refer to the Recommended Reading at the end of this book.)

THE LOBSTER – SIMPLY SERVED

Lobster A La Riseholme – with apologies to E.F. Benson, as the original recipe went to sea on a kitchen table and never returned! (*Mapp and Lucia* by E.F. Benson.)

Lobster is never better than when served quite simply with an oil and vinegar dressing, or tartare sauce, or mayonnaise as an accompaniment. First twist the large claws off the lobster and crack them without injuring the flesh. Remove also the smaller claws, which are only used for garnishing. Then split the lobster right down the middle of the back, from head to tail, using a strong, pointed knife. Remove the intestine, which looks like a small vein running through the centre of the tail, the stomach, which lies near the head, and the spongy-looking gills, which are not good. To serve, stand the head upright on the dish, arrange the cracked claws and split tail round it and garnish with parsley or salad.

Another popular way to serve lobster is en salade. For this, the meat should be removed from the claws and shell cut into small pieces, mixed in a mayonnaise dressing, and returned to the shell for serving with salad vegetables.

L'Exposition De L'Art Decorativ

The 1925 Paris Exhibition of Decorative Arts was the first international exhibition in 150 years to be solely devoted to the applied arts. It was also the first in which all exhibits had to be a reflection of contemporary ideas. Nothing was allowed to exhibit which had its inspiration or derivation from the decorative arts of the past. The pavilions themselves were unique examples of simple, bold structures reflecting the extreme ideas of the most avant-garde architects and designers of the time. The gardens and sculpture parks surrounding them gave an almost shocking look to the exhibition. This was something completely new – it had never been seen before.

Although many European countries were represented at the exhibition, it was dominated by the work of the French designers who were leading the field of decorative arts throughout the 1920s. France was the centre of the artistic world, with Picasso, Braque and Matisse painting in Paris. Writers such as Hemingway and Sartre were dining at Le Boeuf sur le Toit to the music of Saint Saens and Faure. It was inevitable that this confidence should be echoed in the applied arts.

Ruhlmann, Dunand and Dufrene were dominant in interior design and furniture, alongside textiles by Benedictus. Glass was exhibited by some of the greatest makers of the 20th century – Lalique, Daum, Argy-Rousseau and Maurice Marinot. Boucheron and Cartier designed jewellery and silverware.

There were, however, a few other Europeans who succeeded in challenging the French! Clarice Cliff was showing her brightly-decorated ceramics with some others from the English potteries. The Scandinavian Pavilion designed by Saarinen and showing glass designed by Simon Gate and Edvard Hald for Orrefors, showed the first indication of a style which was to dominate design in the applied arts later in the century. Many of the exhibitors were so inspired by the quality of work shown at the exhibition that it dominated their own work for many years.

The Art Deco influence was brought to maturity in the 1930s, and was a style which did not outlast its decade, apart from a fleeting resurgence during the 1970s. It remains one of the most charming and collectable periods, particularly in ceramics, of the 20th century.

LALIQUE

Lalique started his working life designing jewellery in the 1890s in the Art Nouveau style, and was acclaimed for his qualities of workmanship and design. By the turn of the century, he was working out of luxurious premises in the centre of Paris. It was to develop his own style in a new idiom that he looked at the medium of glass for inspiration. At first he worked with the perfume manufacturer Coty to make wonderful, wildly-decorated bottles for their goods. He then started to make glass lamp bases, flat in form and mounted on a bronze base. The images used for these works were sculptural figures and animals, stylised in an elongated, simple form, using the elegance of the best of Art Nouveau in a modern, uncomplicated way.

Lalique's sculptures were moulded in opaline glass, often acid-etched and produced in large quantities. Lalique himself designed and signed each one with 'R. Lalique', although he had no part in the production. His imagination was boundless. The wide range of items produced under his name, all to his scrupulously high standard of design and workmanship, is impressive. He designed car mascots, jugs, bowls, light fittings and numerous tableware ranges. For the 1925 Paris exhibition, he even designed a glass table.

Lalique had many French contemporaries who worked in opalescent glass – Sabino, Etling, Verlys, etc. His influence was also felt in the glass companies of Eastern Europe, where some of his original mouldmakers went to work. The British companies of Bagley and, in particular, James Jobling were greatly influenced by Lalique, producing some of their best designs after seeing the 1925 Paris exhibition. Lalique's work travelled around the world during his lifetime, and continues to do so as collectors fight with huge amounts of money for a special piece designed by the master.

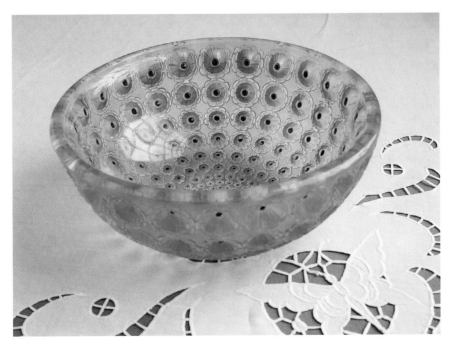

A Lalique bowl in the 'Marguerite' pattern.

THE JAZZ AGE

The 1920s was the era of jazz – a new music style which was born out of the Deep South of America, and which spread after the Great War throughout the USA and Europe. Jazz became synonymous with Art Deco style, and during the 1920s it had its base in Paris, France. Flapper girls dancing in cocktail bars were the image of the era, which still held some kind of hope for a new world after the years of war.

Cocktails were taken at home, as well as in bars, and the cocktail cabinet became the kind of luxurious item of furniture which was desired by everyone. It consisted of a cupboard which was usually made in one of the fashionable woods of the time – rosewood or burr walnut. This held the numerous bottles of liquor and fruit juices required for the great variety of cocktails. On top of the cupboard was some kind of decorative cabinet, often with clever, mechanised openings, which held the glasses, the accessories and a mixing surface. This cabinet could be very elaborate, as it was in full view as the host mixed a drink for his guests. Glass, gilt finishes and painted surfaces were used for accessories such as shakers, measures and holders for cherries, mixing sticks, olives, etc. The wilder the better was the call with cocktail cabinets, and they ranged from the very expensive to do-it-yourself models.

ABOVE Martini glass by Webbs, overlaid cut glass vase by Webb Corbett.

LEFT Lalique - the only glasses for champagne cocktails!

RIGHT 1920s textile design.

COCKTAILS

HARVEY WALLBANGER

45 ml vodka
125 ml orange juice
2–3 teaspoons Galliano

Mix the vodka and the orange juice and shake for 30 seconds. Fill with ice cubes. Float the Galliano on top.

DRY MARTINI

60 ml London Dry Gin
15 ml dry vermouth
A green olive to decorate

Pour the gin and vermouth over ice and stir well. Strain and top with an olive.

TOM COLLINS

Juice of one lemon
1 ½ teaspoons caster sugar
60 ml gin
Soda water to top up
Lemon or maraschino cherry
  to decorate

Shake the lemon, sugar and gin with ice for 60 seconds. Strain into a tall glass and top up with soda water. Decorate with lemon or cherry.

MANHATTAN

½ measure rye whiskey
½ measure Italian vermouth
Dash bitters
Maraschino cherry
Slice of lemon

Stir with ice and serve in an old-fashioned glass with a cherry or lemon.

CLARICE CLIFF

Clarice Cliff was born in Tunstall in 1899, and originally became apprenticed as a trainee hand painter. In 1916, she went to work for the ceramic company of A.J. Wilkinson. When the company purchased the Newport Pottery Company, Cliff was offered the chance to decorate the blank pots in her own style. She was strongly influenced by the fine art and design of her time and with the support of Colley Shorter, whose family had now purchased Wilkinson's, she went to the Royal College of Art in London in 1927. She spent two months at the college and some time in Paris before returning home. She was now inspired to enliven the woman at home by designing brightly-coloured domestic pottery in her own brand of Art Deco.

She commented, 'I noticed how very monotonous the designs of earthernware and pottery had become. They were not vivid or colourful in the modern sense which one demands today. People had become so accustomed to many of the designs that they ceased to ask for anything different. Why not design something quite different as regards colour and form? Something to make our tables brighter and introduce more vivid colour and modern design into pottery which could be produced at a moderate cost. This would bring it within the reach of the people in little homes up and down the country.'

ABOVE LEFT Clarice Cliff '515 shape' vase in 'House and Bridge' pattern.

ABOVE Clarice Cliff vase in 'Picasso Flower' pattern, produced in 1930 only.

Set of six 'Idyll' pattern Clarice Cliff napkin rings, designed to make a single landscape scene.

The 'Bizarre' collection – designed, modelled and painted by Cliff herself – was born. The collection was so popular that within two years she had trained around two hundred women to work with her, painting the pots to her designs. She usually selected young women from the schools of art, but carefully created every design herself before training each woman to copy the original perfectly. Cliff designed breakfast sets, tea and coffee sets, dinnerwares, bridge sets, sandwich sets, table lamps, candlesticks, vases, bowls, ashtrays, flower pots and umbrella stands. Each piece was carefully signed with the 'Bizarre' mark and the signature 'Clarice Cliff'. The designs were bold geometric patterns, stylised in the Art Deco manner and painted with freedom and vigour. The named backstamp was an added selling feature of designers' work during the 1920s and 1930s. 'Look for the original signature', it stated on the advertising material promoting the collection.

ABOVE Clarice Cliff 'Conical'-shape trio in 'Lydiat' pattern with 'Nasturtium'-pattern toast rack and chintz vase.

LEFT Clarice Cliff 'Bizarre'-pattern teapot and plate on an embroidered table-cloth.

BELOW Clarice Cliff fruit basket in 'Orange Secrets' pattern, and rare 'Orange V' clog.

In 1939 Colley Shorter's wife died, and soon afterward he married Cliff. They continued to work together, despite the dwindling orders brought on by the threat of war. After the war, Cliff continued working alongside her husband, still designing and supporting the business. But the market had changed, and despite adapting her work to the change of style and the new production methods, she never reached the quality and originality she had known before the war. The pinnacle of the work of Clarice Cliff was in the late 1920s and the 1930s, when for ten bright years she produced some of the most colourful, original work of the 20th century. Her work is increasingly followed by collectors worldwide, and has reached prices in auction which she would never have believed possible. She has continued to be an inspiration to any designer interested in the very best of Art Deco.

BUYING CLARICE CLIFF PIECES

'We had been buying Clarice Cliff's works for 30 years. Many pieces had been purchased long before her name was known around the world, when a few pounds would buy you a good teapot or sugar shaker. Sometimes the painting left a lot to be desired, but that was part of the charm of Clarice Cliff's work. One could visualise her getting up with a hangover and letting the glaze run a bit more than usual – some of her best pieces have that look about them!

The teapot that we found was not like that – it was well-painted, with good colour on the typical conical shape. The good news was the price – it was a bargain. And the bad news was that there was a bit of dirt slightly obscuring the pattern. The seller obviously didn't know what he had – but we did!

Triumphantly we took it home, with deep discussion about its date and quality, and the first step was a wash. It went straight under the tap, and was beginning to clean up nicely, when suddenly the bowl began to fill up with colour – our beautifully painted Clarice Cliff design was running down the sink, and a pure white teapot was sitting proudly in front of us. So much for being an expert!'

– *An 'expert' collector*

Clarice Cliff 'Bonjour'-shape dinner service with 'Biarritz' plates.

1930 ~ 1939
A Decade of Contradictions

CALENDAR 1934

A needlepoint calendar from 1934.

In 1928 the Wall Street Crash in America heralded in the years of the Depression, making an unproductive start to the 1930s. It hardly seemed the most promising background for a strong period of development, but almost as a contradiction the 1930s turned out to be one of the most creative periods in the 20th century. The huge social and artistic changes that had characterised the previous decade were refined by the realities of the 1930s, as the public responded to new visions in architecture and interior design. The influence of the Bauhaus had now gone beyond Europe and was spreading across the world. With the final dissolution of the Dessau school in 1933, the principal figures from the school – Mies van der Rohe, Joseph Albers and Moholy Nagy – had left Germany, and were working first in England and then in the USA. Their influence on architecture, and interior and industrial design was very important in the development of a 'modern' style.

Although the Depression in Britain meant that unemployment in the working classes was now in the millions, there was a rise in living standards in the middle classes, as building societies made home ownership possible. Car ownership had risen to 2.5 million by 1936, and about half of the population had electricity. Manufacturing had begun again, after an unsteady start, and if you had a job and some money to spend there was plenty around to spend it on. An import tax on foreign goods gave a boost to the British manufacturing industry, and gradually companies began to come out of the Depression with an exciting market to conquer.

New homes were being built for a new market. Neat, often semi-detached, houses with bright kitchens and bathrooms were required for the new, small, middle-class families, for whom the home was the centre of the world. Many of the upper-class ideals were now rationalised to fit a middle class effort to attain a different lifestyle. The functions of the kitchen and the dining room were now considered separately, and these rooms were fitted accordingly. The kitchen became a working unit for the first time, and cookers stood beside custom-built cupboards and tables, which were designed to make the most of a small space. New kitchen appliances, which had begun to appear during the 1920s, became more user-friendly in the 1930s, as the housewife started to rationalise the requirements of her new lifestyle. Despite all of these improvements in conditions and appliances, though, cooking in Britain was still a little dull.

An Austrian embroidered net table mat.

Elizabeth David, a cook who became prominent two decades later, said of this period, 'During the first half of the century, there was an almost obsessive concern with economy – borne out of necessity in the main part. The Great War had required obvious restraints and after the war there were only a few short years before the Wall Street Crash and the following years of the Depression. The assumption was for the most part that cookery was a burden to be dealt with as quickly as possible.'

There was still a big division in restaurant food. For the better off, there was a simplified *haute cuisine* left over from the 1920s, for which the look of the food in the hands of the unskilled chef took priority over the taste. For the rest, there was plain, wholesome cooking. 'Wholesome' frequently meant heavy main courses cooked in suet and dripping with butter or oil, often served with boiled vegetables and followed by steamed or baked puddings. In the words of P. Morton Shand in his *Book of Food* (Cape 1929), 'For the past hundred years our national cuisine has provoked the world's grimace.'

In Europe, however, cooking was something to be enjoyed! Marcel Boulestin, owner of a successful London restaurant, suggested that the difference between French and English cooking lay in the way that the French regarded preparing and serving food as a creative task which depended on inherited skills, time spent and thoughtful consideration. The BBC did its best to help bring about a change in the British approach to food by broadcasting a number of weekly programmes on the radio covering all aspects of cooking, from basic knowledge of ingredients to dinner party fare. An accompanying leaflet gave either a full transcript of the programme, or at the very least recipes and instructions on preparation. The presenters became popular celebrities almost in the same way that celebrity chefs do today.

Ambrose Heath was a journalist who became a notable food observer. He wrote many books and magazine articles, as well as broadcast on the radio, throughout his life. He felt that good cooking should be neither difficult nor expensive, and that too much time was spent on overdone dishes. If all of the ingredients were allowed to play their part, then simple food could taste wonderful. In his opinion, two essential ingredients were necessary: time and effort. He once wrote, 'Food that is worth eating cannot be flung together.' In his book *Good Food*, which was published in 1932, he recommended foods for those whom 'Possibly from sentiment … would like to taste again some of the dishes which they remember having eaten with delight on a holiday abroad.' The artist Edward Bawden illustrated Ambrose Heath's cookery books with the same humour and style he used on the Shell advertising posters of the time.

New shops were required for the new consumers. Gordon Russell, who had a Cotswold School business, had opened an architect-designed modern shop in London that sold his simple but beautiful furniture. Ambrose Heal was selling modern designs in the Applied Arts section of his old, well-established London shop.

Trends in ceramics and glass in Britain were mainly a continuing refinement of the brightest ideas of the 1920s and reflected a much more exciting background for food than ever before. Clarice Cliff and Susie Cooper were producing their best, most mature work in their highly colourful, decorative

Poole 'Bluebird' vase, designed by Truda Carter.

styles. Serving dishes were often designed to hold specific foods. Cliff had designed an amusing fish service for the ceramic company Shorter during the 1920s which was so popular that it was produced in various colours for about 40 years. There were similar items produced in America; 'Dishes for Fishes' were offered by Mitteldorfer Strauss on Fifth Avenue in New York City. Other companies such as Carlton and Royal Winton were making celery and asparagus dishes in the forms of the appropriate vegetables.

In the main, the pressed glassware producers Davidson's, Joblings and Bagley were following the European designers Lalique, Sabino and Marinot with their own brands of Art Deco styling for the table. At the other end of the glass market, the Stourbridge cut crystal companies were beginning to move from the traditional cutting to a simpler, more modernist look. Many of the other large ceramics companies in Britain were starting to produce a range of Art Deco-inspired china for every level of the market. During the 1930s, Art Deco lost its elitism and became a popular, everyday style. Shelley, Crown Devon, Carlton and Burleigh were leading the way with tea and coffee sets in every shape and size, as long as they had geometric shapes and hand-painted finishes! Afternoon tea was essential, to show off your most interesting china as well as your hand-embroidered tablecloth, which could complement the design.

Women's magazines such as the *Embroideress* and the *Needlewoman* gave detailed instructions and diagrams for decorating everything in the home. They were sponsored by the thread and fabric companies, in part as a promotion of their goods, but along with the Women's Institute they played an important role in the social development of women's lives during the 1930s.

At Barlaston, there was a completely different story from Wedgwood. The company had employed the architect Keith Murray to design a new range of ceramics that owed more to the influence of the Bauhaus than Art Deco. The new pots were modernist in style: simple, self-coloured and with very little surface decoration. They were exhibited to the trade as modernist pieces and sold surprisingly well. This started another trend for the cheaper companies to copy. Carlton made a poorer-quality version in a much softer range of colours, which bore a passing resemblance to the Wedgwood originals but were popular in their own right. These pieces sold well in Europe, where the modernist ideals were accepted, and went on to kick-start the postwar design revolution, but in Britain during the 1930s there was still a huge market for traditional flowers and gold leaf.

By the middle of the decade, the threat of conflict in Europe had once again created a lack of security in the financial and manufacturing worlds, dampening many of the more creative modern views. After 1935 the mood in Europe became more cautious, as the political scene became more unsure. By the end of the decade, there was a strong feeling of retreat back into traditional values, as the world waited for the outcome of the unsettled political situation. Art Deco styling had virtually disappeared by 1939, and would have to wait for a revival during the 1970s, as the period immediately after the war produced a completely different story.

'Linton'-shape coffee set by Clarice Cliff.

'Dressed Crab and Black Coffee.'
Green Monart vase, Denby coffeepot,
Wedgwood shell plates with crab,
inspired by E.F. Benson's *Mapp and Lucia*.

Dishes for Fishes

The 1930s saw a new kind of fun aspect to ceramics. Serving dishes were very often produced in the shape of the fruit, vegetable or recipe that they were holding at the table. There were cauliflower dishes, asparagus, celery and, most interestingly of all, fish dishes!

Fish-shaped services went back well into the 19th century and were produced in very grand forms by most of the best European companies. Sarreguimine, the French ceramic company, was a notable example. In Britain, the most popular fish service was produced by the company of Shorter. The firm of Arthur Shorter was established in 1878 and until the 1920s it had concentrated on producing decorative majolica and coloured, low-relief, patterned ornamental ware.

During the 1920s, Shorter took over several smaller companies, retaining some of their original names. A.J. Wilkinson was one, and this company started designing for the new Art Deco market under the management of Colley Shorter, the son of Arthur Shorter. It was Colley Shorter who set up a design studio at Wilkinson's for Clarice Cliff, an already successful paintress, and it was he who encouraged her to design the first patterns for the fish-shaped dinnerware which became one of Shorter's most important products.

The fish service went through various colour and textural changes during its 40 years of production, but it never lost its original style and decorative humour. The glazes were soft and matte during the 1930s, changing to a much harder, glossy finish by the 1950s. The colourways were numerous and ranged from a creamy white with peachy highlights, through various blue and green combinations to a very shiny, bright, multicoloured

Shorter cruet set in the form of two fish on a dish.

FISH ROAST

2 lb. middle cut of cod
8 oz. tomatoes
1 oz. fat or dripping
1 teaspoonful salt
Pinch of pepper

Remove any fins and make about four shallow slashes across the back of the fish. Cut one of the tomatoes in thick slices and place one of the slices in each slash. Dot the fish with fat or dripping, sprinkle with salt and pepper and put in a baking tin. Place the rest of the tomatoes around the fish and bake in a hot oven for half an hour or until the fish is cooked. Baste once or twice during the cooking.

Shorter fish plate designed by Clarice Cliff during her time with Shorter in the 1920s.

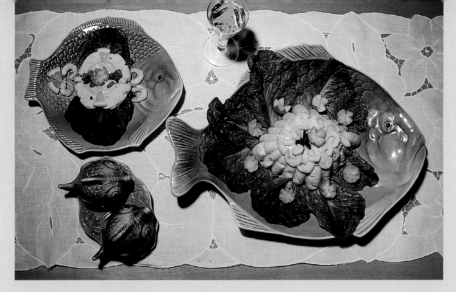

LEFT Salmon Mousse placed on a Shorter fish set, created c.1930.

BELOW Fish recipes from the BBC in 1933, in a twopence booklet encouraging economy in the kitchen.

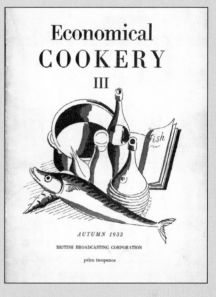

service made during the 1950s. The service included two sizes of plates and several serving plates, fish-shaped soup bowls, a circular hors d'oeuvre platter, an oyster or possibly a mixed fish dish, covered tureens, a sauceboat and a fish-shaped cruet.

In the USA, the Californian Pottery made fish plates which were very similar in shape to Shorter's, although self-coloured. Although the shape was identical, the American company claimed that Inez Donov designed them. The company also made a tuna baker with a stand, which was an Altantic cousin to the humorous Shorter condiment set! Mitteldorfer Strauss, a store on Fifth Avenue in New York City, was selling various 'Dishes for Fishes' for those who liked their fish on an appropriate dish in 1935. Shorter continued to produce the fish service alongside many other decorative wares until the 1950s.

This postwar period was a difficult time for many of the traditional ceramics companies. Once again, Shorter successfully followed current trends by producing a range of matt-glazed vases and dishes in pastel contemporary colours and soft, matt-glazed styles. This range kept the company going until the 1960s, but by 1964 the company's sales had plummeted, and their ranges looked old-fashioned. Shorter was finally taken over by Fieldings Crown Devon, and the company moved to the Fieldings factory in Stoke, where some of the Shorter wares were still produced for a few years, but under the Crown Devon backstamp and name.

SALMON MOUSSE

9 oz. (250 g) salmon
3 oz. (100 g) unsalted butter
¾ oz. (20 g) smoked salmon
The white of an egg
Salt and pepper
¾ pint (450 ml) whipping cream

Cut the raw salmon into pieces and place in a food processor. Add the smoked salmon and the egg white and season well.

Process until smooth and then add the butter until thoroughly mixed. Chill for half an hour. Add the cream slowly while still processing and then adjust the seasoning. Line the bottom of some small ramekins with grease-proof paper, and fill with the mixture. Bake in a bain-marie in a fairly hot oven (160ºC) for 15–20 minutes. Serve warm or cold with salad and garnish.

SIMPLE FLAVOURINGS

As a change from the usual accompaniments of parsley sauce, tomato sauce and so on, have you tried these? With boiled, steamed or baked white fish, serve horse-radish sauce or mustard. Mix a tablespoon of chutney with the sauce when making fish pie. Sprinkle grated cheese over white fish before baking or grilling it. When making a white sauce to go with fish, add paprika pepper to the flour before combining it with the other ingredients. 1 teaspoonful of paprika will mix with 3 teaspoonfuls of flour.

THE JOY OF COOKING

The Joy of Cooking is a volume of recipes which were written during the 1930s by an American woman who had brought up her family and needed a project to fill her time without her children. Irma S. Rombauer has basically given us her life in recipes – a private record of her family's likes and dislikes, food from friends, adaptations from travels and foods inspired by dining out. Although she was encouraged to write these recipes primarily by her children when they left home as a record of 'what Mother used to make', she herself says that her 'roots are Victorian'.

There are shades of Mrs Beeton in the work, as Rombauer illustrates all aspects of the kitchen and food from her own experience and her own time. However, the easy writing manner of the book, 'written so that a child may understand it', and the practicality of all the recipes makes this feel like a much more modern volume. *The Joy of Cooking* was first written in 1933 and published by a private printer in the USA. The book was so popular that it was reprinted numerous times on both sides of the Atlantic in a larger volume with a few updates to make it more contemporary. At the start of the 21st century, it has even been produced in CD-ROM format, and it has its own Internet site!

Irma Rombauer has inspired the Creamed Seafood Au Gratin recipe here, and on her recommendation, 'Do not overlook this delectable luncheon dish!'

CREAMED SEAFOOD AU GRATIN

Prepare some thinly sliced, sautéed mushrooms. The amount should be about the same as a mix of raw fish – small pieces of white fish, some prawns, crab or lobster – whatever is available. Prepare a cream sauce with butter, flour and cream. When the sauce is smooth, fold in the fish and the mushrooms. Fill some ramekins or scallop shells with the mixture, cover the tops with breadcrumbs, dot with butter or cheese and bake for about 15 minutes in a medium oven. Season the dish with a spoonful of sherry before serving.

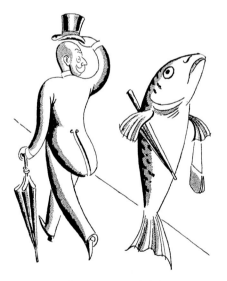

'Know your fish!'

Creamed Seafood Au Gratin on Wedgwood shell plates, candlestick by Bagleys Glass of Knottingley, Monart vase and green table glass by Whitefriars Glass.

ALICE B. TOKLAS

Alice B. Toklas was born in 1877 in San Francisco to a middle-class Jewish family. After the death of her mother, Toklas worked as a housekeeper, but at the age of 29 she came to Paris to escape from looking after her brothers. There she met Leo Stein, the art critic and collector, and was offered the position of cook and housekeeper at the salon of Leo's sister, the noted writer Gertrude Stein. In their house at the Rue de Fleurus, Stein and Toklas soon established a relationship that was to last for the remainder of their lives. Toklas said that when she met Stein, 'Bells rang !' This only happened to her in the company of genius. They also rang for her when she met Alfred Norah Whitehead, the philosopher, and Picasso, whom she deemed a decent dinner companion as well as a genius.

Toklas and Stein agreed that their life together should be based on plenty of food, the company of writers and artists and avoiding doing things that displeased them! Stein took the position of the breadwinner, while Toklas became the gardener, cook and general housekeeper. They travelled widely from their home in France, including several trips before and during the Second World War to America, where Stein's writing was very popular. Toklas collected recipes from these trips, as well as from friends and acquaintances, and finally published them in a conversational recipe book in 1954, which she described as a 'mingling of recipe and reminiscence'. *The Alice B. Toklas Cook Book* was made famous by the recipe for Hashish Fudge (which 'anyone could whip up on a rainy day'), given to her by a friend and described by her as, 'The food of Paradise ... it might provide an interesting refreshment for a Ladies' Bridge Club ... Euphoria and brilliant storms of laughter, ecstatic reveries, and extensions of one's personality on several simultaneous planes are to be complacently expected...' This recipe was actually left out of the original book published in America, but it was included in each successive English publication.

Toklas's cooking developed with the lifestyle she led. One day when Picasso was coming for lunch with them, she cooked a sea bass, coated it in mayonnaise, and decorated it with red, tomato-paste-coloured mayonnaise and a design of finely-chopped egg yolks, whites and green herbs in a style she thought would amuse him. He appreciated the 'chef d'oeuvre' but said that it should have been made for Matisse and not for him!

Stein and Toklas lived together for 21 years, and were legendary during the 1930s for their salon and entertaining. During the war, they were decorated by the French government for their work with the American Fund for the French Wounded. Gertrude Stein died in 1946, and Alice B. Toklas in 1967. After a lifetime of living with and cooking for the literary elite, Toklas finally published her own book at the age of 77. It has become her epitaph, and denies what she says herself at the end of the book: 'As if a cookbook has anything to do with writing.'

Oysters on a glass 'Shell' plate.

OYSTERS ROCKEFELLER

Alice B. Toklas insisted that this was a dish which had made more friends in France for the United States than anything else!

Place oysters on an ovenproof dish, held in position, if necessary, by some sand. Chop together some parsley, raw spinach, tarragon, chervil, basil and chives. Cover the herbs with fine breadcrumbs, salt and pepper and dot with melted butter. Cook in a preheated, hot oven for 5 minutes and serve immediately.

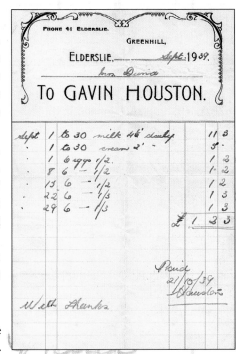

Shopping and Cooking, a leaflet from the BBC in 1935, containing suggestions for the week's meals and recipes.

A menu list from *Shopping and Cooking,* helpfully provided next to the appropriate shopping list.

The *Shopping and Cooking* leaflet was designed to coordinate with the morning chat programme on the radio.

SHOPPING AND COOKING

Shopping and Cooking was the title of a booklet which coordinated with an early morning talk programme given by the BBC on managing the household budget. Different financial backgrounds and budgets were discussed with lists of recommended menus, shopping lists with prices and recipes for a week laid out in detail. The list illustrated shows the weekly budget for this family could be £1 7s 6d.

The government was keen to encourage this kind of financial advice. The Depression had left many people a lot poorer than they had been, and the unsettled political situation in Europe brought the threat of war closer as the decade progressed. The BBC was happy to start taking on an educational role which would become much more important during the next decade.

Magazines were also keen to promote good cooking, and pages such as 'Readers' Recipes' gave prize incentives for sending in your favourite recipe. One week's prize was a 'handsome hatbox'!

RIGHT Mrs Dunn's account from the dairy Gavin Houston for the month of September shows she spent £1 2s 3d on milk and cream.

Afternoon Tea

Afternoon tea was a peculiarly English institution until the Second World War. The ingredients had been laid down in the Victorian era. Sandwiches (preferably wafer-thin slices of cucumber on thinly sliced bread) were followed by scones, pancakes or teacakes. In the 1930s, sponge cake, walnut cake or Viennese fingers were favourites to follow and were washed down with copious cups of tea. This feast was usually served around 4 o'clock in the afternoon in the drawing room of the home or in the garden in good weather.

The tea was served from a teapot which was topped up regularly with hot water and held on a silver tray with milk and sugar. This of course was tea in upper- or middle-class households, but in even the most humble homes a form of afternoon tea was very often available.

Advice on afternoon tea was given in most contemporary magazines. In the early 1930s, *Good Housekeeping* gave a free booklet to its readers entitled *The Summer Cookery Book*. In it, the merits of the sandwich were discussed at length: 'The virtues of the sandwich have not yet been exhausted. They form an interesting addition to the tea table. In a whole-day picnic they are convenient to carry and convenient to eat, and they form an economical part of a refreshment at a dance.'

The following sandwich fillings to be served on thinly sliced bread were recommended:

Silver Lustre coffee set by Gray's, possibly designed by Susie Cooper.

'Dawn' pattern tea service by Burleigh.

Chicken cut in small pieces, shredded lettuce, mayonnaise, chopped celery
Beef and finely-chopped chives
Salmon, mayonnaise, lettuce leaf
Gruyere cheese and chopped walnuts
Mustard, pickle and chopped walnuts or chopped celery
Scrambled egg and chopped watercress
Chopped ham and hard-boiled eggs
Tomato, chopped chives, sliced cucumber
Cream cheese and finely-chopped parsley

Sweet fillings included:

Chopped dates and nuts
Preserved ginger or figs
Strawberry jam and cream
Honey and nuts
Quince jelly

In 1934, the BBC was broadcasting cookery talks each morning for 15 minutes. In the *Radio Times*, a small booklet was issued called *The Wise Penny*, which gave details of the broadcast and the recipes in advance. Emelie Walker gave one talk entitled 'The Sixpenny Cake and Others' and the Gingerbread recipe on page 75 was adapted from her original recipe.

WALNUT CAKE

8 oz. butter
8 oz. caster sugar
3 eggs
8 oz. flour
½ teaspoonful salt
1 teaspoonful baking powder
2 oz. walnuts
3 tablespoonfuls milk or water

Beat the eggs and the sugar. Add each egg separately and beat well in. Sift the flour, baking powder and salt together and stir lightly into the creamed mixture, add the broken walnuts and lastly fold in the milk. Transfer to a tin lined with greaseproof paper, and bake for 1 hour at gas mark 3 (160°C).

COFFEE ICING

Put 6 oz. icing sugar in a basin and pour in a little boiling water, mixed with some instant coffee. Mix smoothly, adding sufficient water until of a coating consistency.

CLOCKWISE FROM ABOVE Walnut Cake served on a Silver Lustre coffee set by Gray's. Gingerbread on a Crown Ducal plate. 'Yellow Gold Lustre' tea service and sandwich plate by Gray's. Susie Cooper 'Dresden Spray' plate with Coffee Kisses. Hand-painted tea plate by Crown Ducal with Viennese Biscuits.

VIENNESE BISCUITS

4 oz. butter
1 oz. icing sugar
4 oz. flour
½ egg
A few drops vanilla essence

Beat the butter, add the sugar and beat together to a cream. Mix in the flour and the vanilla essence. Pipe the mixture into 3-inch lengths onto a greased baking tray and bake for 15 minutes at 160°C. Leave until cold. Put two biscuits together with the chocolate filling in between. To make the filling, break up 2 oz. chocolate and soften over a pan of hot water. Cream together 4 oz. butter and 8 oz. icing sugar and gradually work in the softened chocolate.

COFFEE KISSES

6 oz. self-raising
  flour
3 oz. sugar
3 oz. margarine
1 egg beaten with some made-up
  instant coffee or coffee essence

Mix the flour and sugar and rub in the margarine. Stir in the egg and the coffee essence, and mix well. Form into balls about the size of marbles. Place on a greased baking sheet and bake for 15–20 minutes at 160°C.

Filling
2 oz. icing sugar
1 oz. butter or margarine
A few drops coffee essence

Beat all ingredients together to form a cream.

When kisses are cool, sandwich together with filling.

GINGERBREAD

³/₄ lb. flour	1 teaspoon
4 oz. butter	ground ginger
4 oz. sugar	1 oz. sultanas
1 teacup treacle	
1 ¹/₂ teaspoons	
bicarbonate of soda	
1 egg	

Mix all the ingredients together, except for the bicarbonate of soda. Dissolve the bicarbonate of soda in a cup of boiling water and add to the mixture. Place in a large, greased baking tin and bake in a moderate oven for ¹/₂ hour.

DROP SCONES OR PANCAKES

¹/₂ lb. plain flour
¹/₂ teaspoonful bicarbonate of
  soda
1 level teaspoonful cream of
  tartar
¹/₄ teaspoonful salt
1 egg
¹/₂ pint milk, approx.
1 tablespoonful sugar

Sift together the cream of tartar, bicarbonate of soda and the flour. Make a thick batter with the other ingredients. Heat a girdle or heavy-based frying pan and grease lightly with a little butter. Pour spoonfuls of the mixture on the hot surface and cook until the bubbles which form start to burst. Turn and cook the other side until golden brown. Keep warm, covered with a teacloth, to stop the scones from drying out.

KITCHEN GADGETS

Gadgets and appliances for the kitchen continued to be popular in the 1930s. Throughout the decade, the Good Housekeeping Institute ran courses, at the request of its readers, on the use of domestic equipment. A few gadgets failed to make the mark. The Thor was an 'electrical servant' which washed clothes and also acted as a food mixer, beater and juicer! And the Atmos claimed to wash, rinse, wring and iron clothes – it also vacuum cleaned! Other kitchen gadgets were not quite so ambitious, and they were all the more useful for that. The Bel cream maker agitated hot milk and unsalted butter to make acceptable thick cream in the days before it came packaged in a carton. It also claimed to make a foundation for ice cream and mayonnaise, and could be used as a cocktail shaker. The butter churn worked on the turn of a handle and the meat press could be used for hams, tongues or meat loaves. Another more traditional product of the 1930s, and certainly more decorative, was the Carlton lemon squeezer – a collectors' item today.

FROM TOP A Bel cream maker. Carlton lemon squeezer. A meat press.

LEFT An advertisement for Bird's Custard in 1934.

Plates, tureens and a condiment set by Crown Devon. Glass with a bull's eye moulded pattern, and posy bowl in amber, wavy, moulded glass by Thomas Webb and Son.

CROWN DEVON

The original pottery company of Fieldings was founded in 1870 by Simon Fielding. It produced mainly domestic earthenware and majolica until 1905, when the company moved to the Devon works in Stoke-on-Trent. Under the new trading name of Crown Devon, the company began to expand its range of production, and by the 1920s it was making pottery in all domestic classes, including nursery wares. Contemporary Art Deco tea wares in bold geometric patterns were produced as well as a range of salad wares in the form of lettuce and cabbage leaves.

By the mid-1930s, Crown Devon was also producing dinner and tea wares with a hand-painted floral look, which was very fashionable in the prewar era. Its designers specialised in producing unusual novelty items like a honey pot in the form of a beehive, and this playfulness was a feature of the company's tea and dinnerwares. New shapes for serving dishes, condiments, jam and cream combinations were used, which gave the ranges an interesting edge over their competitors. The company flourished throughout the 1930s and continued production throughout the war. Under the leadership of Reginald Ross Fielding, the great grandson of the founder, a period of development began immediately after the war. This allowed Crown Devon to retain its position as a leader in modern stylish dinnerware until the 1960s.

By 1964, the company had acquired one of its competitors, Shorter and Son, but it was unable to address the new demands of the market and declined in popularity. The family sold out in 1966 and the company was sold again a few years later, but by this time it was producing only novelty table wares and nursery china. In 1982, the Crown Devon Pottery finally closed after 103 years of continuous production.

An advertisement for Huttons linens, from the 1930s.

Biscuit barrel and conserve pot by Crown Devon. Glasses and decanter in a wavy moulded pattern by Thomas Webb. Flower vase in spiral moulded glass by Stevens and Williams.

THOMAS WEBB

During the 1920s and '30s, the Stourbridge glassworks of Thomas Webb and Son produced some of the most interesting table glass in Britain. The company had started in 1859 and had produced many innovative glass techniques, including: alexandrite, which was transparent glass with amber to red shading; Burmese, which was opal glass in lemon and pink; and satin glass with internal air patterns. In the 19th century, the company led the field in Bohemian-style cameo glass, employing John Northwood and the brothers Thomas and George Woodall. These men produced figurative pieces of cut art glass cameos which are highly prized by collectors today.

In the 20th century, the focus of the company changed to tableware as the market demand grew, but Thomas Webb and Son remained innovative in its approach to design and production techniques. By the 1930s, it was producing a wide range of vessels and drinking glasses which were made by dip moulding to make optical ribbing in different patterns. Some looked like waves, some were diamond-shaped and some had bull's-eye blobs in the glass. Many were flint, but some were also produced in colours such as amber, green and the soft turquoise which even today has a contemporary look.

After the war, under the design management of the Swedish designer Sven Fogelberg, the company followed the fashion in glassware and developed many new styles and techniques to remain at the forefront of modern design. As Webb's Crystal Glass Co., the company survived until a merger with Dema Glass in 1971 and another with Coloroll in 1978. In 1990, the factory finally closed with the bankruptcy of Coloroll.

CHALFONT CREAMS

1 Rowntree's jelly (any flavour)
1 egg
1 oz. cornflour
1 pint milk
2 oz. sugar
1 gill cream

Dissolve the jelly in one pint hot water. Pour a little of this clear jelly into the bottom of custard glasses. Mix the cornflour into a smooth paste with a little milk. Bring the remainder of the milk to the boil, pour over the paste, sir thoroughly, return to the saucepan and bring to boil. Beat up the egg, cream and sugar in a basin and pour on the cooled cornflour. Allow to cool. Add the jelly to the cornflour mixture. When both are cool, stir thoroughly and pour into custard glasses. Leave to set. When set the appearance is improved by sprinkling chopped pistachio nuts over the top.

HIGH TEA

High tea in the upper classes in prewar Britain was usually served in the nursery as a way of allowing children to eat their evening meal around 5 o'clock without the attention of adults. It also allowed adults to eat their evening meal later, without the irritation of children! In the middle classes, it was the option to eat less in the evening after a large luncheon, or when a proper dinner was not required. In the lower classes, it was the normal way to end the food for the day.

High tea consisted of a meal of some kind of meat or fish, chips or potatoes and a vegetable. It was usually served with bread and butter and followed by a selection of scones and cakes or even a Spotted Dick and Custard type of pudding. The inevitable pot of tea accompanied the meal. By the end of the 20th century, high tea, or just tea, was the norm for everyday family life, with dinner being served for a special occasion. A fish tea is still available in many fish and chip restaurants.

Puddings were an important part of high tea for children and adults in the 1930s. Jam Roly Poly, Spotted Dick and many others were made with a base of suet or animal fat. This made the mixture light and rich, but it was reserved for middle-class tea rather than an upper-class dinner. Trifle was another popular pudding, with many different combinations of jelly, fruit and custard. Recipes could be found in all of the popular magazines of the day, as well as in product leaflets.

Strawberries served on a Crown Devon fruit set, with a Crown Devon sugar shaker and jug, and a flower posy of two-coloured, rib-trailed glass by Whitefriars.

INDIVIDUAL TRIFLES

Make up a red jelly with 1 pint of water. Crumble some stale cake or trifle sponge or Swiss roll into individual sundae dishes. Pour jelly over the cake, adding some fresh raspberries or chopped strawberries if desired. Allow to cool completely. Make up 1 pint of Bird's custard according to the instructions on the packet and pour over the cooled jelly. Top with whipped cream or fresh raspberries or a halved cherry and serve.

A dessert set by Stuart Glass, a diamond-moulded glass vase by Whitefriars and a hand-embroidered tablecloth.

ELIZABETH CRAIG

Elizabeth Craig was a cookery writer for about 20 years, and she wrote many books as well as articles for magazines, newspapers and radio broadcasts. She excelled in well-prepared, traditional food and she appealed to the housewife who knew very little about cooking by giving clear, easy-to-follow instructions with every recipe. In *Cookery and Household Management*, published in 1936, she states, 'Many cookery books fail by taking for granted that the housewife knows more than she does about cookery ... even a novice should be able to follow these recipes without any difficulties.'

Delia Smith echoed these words in the 1990s with her *How to Cook* series, and in many ways Elizabeth Craig was the 'Delia of her day'. Although she professed to be a modern cook, Elizabeth Craig was very aware of traditional cooking. She wrote, 'I am glad to be able to present to housewives ... a large number of old favourites which I have found very few books carry. There is one thing husbands won't be able to say any more if their wives use this cookery book, and that is that they can't get the dishes mother used to make.'

She covered all aspects of cooking and entertaining, and in 1932, in *Cooking with Elizabeth Craig*, she wrote about this: 'In planning this book you will notice that I have tried to devote most space to everyday cookery ... At the same time I am being constantly asked to arrange menus and provide recipes for party fare. I thought it well to include quite a number of suggestions which I hope will appeal to the up-to-date hostess, not to mention the host ... After all, I think that a cookery book that ignores the party spirit is as incomplete as champagne without the sparkle.'

CARAMELISED ORANGES

Large oranges
Caster sugar
½ lb. cane sugar
Brandy or liqueur
2 tbsp cold water

Peel the oranges, making sure that all the pith and pips have been removed. Slice thinly and arrange on a dish in overlapping circles. Sprinkle some caster sugar and some brandy over them and leave to steep for 20 minutes. Boil ½ lb. sugar with 2 tbsp water until a caramel has been achieved and a drop in cold water hardens it immediately. Pour the caramel over the oranges and refrigerate until cold. Serve with cream, either spooned over or piped in the centre of each of the oranges.

ABOVE AND LEFT Caramelised Oranges on a Stuart Fruit set.

A Society Lunch

The period between the wars was a time of extraordinary change in British society. The class structure was beginning to crumble, and with it the traditional values of the social world. Money no longer meant breeding, in the old sense. Many of the wealthy Victorian business fortunes had been lost in the stock market collapse in 1928, and the aftermath of the Depression left the hitherto wealthy in a position of having to earn a living. Art patronage of the writer or bohemian painter in the socialite world became more fashionable for those who still had money. Throughout the 1920s and 1930s, there were still 'salons' where society hostesses would invite a mixed group of prominent guests for a luncheon party or dinner, much in the same way as the 19th century 'salons' were held for afternoon tea or evening drinks. The guests were a colourful mix of socialites, politicians, artists and writers, with the occasional businessman for effect.

The hostesses were few but legendary, and they reigned supreme over this section of society until the Second World War, vying with each other to see who could capture the best guest list. These gatherings were attended by some very influential people and every subject was informally discussed, from affairs of state to the latest dress worn by Wallis Simpson – provided that she was not at that particular function! The leading hostesses were Lady Emerald Cunard, Sybil Colefax and Mrs Greville, who owned Polesden Lacy, the house in which King George VI and Elizabeth Bowes-Lyons spent their honeymoon.

Of these, the least affluent but most popular was Sybil Colefax, who started her own interior design business after the death of her husband in 1936. Although she had the smallest means, she was renowned for inviting the most interesting and most artistic groups. She was a well-liked woman with a knack for 'stage managing' a group of people in a congenial way. One of her greatest friends and most frequent guests was the writer and politician Harold Nicholson, and his memoirs include constant references to luncheons with Colefax before and during the Second World War. Her guests frequently included such diverse personalities as Winston Churchill and Oswald Mosely, George Bernard Shaw and the unfortunate American Lindberghs, and the greatest catch for any hostess – the Prince of Wales and Wallis Simpson. Arthur Rubenstein or Noel Coward often supplied the music for these events.

Noel Coward wrote in 1967, 'Sybil ... understood her friends very well. She managed to produce a cast of very interesting people – like Virginia Woolf, for instance. They would sometimes abuse her afterwards but would only rebound on themselves.'

Charlotte Rhead dinnerware with a hand-embroidered napkin in a Bakelite holder.

Cream of Tomato Soup in dinnerware by Charlotte Rhead for Crown Ducal. Bull's-eye design glass by Thomas Webb.

Somerset Maugham, the writer, and his wife Syrie were also frequent guests of Sybil Colefax, although Syrie returned to interior decorating in the USA when her sham marriage to Maugham was dissolved in 1927. Maugham lived most of his life in Europe, travelling with his lifelong companion Gerald Haxton, an American whom he had known before his marriage. Syrie had her own, rather smaller gatherings of socialite friends, but was best known for her stylish, professional work as a decorator in America, where she followed the ideas of Le Corbusier in France by creating a 'white in all its shades' look for the expensive interiors of the rich and famous.

Lady Emerald Cunard was married to the shipping magnate Sir Bache Cunard and was the wealthiest of the London hostesses. She was clever at combining a careless, almost offhand approach to people while skilfully manipulating them. She was notorious for coming down to dinner late because she had spent too long in the bath! She also paid very little attention to the look of her table. Noel Coward wrote, 'There were seldom any signs of festivity like flowers and the food was by no means sensational. She carried on a running battle with her cook and was very funny about it.' Her guests were often more important people in the country, but less amusing than Sybil Colefax's, although she herself was a real entertainer.

During the war, the loss of servants for social gatherings, as well as the lack of availability of food and drink as rationing took over, restricted the entertaining by the hostesses. The stylish new Dorchester Hotel had been built and opened in 1929, and the obvious answer was to abandon their homes and take rooms for parties there. A masterpiece of modern technology and Art Deco styling, the hotel was designed by architect Owen Williams, who used reinforced concrete techniques to create huge public spaces with free-hanging balconies. One of the advantages for the less affluent hostesses

CREAM OF TOMATO SOUP

Simmer covered for about 15 minutes:

2 lbs. tomatoes
1 chopped onion
¹/₂ head chopped celery
2 teaspoonfuls sugar

In another pan, melt 4 table-spoonfuls of butter and add 4 tablespoonfuls of flour. Stir in slowly 2 pints of milk or cream. Bring to the boil, and add the tomato mixture. Season with salt and paprika. Reheat but do not boil after the cream has been mixed in. Serve with chopped parsley and croutons.

RIGHT Chaud-froid of Chicken on Charlotte Rhead dinnerware.

of dining at the Dorchester was that each guest was discreetly handed a bill for 10/6d to pay for their meal. The only person whose invitation included a free dinner was Emerald Cunard – in *The Dorchester: A History*, it is said that as bombs fell around the Dorchester, she would crawl under a table and read Proust and Shakespeare to her imprisoned guests.

The end of the war brought about the end of the reign of the hostesses. The need for them had gone, as class barriers had been broken down during the war years. As people began to restart their lives, with women taking a more active role in every part of the country's business, such activities were no longer appropriate or necessary. During the 1950s and 1960s, different types of social gatherings would replace the society hostesses' parties.

Serving Lunch

This menu for lunch could have been served by Sybil Colefax to her high society friends. The tableware was designed by the ceramics artist Charlotte Rhead for A.G. Richardson and the glassware was Thomas Webb's bulls-eye pattern. Although the dinnerware retains a slightly Art Deco look in the form of the china, the decoration has followed the more modern approach of minimal decoration.

Cream of Tomato Soup is followed by a Chaud-froid of Chicken. A chaud-froid is a rich, white sauce set with gelatine and poured over some cold meat or fish and left to cool. The level of decoration would reflect the quality and importance of the guests. The lunch would probably have been served on a side or buffet table to show off the quality and attractiveness of the meal. A waiter would either have served from the side table or placed the dishes in the centre of the dining table for guests to serve themselves.

CHAUD-FROID OF CHICKEN

Poach 4 breasts of chicken with a bouquet garni and leave to cool in the cooking liquor. Melt 1 oz. of butter in a saucepan, stir in 1 oz. of flour and cook for 2 minutes. Bring ½ pint of milk to the boil and gradually whisk into the mixture. Stir continuously until a smooth sauce is achieved. Season to taste with salt and pepper. Make up a packet of aspic jelly using the cooking liquor, and add 2 level teaspoonfuls of powdered gelatine. Allow to stand until almost set and gradually add the white sauce, stirring until thick but not set. Remove the skin carefully from the chicken portions and pat them dry. Coat each portion carefully with the aspic and leave on a sheet of grease-proof paper, allowing the excess sauce to run off. Leave to set completely. Remove to a serving dish. Serve on a salad platter or a base of chopped savoury jelly.

In the 19th century a chaud-froid prepared, for example, in the Ritz would have been made by a different method of boiling up cows' feet to achieve an aspic jelly. In the 20th century, this is one advance that has been made by using a packet of ready-prepared aspic!

British Glass in the 1930s

Glass production in Britain during the years between the two wars was dominated by the huge 19th century glassworks centred around the town of Stourbridge in the West Midlands. Stevens and Williams, Webb Corbett, John Walsh Walsh and Stuart led the field, but there were also other, smaller firms mainly concerned in producing tableware services of traditional cut glass. The London company of Whitefriars was also a very large glass producer, but it had its own direction in competition to the Stourbridge works. There were numerous other glass companies in Britain competing in a changing and widening market. Monart, Gray-stan and Nazeing were making ranges of coloured tableware and art glass for more exclusive London shops such as Liberty and Harrods. In the North-east of England, the traditional Victorian pressed glass companies were still trying in vain to hold onto the cheaper end of glass production while being challenged by smaller companies like Bagley in Knottingley.

For all of the Stourbridge companies with their roots in the massive 19th century production of tableware, the big change in the 20th century was the emergence of 'art glass', which gave the blower and cutter free reign in the creative possibilities of glass making.

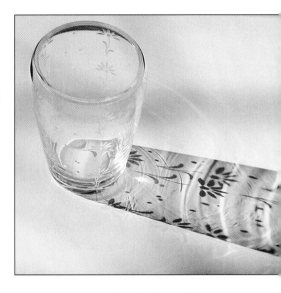

A vase by Ludwig Kny for Stuart Glass.

'Woodchester' pattern for Stuart Glass, based on designs by Eric Ravilious for the Harrods Exhibition in 1934.

Stuart Glass

The Stuart Glass Company started making table glassware at the Redhouse Glass Works in Stourbridge in 1881. Robert Stuart had produced both acid-etched and cut flint glass tableware services, and by the start of the 20th century he had also begun to make some coloured art glass vases and bowls.

Ludwig Kny joined the firm as Chief Designer in 1918, although his father's firm of Bohemian glass engravers had been employed on a freelance basis for some years. He remained in this position at Stuart until his death in 1937.

During the 1920s and 1930s, most of the production at Stuart was of cut glass. This method was combined with a new technique for acid polishing, which replaced the old and time-consuming hand polishing previously employed. Kny also introduced intaglio glass, in which the cutting and etching was made on the underside of the piece and viewed through the glass. This technique enabled more decorative freedom in the designs. Intaglio patterns were popular, and included panels of fruit and different leaf designs, including the acanthus. The patterns of the early '20s were for the most part extensions of the prewar ranges, but in the early '30s Kny began to simplify the designs and bring cut glass into line with modern thinking. Much bolder, deeper cutting lines were used, sweeping across the glass rather than tightly cross-cutting it as in traditional, formal designs. Abstract Art Deco designs such as zigzags and stripes appeared.

When combined with new colours and shapes like cocktail sets, dressing table services and cigarette boxes, these new designs gave a jazzy, modernist look to some of Stuart's '30s ranges.

Between 1921 and 1926, a new range of glassware was registered by Stuart. There were more than 20 new designs in the range, which was simple in style and form and included moulded rings in each shape. These designs often had the registration number etched on the base of the glass. This mark predated the trademark 'Stuart', which did not appear on the base as a mark until around 1927. A new feature in the Stuart range appeared in 1927 with the first designs for coloured, enamelled glass. Many of these designs were floral, bright, cheery, and basically fun – there was even a range depicting 'Winter Sports', with tiny figures shown skiing and skating round the glasses. Some of these patterns were painted freehand, but usually the outline was transferred onto the glass and filled in by hand. Although almost all of the enamelled work was done on clear glass blanks, the ringed ware was also produced in a range of undecorated colours: amber, green and, more rarely, a turquoise blue. This enamelled glass was very popular, and by the end of the decade 35% of Stuart's patterns were for enamelled ranges.

In the years between the wars, Stuart actually added 15,000 new designs to its ranges. Some of these were never put into production, and not all of them were commercially successful, but this was an enormous output of potential new ranges of glass. Earlier designs – some from the 19th century – were still being produced for the traditional market, but Stuart, through Kny, showed real commitment to innovative design.

In 1934, Stuart was asked to take part in two promotional exhibitions: one in Harrods, and the other, 'British Art in Industry', at the Royal Academy. The company invited eight artists, in addition to Ludwig Kny, to submit designs for the glassware project: Gordon and Moira Forsyth, Laura Knight, Eric Ravilious, Paul Nash, Graeme Sutherland, and Dod and Ernest Proctor. All of these artists were working in a new medium, and they responded in typically individual ways. Nash and Sutherland designed abstract swirls and geometric lines and spots. The Procters and Knight used either enamelled or engraved figures with some humorous qualities. Ravilious designed plant and leaf forms.

As an exhibition, it aroused much interest in the buying public and increased awareness of glass design. As a commercial design exercise, it was a failure, with very few of the ideas ever going into production. It served to illustrate the fact that a designer should be sympathetic to the requirements of the manufacturer and have a working knowledge of materials before creating a successful commercial range. Only one design, by Paul Nash, was put into production. A range of glassware called 'Woodchester', loosely based on the Ravilious fern motif, was extremely popular. The exhibition established Stuart as one of the most artistically advanced companies of the 1930s, leading the way with a more modern approach to design in glass.

A vase by Stuart Glass.

A cabinet of 'Woodchester' glassware.

KEITH MURRAY

Keith Murray was born in 1892 in Mount Eden, New Zealand. In 1906, his parents decided to emigrate to England, where he finished his schooling. After the First World War, he decided to train as an architect at the Architectural Association in London, but the Depression of the 1920s had a profound effect on new building, and jobs for new graduates were extremely hard to find. In 1925, he visited the l'Exposition de L'Art Decorativ in Paris and was inspired by the innovative design work shown there. He had kept an interest in old glass for many years, but felt that the current glass production in Europe relied too heavily on Victorian values and that this would be an area to which he could apply some innovative, modernist thinking. After a brief and not very fruitful session with the Whitefriars Glassworks in London, Murray finally met Herbert Williams Thomas from the Stevens and Williams Glassworks in Stourbridge in 1932, who employed him as a freelance designer.

During his period at Stevens and Williams, Murray produced more than 150 new designs a year for glassware, learning all that he could about

Tableware by Keith Murray for Wedgwood. Glass by Ludwig Kny for Stuart Glass. Vase by Webb Corbett.

techniques for blowing, cutting and polishing. These included designs for tableware, which were produced in quantity, as well as vases, bowls and specialised individual pieces. Some of his designs were never produced. In the *Design for Today* magazine of June 1933, Murray discussed what he saw as the basic elements of good glass design:

'The established purpose of the piece must be established by its form. The form is all-important: the profile, the mass, the weight and the colour. Decoration, if used at all, must be used to express the form of the object, not destroy it.'

This statement represented a radical move away from the heavily decorated 19th century ideas about table glass, and related more to the

DESIGNS BY KEITH MURRAY, AND ANIMAL FIGURES BY JOHN R. SKEAPING WEDGWOOD

Wedgwood advertisement for Keith Murray china and John Skeaping animals.

functionalist thinking of the Bauhaus. Murray was keen to exploit the traditional skills of centuries of craftsmanship in glass and to use this to compete in a modern European marketplace. He stated:

> *'The important thing that manufacturers have to decide is whether they are going to progress, or whether they will be content to struggle for another generation against the current of changing tastes and needs.'*

Murray's work with Stevens and Williams ranged from the practical elegance and simplicity of decanters and glasses blown with optical moulding and spiralling techniques to glass cutting which was minimalist and often whimsical in form. His pieces are highly regarded by collectors today.

In the same year that he began working with Stevens and Williams, Murray also met Josiah Wedgwood, and on the same freelance basis he began to design ceramic tableware and single items for Wedgwood. He suddenly was working with two huge companies that were attempting to bring a new, modernist approach to form and decoration in all aspects of tableware during the 1930s.

Designs by Keith Murray, with new glazes developed by Norman Wilson for his shapes, were first shown at the British Art in Relation to the Home Exhibition in London in 1933. They were also shown at the exhibition of new Wedgwood shapes in John Lewis in London in the same year, and 124 of his designs were available for order. He worked tirelessly to produce new shapes that appealed to a well-educated, design-conscious public. With simple, architectural, functional forms, he created everything from everyday tableware items to cigarette boxes, ashtrays, vases, mugs and beakers.

Although his most innovative work for Wedgwood was in the uncluttered forms he designed using the wonderful green, cream, yellow and black glazes of Wilson, Murray also designed many other patterns for the company that were in production from 1934. These patterns were also simple and uncluttered, using a stylised flower motif with coloured bands on a white ground. 'Weeping Willow' and 'Iris' were two of these. The paintress Millicent Taplin designed several lustre-relief patterns that were also applied to Murray's shapes. His work for both companies was shown at a number of major exhibitions during the prewar years: Milan in 1933, London in 1935 and Paris in 1937. He was soon established as a pioneering figure in European design.

By the end of the decade, Murray, along with his partner Charles White, was also established as an architect and was commissioned to design the new factory for Wedgwood at Barlaston. Unfortunately, work started on the factory at the beginning of the Second World War, and due to wartime restrictions the original concept of a modernist white façade had to be modified and replaced by an ordinary red brick facing. Murray increasingly continued to work as an architect after the war, when there was an increase in demand for new buildings. He finally retired from Wedgwood in 1948. With his partners he established a very successful practice specialising in industrial buildings; they designed Hong Kong Airport in the 1950s. Murray retired from practice in 1967, and died in May 1981, aged 89.

Tableware by Keith Murray for Wedgwood and Stuart glassware.

Keith Murray patterns from a Wedgwood pattern book.

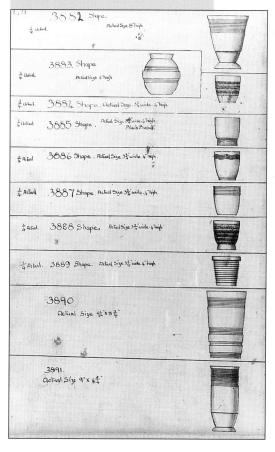

WHITEFRIARS IN THE 1920S AND 1930S

Whitefriars was the name adopted by the original company of James Powell and Sons, which opened in 1834 in the Whitefriars district of London. Throughout the 19th century, the company produced table glass, art glass and some industrial glass, as well as stained glass windows for such people as William Morris and Philip Webb, as well as for companies such as Liberty and Harrods. In 1923, the company moved out of its original building in St Paul's in London and into a purpose-built factory in Harrow, Middlesex. Some of the designs produced during this period of change seem to have been taken from a stockpile of designs left over from the prewar period, and new ranges were required to keep the company at the forefront of glass design.

During the 1920s, either Harry Powell or his cousin James designed all of the main ranges. They travelled widely, and many of their pieces in the early part of the century were based on historical and museum sources in Europe. By the time these pieces reached production, they were modified to meet both the contemporary market and the technical ability of the blowers, and they were distinctly modern in character. Technique inspired some of the best Whitefriars ranges.

Throughout this period, unlike other glass companies, Whitefriars did not use outside designers for its glass ranges. It employed in-house designers at all times, and this allowed for an understanding between the designer and the maker. Barnaby Powell joined the company before the First World War, and he was responsible for much of the decorative art glass of the period. He was interested in effects within the glass, such as the 'Cloudy' range from the 1920s, with its bubbly, semi-opaque glass, and the 'Streaky' range, for which multi-coloured 'streaks' of glass were drawn around the piece in watery lines.

During the 1930s, the lightweight glass of the '20s was replaced by much heavier glass, some of which, called optical glass, had internal ribbing. This glass was practical, substantial and popular, and it was produced in the full colour range. The 'ribbon-trailed' designs of the 1930s were a direct collaboration between Tom Hill the glassmaker and Barnaby Powell the designer. Powell produced his first 'ribbon-trailed' range in 1933. It was eventually produced in all colours, including twin colours from 1933 to the mid-1940s.

Whitefriars produced some of its most innovative work between the wars. Unlike at some of the other major British glassworks, the bosses at Whitefriars were not happy to continue producing designs which had been popular since the 1900s. They were also more individual in their approach to design. Their ideas were not obviously derivative, and they did not rely on the Art Deco movement, which many companies were following in the hope of finding a popular answer to contemporary glass. Whitefriars preferred a more honest approach, looking to in-house designers who had the knowledge and understanding of the medium to take them through this creative period with integrity.

Tea ware by Keith Murray for Wedgwood, vase by Stourbridge.

Cigarette box by Keith Murray for Wedgwood. Sherry set by William Wilson for Whitefriars Glass.

1940 ~ 1949
Wartime

By 1940, life in Britain was completely dominated by the war with Germany. A nationwide poll had shown that the country's agreement to rationing was the fairest way to share resources. Petrol had already been rationed since September 1939, and January 1940 saw the beginning of food rationing. Gradually, travel ceased, and all food became scarce. As the war progressed, entertaining and dining out became increasingly difficult. People struggled to find enough basic foodstuffs to satisfy their families' hunger, never mind entertain!

The Ministry of Food controlled the supply and movement of food across the country, under the direction of Lord Woolton. The country rallied in support, but he bore the brunt of any humour there was to be found in the situation.

Those who have the will to win
Cook potatoes in their skin
For they know the sight of peelings
Deeply hurts Lord Woolton's feelings – THE MINISTRY OF FOOD

TOP Sapphire lobed bowl designed by James Hogan for James Powell Glass, 1940–1946.
ABOVE Commemorative jug with the heads of Winston Churchill and Franklin Delano Roosevelt by Stuart Glass, 1945.
BELOW Green posy bowl made by Stuart Glass and shown in the 'Britain Can Make It' Exhibition in 1946.

There were certain priorities for the Ministry of Food; consumption of potatoes was an important one. Oatmeal, cheese and green vegetables were obtainable throughout the war. Ministry of Food cooks turned them into every conceivable combination, and recipes were published in free leaflets. Daily milk for children and expectant mothers was encouraged. Extra vitamins and calcium were made available to everyone to make up for shortages of certain natural food. Inventiveness was the order of the day. In the city there were fewer natural possibilities for adding to rations. If you lived in the country, there were more natural options to add to food rations. People near the sea were even reduced to considering seabirds as a possible source of nourishment – Cormorant Casserole seems to have been a favourite!

Millions of tons of processed meat were imported from North and South America for British consumption. 'Spam' had just arrived in the shops, and despite being introduced in times of dire need, it is still on the supermarket shelves today. As the war continued, the merchant navy came under increasing threat as many ships were destroyed with their vital cargos of foodstuffs. Increasingly, Britain had to look to her own resources to feed the people. Propaganda was used to encourage a strong 'Home Front'. Newspapers and radio stations published and broadcast encouragement in different ways for preparing and serving food. Public meetings were held,

and guest speakers travelled throughout the country to promote the Ministry of Food's instructions. Gardening was the nation's most popular recreational activity, and much waste ground was converted to cultivation for the first time. The 'Dig for Victory' campaign had some beneficial effects which lasted long after the war was over.

There was no shortage of food in the USA after the Americans joined the war in 1941, but there was petrol rationing. This affected the distribution of produce over the vast distances in the country and caused some problems. Recipe leaflets produced during the war show the difference between the eating habits of the two nations. While Britain was encouraging consumption of the potato in all shapes and forms, Betty Crocker's America was still frosting birthday cakes.

The Board of Trade was set up to control manufacturing in Britain, and many companies were forced either to stop production during the war or to work under the direction of its Utility Committee. Gordon Russell the furniture designer, Enid Marx the textile designer and a number of other prominent manufacturers and designers were involved to maintain a 'no frills' approach to the manufacturing needs of the country. China became plain white and glass was undecorated, but there was always someone trying to push the rules to the limit. Many decorative vases made during the war had a very small celery pattern either impressed or moulded into some part of the glass, but how many celery holders does a country need during wartime! Designs produced under wartime restrictions were often very acceptable, and after the war many companies used the ideals of the Utility Committee to start a new, minimal approach to the design of tableware.

Although the war ended in 1945, it took many years for the effects of wartime scarcity to disappear for everyone in the country. For some, the possibility of constant shortage was never to leave their thoughts. To try to help kick-start manufacturing again, the government organised the 'Britain Can Make It' Exhibition in 1946, followed by the Festival of Britain in 1951. British manufacturers also took part in European trade exhibitions. At the time, these were dominated by Scandinavian designers, who had been less restricted during the war. New manufacturers were introducing new production methods. Traditional prewar companies were looking at methods of modernisation. With huge investment in machinery and techniques, and with an educated mass market opening up for the first time, by 1949 the future was beginning to look very exciting.

Leaflet published by the Good Housekeeping Institute in 1940.

Booklet sold by the Good Housekeeping Institute with the approval of the Ministry of Food.

LEFT 'Utility' Chocolate Ware pot by Denby.

LORD WOOLTON AND THE MINISTRY OF FOOD

In April 1940 Lord Woolton, a businessman who had started his working life as a social worker in the slums, was put in charge of the Ministry of Food. As Sir Fred Marquis before the war, he had been a successful businessman, eventually acting as the controlling power behind the popular Lewis stores. He called the Ministry 'the greatest shop the world has ever known' and himself the country's grocer. This huge bureaucracy effectively controlled the manufacture and equal distribution of almost all foodstuffs in the country throughout the war and for a period after.

Lord Woolton was also committed to improving the health of the men and women on whom the outcome of the war depended, and to ensuring that the future generation of children would grow up into healthy adults. During the period of conscription in the First World War, only three out of every nine adults were considered fit for service due to chronic illness and undernourishment. Already in the 1930s free milk had been introduced in schools, and vitamins and cod liver oil were given to mothers and young children.

Lord Woolton's Pie served in Denby 'Manor Green' tableware with Parsley Sauce in a Pyrex™ gravy boat.

The Ministry of Food concentrated on three main areas:
1. Civic canteens and restaurants, to make sure that every person had at least one nutritious meal a day;
2. Introducing rationing to control the fair distribution of food to the whole community; and
3. Educating housewives about the best ways to feed their families with the available foodstuffs.

The canteens and restaurants were set up in every workplace and on busy streets to ensure that no one went hungry. They catered for everyone, from schoolchildren to civil servants, and served meals and hot drinks from 7 o'clock in the morning to 10 o'clock at night. The 'British Restaurants' encouraged communal eating for all classes of society for the first time. In 1941, there were around 70 million lunch meals a week being produced in canteens, school dining halls and civic restaurants. By 1944, there were 170 million. This shift away from breaking the day for lunch at home became a permanent feature of life after the war. Efforts were made to make the local restaurant or canteen a 'home from home', with pianos, tablecloths and libraries often in place for the customers' use. The canteens and restaurants provided a much-needed respite for women, who were either involved in war work or looking after young children.

Wise Eating in Wartime was a booklet produced by the Ministry of Food to support a 'Kitchen Front Broadcast' by the BBC.

RATIONING

Ration books were introduced in October 1939. Everyone had to register with a butcher and a greengrocer, and use them exclusively. A ration book was issued to each person, including children and royalty, and time limits were set for using the ration book tokens.

From the beginning, sugar, meats, fats, bacon, tea and cheese were rationed, but other staple items like bread and potatoes were not rationed until the late 1940s; bread was rationed in 1946, and potatoes in 1947. In 1941, a system of exchangeable points was introduced for dried and canned goods such as dried peas, cereals and treacle. Cod liver oil and condensed orange juice, as well as extra milk and eggs, were available for children, pregnant women and the infirm. The diet was nourishing but very boring, and endless queues would form at any hint of something more than basic foodstuffs being delivered to a grocer's shop – particularly chocolate or bananas. Being in the right place at the right time was very important.

'Time flies like an arrow – fruit flies like a banana.'

This comment by Groucho Marx would have been popular during the war, when bananas were at the end of the longest ration queues!

Offal and sausages were unrationed but not always available, and many recipes were available for using these cuts of meat, for example: Pigs' Feet in Jelly, Calves Head Hash and Skirt Pudding. Fish was unrationed but scarce and expensive. Fish supplies increased by seventeenfold by 1941, and unheard-of varieties were appearing on the market: ling, saith, salt cod, an unknown fish by the name of snoek and, later, whalemeat. Each person was allowed 16 points per month for other extras such as biscuits, cornflakes, Ovaltine, rice, canned salmon, honey, beer, gin or whisky, orange juice, baked beans, salt, vinegar and dried fruit.

The Ministry of Food made the first really effective use of media and advertising to alert the country to the inevitable restrictions of the war. It also tried to install a feeling of solidarity and unity on the Home Front, however, which gave people a feeling of working together for a common good.

Doctor Carrot and Potato Pete were Ministry of Food cartoon characters that appeared regularly in newspapers and leaflets urging their own consumption, as well as the consumption of any other home-grown vegetables, which were plentiful. They proclaimed, 'We'll put pep in your step' and 'I'm an energy food'. Other cartoon characters were created, such as the aptly named Squanderbug, which encouraged people to change their eating habits. Everyone

WEEKLY RATION FOR ONE ADULT	
Meat: 2 lamb or pork chops, or 12 oz. mince, or 12 oz. stewing steak. It worked out to about 2 oz. of meat per person per day.	
Full fat milk	*2–3 pints*
Sugar	*8 oz./225 g*
Butter	*2–4 oz./50 g*
Margarine	*2–4 oz./50 g*
Cooking fat	*3 oz./85 g*
English cheese	*3 oz./100 g*
Bacon or ham	*4 oz./100 g*
Fresh eggs	*1*
Dried eggs	*¼ packet*
(equivalent of 3 eggs)	
Sweets	*2 oz./50 g*
Jam	*2 oz./50 g*
Tea	*2 oz./50 g*

Oatcakes, celery and cheese served on a United Glass Bottle Company 'Waverley' plate.

was urged to avoid wasting food and to eat things that were both plentiful and nutritious.

A Battle of Britain pilot, Cat's–eyes Cunningham, claimed that it was eating carrots that allowed him to make accurate hits. This claim was made to hide the new British invention of radar from the Germans. Carrots are supposed to keep you fit, and they contain sugar, but they have no ability to help you see in the dark. Nonetheless, many people still believed this long after the war was over.

As well as publishing leaflets and booklets, the Ministry of Food used the BBC to broadcast a popular programme, 'The Kitchen Front', on the Radio Home Service every morning at 8.15. This informative and entertaining programme was transmitted throughout the war years, and many people took part in it. Marguerite Patten had a regular slot, and so did the cookery writer Ambrose Heath. All recipes were tested in the Ministry of Food's kitchen, and attempts were made to bring a little humour into what was obviously a very serious and important subject. It was a forerunner to the many radio and television food programmes that were to follow during the rest of the century. Listeners were encouraged to take part in the programme by sending in recipes, tips or questions. Recipes with names like Fighter's Pie and Skinflint's Pudding were encouraged; interactive media was born. The broadcasts and recipes were published in the media of the time. *The Listener* was a favourite to help people cope with the limited food available, and it was a test of ingenuity to find new and appealing ways of using dried eggs and carrots. Carrots were used in everything from soup to marmalade. There was even a recipe for Carrot Meringue Pie.

Lord Woolton's Pie was the most famous wartime dish of all. It was supposedly devised by the man himself, but in reality it was a concoction made by an underchef at the Savoy Hotel. It was a vegetable pie made with whatever vegetable was available (almost always carrots), then thickened with oatmeal, covered with potato or potato pastry and topped with cheese – if you had any. The cost of mince in 1940 was 10d and shoulder of lamb was 1s 2d per lb. Although the price was fixed, the quantity changed; in 1940, a person was allowed an amount worth 2s 2d, but by the following year you were allowed only an amount worth 1s. Given the scarcity of meat, Lord Woolton's Pie was very common.

Living in the country was much easier than living in the towns. Besides the nearby farms and farm produce, there were fields to grow your own food, and hedgerow fruits and greens. Every family in the country felt the scarcity, however. After the war, things did not immediately improve; in fact, many things were even more difficult to come by in postwar days. Britain had lost more than 25% of its national wealth during the war, and many things did not come off of rationing until well into the 1950s.

BOVRIL
makes dishes more delicious

Bovril is a great help in the kitchen. Its rich beefy flavour makes your dishes far more tasty, much more appetising. The war has changed many familiar things, but the high quality of Bovril remains the same.

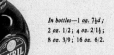

In bottles—1 oz. 7½d;
2 oz. 1/2; 4 oz. 2/1½;
8 oz. 3/9; 16 oz. 6/2.

A magazine advertisement for Bovril.

A Wartime Dinner

During the war, vegetables were used as a substitute for all kinds of other ingredients. Carrots in particular were easy to grow in Britain and were often used in baking to replace sugar because of their high natural sweetness. They were also used as a side vegetable to accompany almost every meal. A wartime dinner consisted mainly of infinite varieties of potato and carrot dishes! Soup was encouraged at all times, as it was easy to prepare and nourishing.

> *'I used to think one didn't oughter*
> *Make a soup from vegetable water*
> *But my dear this is a snorter!'* – MINISTRY OF FOOD LEAFLET

Carrot and Potato Soup or Beetroot Borscht would have been a typical first course to a meal. Often, it was just made with potato peelings, bacon rinds and any vegetables which were not rationed and were available throughout the war. The main course would again contain root vegetables, perhaps in the form of Lord Woolton's Pie, which covered any cooked vegetables with a pastry top, or Corned Beef Hash, which could have infinite additions to turn a tin of corned beef into a family meal. Welsh Rarebit or toasted cheese would have made a high tea meal, or people ate Bubble and Squeak – a delicious combination of potatoes, marrowfat peas and cabbage or brussel sprouts, chopped together and fried in dripping until brown.

Fish was never rationed, but it was scarce. Some very unusual fish appeared which had seldom been seen in fishmongers before. Salt cod was the easiest fish to find, but it lacked taste and flavour. Whalemeat later came on the market, which when carefully prepared had a very meaty flavour. A mysterious tinned fish called 'snoek' appeared, and remained unidentified.

Home-grown rhubarb, plums or apples made a pudding when cooked in pies and tarts. Apple Crumble was a delicious recipe which was created in wartime and has remained a basic family recipe to this day. It was best served with custard or cream, if you were lucky enough to live near a farm.

BORSCHT

1 lb. raw beetroot
2 oz. butter
2 medium carrots
2 medium onions
2 sticks celery
3 medium tomatoes
2 pints stock
2 bay leaves
Salt and pepper
1–2 tablespoonfuls red wine
Vinegar or lemon juice

Peel and grate all of the vegetables. This soup was originally not sieved or liquidised. It is equally good when smooth, though. Heat the butter in a pan, and add all of the other ingredients. Simmer for about one and a half hours. Serve with a spoonful of yoghurt and a little chopped beetroot or a spoonful of sour cream with a finely chopped hard-boiled egg.

ABOVE Borscht in Denby 'Manor Green' tableware.

LEFT Table set for a wartime dinner with Denby 'Manor Green' tableware, James Powell glass and 'Utility' cutlery.

LORD WOOLTON'S PIE

Lord Woolton's Pie was the name given to a concoction of mixed vegetables with either a potato topping or a pastry crust. It was named after the Minister for Food and contained only things that were not rationed.

Chop and cook a mixture of the following vegetables:

Cauliflower
Swede
Carrot
Potato
Spring onions

Cook about 750 grams of potatoes and mash until smooth. Put vegetables in a pie dish and cover with mashed potato. Top with grated cheese, if you have any, and garnish with parsley. Lord Woolton's Pie can be served with Parsley Sauce.

PARSLEY SAUCE

Melt 2 oz. of butter in a pan. Add 1 oz. of flour and cook gently for several minutes. Add about a pint of hot milk, stirring constantly, and stir in several tablespoonfuls of chopped parsley.

CORNED BEEF HASH

Combine equal amounts of chopped canned corned beef, diced and peeled potatoes and chopped red onions in a pan. Cover the pan and add 2 or 3 tablespoons of water, salt and pepper. Cook until the onions are tender and the beef is dry, then add 3 tablespoons of butter. Brown over a slow heat and serve. Delicious with poached eggs.

RHUBARB CRUMBLE

Cook 1 lb. of rhubarb gently in water with 3 oz. of sugar until barely tender, and place in a pie dish. For the crumble: rub 3 oz. of butter or margarine into 6 oz. of flour until the mix resembles fine breadcrumbs. Add sugar and sprinkle over the fruit. Bake in a moderate (180ºC) oven for approximately 35 minutes. Serve hot with custard or cold with cream.

ABOVE Corned Beef Hash.

LEFT Lord Woolton's Pie.

BELOW Rhubarb Crumble.

A Woman's Working Day

A woman's routine day in wartime consisted of: cooking breakfast and washing up; getting to the shops early; collecting rations; and starting to queue. Then she went back home to cook lunch and prepare the evening meal, which was usually three courses and included a cooked pudding. Afternoon tea was around 4 o'clock, with cakes, tarts or scones. As well as this, there was jam and chutney to prepare and fruit to bottle. Housework included cleaning the main rooms every day, cleaning out fires, washing, ironing, dressmaking (another necessary skill), mending and gardening, to say nothing of general odd jobs and household upkeep.

Marguerite Patten

An advertisement for Bird's custard.

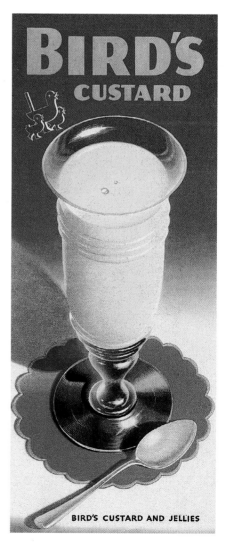

Marguerite Patten was a home economist who had worked in the electrical industry before the war. One of her jobs was to give cookery demonstrations – usually with plenty of time, equipment and expensive ingredients. During the war, her energies were devoted to suggestions for keeping a wartime family well-fed without much time or many ingredients.

She joined the Ministry of Food in 1942 as one of hundreds of food demonstrators who travelled all around the country. Her job was to show people how to make rations go further, and how to use limited ingredients to make nutritious meals. At first she was based in Cambridge, where she gave her first demonstration outside in the marketplace. The Food Division of the Board of Trade had set up centres in markets, canteens, hospitals, clinics and even at shop counters. The public's reactions to this advice varied widely. Experienced cooks felt that they needed no advice on how to feed their families, while others refused to accept that their diet now had so many gaps in it.

In 1943, Patten was put in charge of the Ministry of Food Bureau in Harrods. She demonstrated cooking daily, often to upper-class women who had never needed to cook for themselves before. Demonstrations included recipes for:

Mock Crab: margarine, dried egg, 1 oz. cheese, salad dressing and vinegar, salt and pepper. Use to spread on toast or mashed potato.

Mock Banana: parsnips with milk and banana essence.

Mock Cream: margarine, sugar, dried milk powder and a tablespoon of milk, served with the wartime invention Fruit Crumble, which was created as an alternative to making pastry.

'Murkey': stuffed mutton. For Christmas in 1941, this was a replacement for turkey!

POTATOES

There is no vegetable more useful than the homely potato. Potatoes are a cheap source of energy, and they are one of the foods that help to protect us from illness. They contain the same vitamin as oranges and ½ lb. of potatoes daily will give over half the amount of this vitamin needed to prevent fatigue and help fight infection.

Potatoes save Shipping

Potatoes, which are home-grown, give us the same kind of energy-food as cereals, which are imported. Eat them in place of bread and other cereals wherever possible, and you help to save shipping space.

So don't think of potatoes merely as something to serve with the meat. They can be much more than that. A stuffed, baked potato can be a course in itself. Potatoes can be used, too, for soups, bread-rolls, pastry, puddings and even cakes, as the following recipes show.

Hints on cooking Potatoes

1. Always cook them in their skins.
2. If you must peel them, peel thinly.
3. After peeling, cook at once. Avoid soaking in water if possible.

Boiled Potatoes

Scrub the potatoes, and put into boiling salted water using just enough water to cover.

Cook with the lid on. Boil rapidly but do not let the potatoes break up and become 'mushy.' When tender (this should be after 10-15 minutes cooking) drain carefully. Shake the potatoes gently in the saucepan over a low heat for a minute or two. This dries the potatoes and leaves them deliciously floury.

SALADS

Let Your Slogan be "A Salad a Day"

OATMEAL

Oatmeal is such an important food that the Government has undertaken to subsidise it. There are plentiful supplies of Oatmeal and rolled oats at a price which is now within the reach of all.

SCOTLAND gives us oatmeal, the most valuable of all our cereals, more nourishing even than wholemeal flour. Oatmeal is one of the simple foods on which our forefathers lived and throve. The cakes that King Alfred burned were, in all probability, oaten cakes and for many a century oatmeal played an important part in the countryman's diet. During the last hundred years other cereals have tended to oust it from the Englishman's table but to-day it is coming into its own again.

Why is oatmeal valuable? Because it not only builds our bodies and gives us energy but also helps to protect us from illness. Oatmeal contains even more of that elusive vitamin B1. than wholemeal bread and far away more than white flour. That is one reason why it is a 'protective food.' Another is that it gives us the elements that make bone and blood.

What can we make with oatmeal? Porridge and oatcakes certainly, but there are many other ways of using it. It is excellent when added to many meat and vegetable dishes and can be used to thicken soups and stews. It makes a delicious stuffing for meat and poultry. Fish, especially herrings, are very good cooked in oatmeal. It can replace some of the white flour in scones, cakes, biscuits and puddings. Last but not least, oatmeal water is a refreshing drink.

Choose medium oatmeal or rolled oats for porridge, biscuits, and puddings. Fine oatmeal is excellent for coating fish and rissoles, while the coarse is usually preferred for stuffings. When making scones and bread you will need some flour to supply the necessary gluten.

Don't forget that oatmeal contains fat so that it will not keep indefinitely. It will keep for a month or two if stored in a tightly lidded container, but take care to use it all up before you put in a new supply.

War cookery leaflet — Number 3; War cookery leaflet; War cookery leaflet — Number 1. Ministry of Food.

Patten went on to work in radio programmes during the war. After the war, she had an astonishing career in the media which lasted until the end of the century; she was still demonstrating cooking in the Imperial War Museum in 2000! She wrote many cookery books and made television programmes, on some of which she hosted as well as demonstrated. She played a significant part in the work of the Home Front during the war years, and since then she has established herself as one of the most popular figures in the world of domestic cooking.

In one of the Ministry of Food leaflets above, the highlight is the potato, another vegetable that grows prolifically in Britain. Here the public was encouraged to use potatoes as an alternative to fat in a basic recipe for steamed pudding, and as a pastry base for sweet tarts, and in a chocolate sandwich spread.

Try it if you dare – perhaps with a little custard.

Some of the many Ministry of Food leaflets published to educate people in wartime ways of cooking.

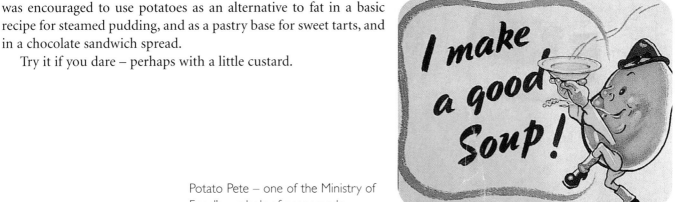

Potato Pete – one of the Ministry of Food's symbols of propaganda.

THE BAGLEY CRYSTAL GLASS COMPANY

The Bagley Company was founded in 1871 by William Bagley and John Wild in Knottingley, Yorkshire, as a bottle works. In 1912, the Crystal Glass Company was formed as a branch of Bagley, to change the company's direction towards lead crystal and pressed table glassware. It soon stopped producing true lead crystal, but continued producing pressed 'crystal' glassware until 1975.

The range of luxury items produced in Bagley 'crystal' was very popular, as this material had many of the qualities of expensive lead crystal at a fraction of the price. At first, the production was limited to everyday articles in clear 'flint' glass: glasses, jugs and simple table sets. Production developed during the 1920s to include art glass and fancy shapes and patterns for the table. The skill of production in the 1920s was a compromise between the glassblower's craftsmanship and the mechanised production of the day.

The company produced a full range of designs, but was keen to keep production costs and therefore retail costs at the lowest possible level. During the 1920s, the company was able to produce 2,400 perfect pieces of glass for a fruit set in one shift, which was a huge number for a manufacturer of the time. In 1933, Bagley introduced a new range of moulded glass called 'Crystaltint', inspired by the glass of Lalique, in a range of pastel colours. The designs were influenced by Art Deco shapes, using the fans, shells and fish motifs that were typical of the French glass of the period.

In 1933, the Bagleys introduced the freelance designer Alexander Hardie Williamson to the in-house company design team. Williamson created a group of designs which included the 'Marine' bowl and plate, as well as the 'Bamboo' range, which were manufactured in 1933 and 1934. Many of the pieces produced at this time were made in coloured, frosted and acid-etched glass, and pieces were often decorated for the souvenir trade, with hand-painted flowers or place names enamelled on the side of the glass. During the 1930s, the company also produced a black glass known as 'Jetique'. This was reintroduced in 1945 and became highly popular in the 1950s, with the addition of some fashionable enamelled spots in white or red.

The war brought an end to the production of fancy glass, and the company was involved in other war work, including a contract for the beer glasses in the NAAFI. They were unable to keep up with NAAFI demand, however, owing to the high number of breakages! In wartime, glass needed to have a use, and so ashtrays were disguised as butter dishes, and narrow flower vases were stamped with the word 'celery' to confuse the enforcers of restrictions put upon the glass industry in the immediate postwar period; these tricks implied food use! After the war, the company went into other areas of industrial glass, as it had the technology for mass production. The designs of the art glass and fancy tablewares did not keep abreast with the fashions of the time, and were gradually discontinued. The Crystal Glass Company finally closed in 1975.

A Bagley 'celery vase' – a frivolous flower vase in disguise!

Custard in a Bagley dessert set, with flowers in a Bagley 'celery vase'.

'DIG FOR VICTORY'

At the outbreak of war in 1939, the experiences of the First World War had made it apparent that food shortages were once again going to become a serious problem. Before the war, a government leaflet had declared that the country depended on 20 million tons of food per year that was imported from all parts of the world: 70% of cheese and sugar; 80% of fruit; 90% of cereals and fat; and 50% of meat. The inevitable restrictions on the sea trade caused by the war meant that these figures would have to be turned around, and the country would have to become as near to self-sufficient in raw materials as possible.

The Ministry of Agriculture was given the power to allow councils to hand over any unused or unoccupied land to the public for food cultivation. 'Dig for Victory' – the most famous campaign of the war – was launched properly in 1940 with the *Growmore Leaflet No. 1*. The campaign encouraged everyone to grow food wherever they could, from window boxes to allotments to gardens. By 1942, there were 10 million copies of the first 'Dig for Victory' leaflet in circulation. It was one of 25 different leaflets, each one of which advised on some aspect of growing food, from tree pruning to potato blight.

Every possible space was utilized for growing vegetables and other edible crops. Even the Kings Great Park in Windsor was cultivated; it became the biggest cornfield in Britain. 'Dig for Victory' weeks were held in all major cities and towns, with posters illustrating lectures, demonstrations, 'Brain Trusts', competitions and prizes. By 1944, there were around 2 million allotments in cultivation, in every situation from tennis courts to railway embankments. Wild plants were gathered to eat, and salads included wild herbs and nettles, which were used as cooked vegetables not unlike spinach. Hedgerow fruits such as brambles and rosehips were gathered and made into preserves. A 35 x 100 foot garden was reckoned to provide most of the needs of a family for the best part of one year. The output, by 1944, of the millions of allotments, gardens and non-professionally produced food was 3 million tons, or 10% of all food produced in the country.

After the war, this enthusiasm for gardening remained while there were still food shortages, but garden plots gradually disappeared as the need for food was replaced by the need to build new houses on temporarily cultivated land. During the late 1960s and the 1970s, there was a revival of self-sufficiency as people began to seek alternative lifestyles, but the widespread enthusiasm created during the Second World War for vegetable growing has never been achieved again.

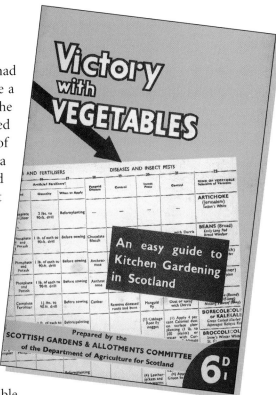

Cover of a leaflet produced by the Department of Agriculture for the Scottish Gardens and Allotments Committee encouraging the 'Dig for Victory' campaign.

Doctor Carrot – one of the Ministry of Food's symbols of propaganda.

AMERICA AT WAR

On 7 December 1941, the Japanese military bombed Pearl Harbor and America officially joined the hostilities of the Second World War. The West Coast of America was immediately affected by its proximity to Japan and its possible vulnerability to attack. Volunteers were called upon to act as fire fighters, police, civil defence guards and home guards. Elsewhere in America there was not the same sense of fear regarding attack, but shortages rapidly began to occur. America rallied to help the war effort through various nationwide collecting programmes. One of these was the 'Keys For Victory' drive, through which old keys and tools were collected in stores across the country and turned into munitions.

In the USA, petrol shortages hit the car-conscious Americans very hard indeed. No new cars were sold, and tyres and spare parts for vehicles were rationed. Women even began to ride bicycles for their shopping trips. Although many foods were grown in the USA, the country still had problems regarding the distribution and processing of produce. Transport was needed to move more important things than food around the country. Soon sugar, petrol, coffee and many other items were rationed.

The most highly recommended Christmas present in America in 1941 was War Bonds! After the war, things slowly returned to normality, although it was normality of a new kind. The most exciting Christmas present in 1948 was a sensational new invention – a television set. Television programmes began in 1949, and the cost of a TV set ranged from $99.50 for a barely viewable 3-inch screen to $670.00 for a 12-inch super screen model.

FIRE KING JADEITE

Fire King glassware was made by the Anchor Hocking Glass Corporation from 1940 to 1970. Fire King glass was called 'miracle glass' because it was made by a formula which produced heatproof, durable oven-to-table ware. The Fire King brand guaranteed that the glassware was unbreakable from heat for two years. Some items were embossed with the Fire King title, and others simply had an identification label.

The glass was produced in a range of colours which included Jadeite, a milky, opaque green, as well as Azurite, Turquoise, Sapphire Blue, Ivory, Royal Ruby, Forest Green and Milk White. There were also various fired-on decorations in other colours. Jadeite was made in sets of 53 pieces, and in the 1940s a set would cost you $6.95.

The *Ladies Home Journal* of June 1948 wrote, 'The (Jadeite) glass is both charming and practical for your dining room, breakfast nook, camp lodge or summer retreat!'

An American booklet from 1944. The cover illustrates the difference between the availability of raw ingredients in Britain and the USA during the war.

CORN CHOWDER

4 or 5 slices of bacon, chopped
1 onion, finely chopped
2 potatoes, chopped into cubes
1 can creamed corn
1 can of corn kernels
1 pint milk (or more if necessary or to preferred thickness)
Salt and pepper to taste

Cook bacon and onion together in a pan until soft. Add all other ingredients, and cook for 15 to 20 minutes, until potatoes are tender. Season and serve. Crisply fried bacon can be served as a topping.

'SYRACUSE ECONORIM'

Syracuse China was manufactured by the large Onondaga Pottery Company in Syracuse, New York. It was the first really fine china produced in America at the end of the 19th century, and was thinner than earthenware but not so thin as bone china. During the first part of the 20th century, the main market for Syracuse China was in the catering trade, but in the late 1930s there was a move to gain part of the domestic market. There was more interest in American tableware during the 1930s due to a 'Buy American' campaign, and also to the political unrest in Europe.

The 'Econorim Shape' range was introduced to the company in 1938 and was used for more than 300 patterns. In 1933, the company pioneered a technique for hand decorating china with stencils and airbrushed glazes called 'Shadowtone'. 'Western Ware' was an example of this technique. Rodeo images were popular for the great American barbecues and picnics, and were produced by a number of the big American pottery manufacturers just before and after the war. These pieces were very cheaply made and marketed, and they were widely available everywhere from department stores to petrol stations.

An American table set with Fire King Jadeite glass dinnerware, with a three-tiered cake stand and cruet set in Bakelite™.

Rodeo design cup and plate by Syracuse China.

RAYMOND LOEWY

Raymond Loewy was born in 1893 in France, where he grew up with a strong interest in model aeroplanes and steam trains. He served in the French Army during the First World War, winning the Croix de Guerre. After the war, he moved to the USA. In 1919, almost by accident, he joined a firm of commercial artists. Loewy was an energetic and attractive character who was very confident of his own ability. He quickly made a name for himself in the graphic window displays of the large department stores on 5th Avenue in New York City.

In 1929, the Gestetner Duplicating Company invited Loewy to redesign its duplicating machine. The result was a streamlined and more hygienic design, and at the start of the 1930s this had a very modern appeal for customers. Other similar projects followed, and by the mid-1930s Loewy had established himself as a leading consultant in the field of industrial design. He was a very single-minded, modern-thinking man with no belief in the roots of past design. He was also an excellent self-promoter, as well as a good businessman, and by the end of the 1940s he had offices in London and Paris.

During his long and very successful career, Loewy redesigned many everyday objects, from the pencil sharpener and the Coca-Cola™ bottle to a locomotive and a Studebaker™ car. His success was underpinned by his name, and every design that left any of his offices had his facsimile signature on the bottom, whether he had designed it or not.

During the 1930s, the giant German ceramics company Rosenthal was trying to establish a hold on the huge USA market. After the Second World War, this was even more important, and after a series of company moves, a link was established with Loewy Design Associates. For a share in the company, Loewy agreed to work with Rosenthal to create modernist ranges for the American market. The most popular range was called 'Model 2000', and by the mid-1960s more than 20,000,000 pieces had been sold using over 200 surface patterns.

In the 1960s, Philip Rosenthal re-established control over the American market and expanded his 'Studio-Linie' collection. Loewy's designs fitted perfectly into the Studio Linie concept:

> *'The true contemporary is neither ugly, crude nor boring. It is varied, warm and elegant but in contrast to the often hollow imitations of the great styles of the past, always a genuine expression of the artistic forces and the spirit of our time.'* – PHILIP ROSENTHAL, 1960

Raymond Loewy went on to expand his fields of design until his death in 1986. In his lifetime, he had become the best-known designer in the world by changing the face of products at every level of society. He transformed many everyday objects by bringing them into the shapes and styles of the 20th century.

CREAM CHEESECAKE

This is a recipe from the USA in 1941. No rationing here!

1 ½ cups digestive biscuits, crumbed
½ cup sugar
2 tablespoons butter
2 tablespoons flour
½ teaspoon salt
1 pound cream cheese
1 teaspoon vanilla
4 eggs, separated
1 cup cream

Combine biscuits with butter and 2 tablespoons of sugar, and line the bottom of a spring-release cake tin. Mix the remaining sugar with the flour and salt and blend with cream cheese. Add the vanilla and egg yolks and beat thoroughly. Whisk egg whites until stiff and fold into cheese mixture. Pour the mixture over the crumbs and bake in a moderate oven (160ºC) for about 1 hour or until firm. Turn off heat but leave to cool in the oven for a further hour or until cold.

Raymond Loewy china for Rosenthal, with Cream Cheesecake.

'BRITAIN CAN MAKE IT'

The years immediately after the war were still difficult times in Europe as life slowly began to return to prewar normality. In Britain, rationing was only gradually lifted as goods became more readily available, but there was an underlying eagerness to move on and an excitement about the direction manufacturers were going to take. The market had been deprived of new goods for so long that a consumer boom seemed inevitable. To help kick-start the new era, the Board of Trade, under Sir Stafford Cripps, organised an exhibition in London as a showcase to illustrate the production of the best of British industry immediately after the war. The exhibition was held at the Council of Industrial Design and was called 'Britain Can Make It'.

Some of the work shown had been designed during the 1930s but had been put on hold because of wartime restrictions. Other work was completely new. Although the war allowed only limited production, its restrictions also stretched designers' ideas and imaginations, as they had to make goods in different ways and with different materials. Some of these ideas, particularly in the diversification of plastics, metals and laminated wood, were being developed into a new form of design that would blossom in the 1950s.

The exhibition was very successful. It was one of the first in Britain to consider the simpler requirements of image and form necessary for the new industries to appeal to a modern public. It was also one of the first to recognise and acknowledge the more significant role played by the designer in the success of a company. In his introduction to the catalogue for the exhibition, Sir Stafford Cripps explained that the market no longer demanded a few well-made and beautiful pieces to grace the homes of the rich. The new buying public wanted ordinary household goods to have beauty as well as fulfil their functions, and they wanted them to be affordable for everyone. This was what postwar trade needed to aim for both at home and abroad.

In *An Attempt to Define Design*, Bernard Hollowood looked at the factors which influenced the design or style of any period. He recognised that political events, social and economic circumstances, technical innovations and the influence of the fine arts all affected the way in which designers approached problems. As he wrote, 'Designers create fashion ... style evolves in spite of them.' This point was illustrated by the range of items on view at the exhibition. In the Pottery and Glass section, traditional tea wares by Royal Worcester and Mintons sat alongside new Wedgwood designs by Eric Ravilious and Keith Murray. New designs by Susie Cooper, which had a modern, sophisticated lightness of touch, were there, as well as some of her 1930s lustrewares that had been discontinued during the war.

In glassware, there was a similar story. The traditions of cut glass in the great Midlands glassworks were being challenged by the uncut services of plain and coloured table and art glass from the London-based company Whitefriars. Its designers James Hogan and William Wilson were influenced by the Scandinavian glassmakers of Orrefors and Iittala, who were beginning to make strong marks on the European industrial exhibitions. The

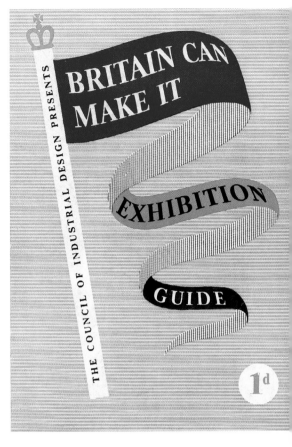

The cover for the 'Britain Can Make It' Exhibition guide.

The postwar tea table, shown in a pencil drawing by Danny Ferguson.

A tea setting in Gray's lustreware.

Stourbridge Company of John Walsh Walsh was exhibiting the work of Clyne Farquharson, a young designer who produced a number of glass services whose elegant simplicity broke with the traditions of British cut glass. Although there was still a traditional market to service, the modern movement was acknowledged by most companies, at least in a small way. The United Glass Bottle Company was beginning its challenge for the cheaper end of the glass trade with new, modern designs that echoed the new technology in pressed glass.

Metalwork during the war had evolved through innovative techniques that could now be directed towards domestic use. With the development of stainless steel, new household items were shown which gave a taste of things to come. The exhibition set out to prove that Britain had picked itself up after the six wartime years of hardship. Manufacturing was standing on the edge of an unlimited consumer demand, and was ready to meet the challenges of mass-market production. This was an unknown field for the industrialists of the 20th century, and there was some question over the need to provide variety and breadth within each area. The designer who understood the potential of his manufacturing process had never been more important.

VICTORY WARE

Wedgwood had moved into its new factory in Barlaston in 1940, and was ready to use its new production methods to introduce a range of modern ceramics that would fit into the government's 'Utility' criteria. Although pottery wares had never been rationed, there were strong restrictions on pottery production. Decorated ware and non-essential 'art' pieces were prohibited, although some companies got around this by embossing or printing functional labels on the items. A glass flower vase produced before the war became a celery holder, with 'celery' inscribed on it, during the war.

Apart from these restrictions, wartime ceramics were not strictly 'Utility', since there were no specifications for design or materials used. 'Simplicity of manufacture, natural colours and the possibility of buying individual items rather than whole sets' was encouraged by the Board of Trade. Victor Skellern was the Art Director at Wedgwood at this time, and he designed a range of tableware which adhered to these guidelines. It was also easy to store, clean and use, with multi-purpose lids on dishes, bowls and pots. He stated that, 'Good design, or the lack of it, has never been so apparent as it is under the new restrictions, and Wedgwood have come unscathed through the Utility acid test.' The new ware was never called 'Utility', but was named 'Victory Ware', a name which was felt by the company to be more appropriate to their forward-looking production.

CLYNE FARQUHARSON

William Farquharson was born on 14 February 1906 in Birmingham. The name Clyne, which appeared as the signature on all of his glass, was his mother's maiden name and was used as a marketing ploy to help sell the glass during the 1930s. After some fairly brief but formal art school training in Birmingham, he joined the glass company of John Walsh Walsh in 1924. Although he spent the next seven years still attending day release classes at the Central Art School, he was employed as chief draughtsman, and for his first few years he worked on full-scale, technical working drawings for factory use. The first design that can be attributed to Clyne Farquharson dates from 1935, but he would certainly have been part of the design team before then, and at least partly responsible for earlier designs. 'Leaf' and 'Kendal' were his most popular ranges, and they made his name as an innovative designer of cut glass. The patterns were free-flowing, with deeply cut leaf shapes and swirling lines, and were unlike any other patterns on the market at that time. They were neither traditional nor modernist, but very beautiful, timeless and original, appealing to a wide market. They still stand as works of art today.

Farquharson married in 1939, and in the same year he was elected to The National Registry of Industrial Art Designers alongside such names as Keith Murray and Eric Ravilious. He was a very private man and very little is known of his personal life. After the war, he went back to John Walsh Walsh and stayed there until the company closed in 1951. He was then employed by Stevens and Williams and moved to London, where he joined another company before disappearing from public view before his death from lung cancer in 1972. Since then, the work of this very private artist from the 1930s has received critical acclaim and has been collected by glass enthusiasts all over the world.

A vase designed by Clyne Farquharson for the Stourbridge glass company John Walsh Walsh. The publication next to it accompanied the 'Britain Can Make It' Exhibition in 1946. It contains illustrations of the exhibits and a number of essays written by members of the wartime Board of Trade as a propaganda exercise in support of British industry.

ERIC RAVILIOUS

Eric Ravilious was born in 1903 in Acton, South London, but was educated in Eastbourne, where his family moved in order to set up an antiques business. He attended Eastbourne College of Art and in 1922 he won a scholarship which allowed him to continue his education at the Royal College of Art in London. His fellow students at the time were the generation following the end of the First World War, and they were a talented group filled with creative enthusiasm. Ravilious immediately became friendly with the wood engraver Edward Bawden, and they worked together for the rest of Ravilious's life.

Various successful exhibitions followed for Ravilious after he left the Royal College of Art, both for wood engraving and watercolour painting. In 1933, he was invited by Stuart Glass in Stourbridge to design a range of table glass for an exhibition at Harrods entitled 'Modern Art for the Table'. Other notable names were also invited to exhibit, including Dame Laura Knight and Ravilious's old tutor, Paul Nash. Ravilious went on to design four ranges for Stuart which were put into production.

In 1935, he received his first request for designs for tableware from Wedgwood. The company wanted new designs with a contemporary feel. Ravilious researched old patterns and adapted them to his own very personal style. At first, Wedgwood was cautious about the designs. The directors liked them, but they felt they were too avant-garde for their traditional market. The design for the coronation mug of Edward VIII was accepted, and eventually it was successfully adapted for the Coronation of George VI. The design was reworked and reinstated for the Coronation of Elizabeth II in 1953. Following the success of these mugs, Wedgwood retained Ravilious as a freelance designer, paying him for six weeks of designing a year. His tableware designs for Wedgwood during this time were mainly put into production immediately after the war, and they contain all of the elements that typify his work. They are beautifully drawn engravings illustrating travel, the garden and various other gentle scenes. Ravilious became an official war artist in 1940 and died at the age of 37 when he failed to return from an air-sea rescue mission off the coast of Iceland in 1942.

The originality of the work of Eric Ravilious in ceramic tableware helped Wedgwood to establish a contemporary edge in postwar design. The company has now become legendary in the field of collecting at the end of the 20th century.

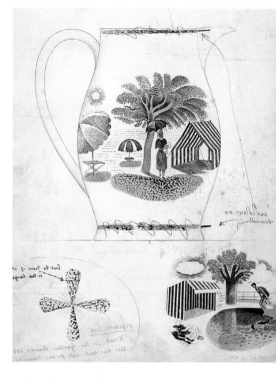

A jug design by Eric Ravilious from the Wedgwood archive.

An illustration for the 'Travel' series by Eric Ravilious.

POSTWAR PRESSED GLASS IN BRITAIN

A selection of pressed glass from the 'Britain Can Make It' Exhibition catalogue.

'Ripple' jug and glass, designed by Alexander Hardie Williamson for the United Glass Bottle Company.

After the war, the restrictions imposed on the glass industry were not immediately lifted. Ornamental glass production was still on hold, and in fact its restriction was not repealed until 1952. The market for domestic pressed glass was reopened in 1948, however. Several forward-thinking companies seized this opportunity to bring a contemporary approach to the design of mass-produced glass items for a market that had been starved of any luxuries for four years.

The postwar encouragement to British companies to restart production provided an opportunity for a new type of tableware. This new tableware was made of inexpensive, well-designed pressed glass, produced by the most modern techniques. These techniques would give most people in the country access to new and exciting tableware designs for a modest amount of money. The most important feature of this glass was that it in no way resembled the heavy, clumsy appearance of prewar pressed glass. The designer was now required to consider the weight and density of the glass, as well as the colour – considerations which had been forbidden during wartime restrictions.

ALEXANDER HARDIE WILLIAMSON

'Doric' bowls by Alexander Hardie Williamson for the United Glass Bottle Company.

Alexander Hardie Williamson was born in Hull in 1907. After graduating from the Royal College of Art, where he specialised in textile design and murals, he joined the staff in 1933 as a part-time lecturer in the design school. During the Second World War, when the college was evacuated to the Lake District, he led the fabric design course in Ambleside. After the war, he became Head of Printed Textiles for the Royal College of Art back in London, from 1951 to 1955.

Throughout his teaching career, he worked on a freelance basis for a number of companies: creating textiles for Warner Brothers; making ceramics for Royal Worcester; and, during the 1930s, working as a design consultant for Bagley Glass of Knottingley. His most singular contribution to 20th century industrial design, however, was his work with United Glass from 1944 to 1974, when he designed 1,711 different pieces for the Sherdley and Ravenhead works. The United Glass Bottle Company was a progressive company that became United Glass in the separate works at Sherdley and at Ravenhead. The company had installed the most modern machines for producing stemware before the Second World War, and now it was beginning to reap the benefits of its investments, as a more discerning public demanded new forms of modern glassware.

People wanted lighter and simpler glasses which could be produced quickly and cheaply, making inevitable breakages easy to replace. The Sherdley plant had begun to meet this demand, but the company needed some contemporary design ideas to expand its ranges. Williamson understood the principles of contemporary design and the modern market, and in 1947 he designed the 'Doric' and the 'Regency' ranges, which had a simple, contemporary appeal. These popular designs were produced until the late 1960s. Williamson spent time learning about the limitations of manufacture, so he was able to design to the full potential of the production capabilities of the factory. Many of his designs were never out of production; the 'Worthington' and 'Club' suites of stemware are still produced today. The 'Paris' goblet for Ravenhead is still in mass production today, and must be the most commonly used wine glass of all time.

In the mid-1950s, Williamson designed a distinctive range of tumblers which had applied, screen-printed, transfer designs on them. They were marketed under the names 'Slim Jims', 'Chunkies' or 'Tubbies', and their colourful, fun designs were matched by lively advertising. They were packaged in bright, coloured boxes in the dominant 1950s style, and were completely new to the British market.

In a talk given to glass designers and teachers in 1964, Williamson showed how clearly he understood all of the detailed production methods involved in making everyday table glass. Only this thorough understanding of materials and production would have allowed him to successfully design so many of the bestselling, mass-produced drinking glasses in Britain in the second half of the 20th century.

'Ripple' bowls.

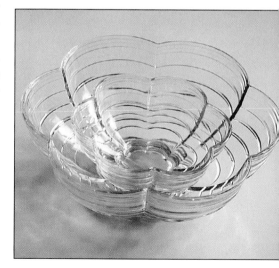

ABOVE: LEFT 'Spiderweb' bowls made by Chance Brothers in the late 1940s.
RIGHT 'Britannia' dishes.

THE UNITED GLASS BOTTLE COMPANY

The United Glass Bottle Company started production of pressed glass tableware in 1932 at its plant in Sherdley. After the war, the company's approach to the new industry was similar to that of Chance Brothers. The company attempted to take new directions in modern design and apply them to the mass production of tableware, resulting in popular, modern glassware. Unlike at Chance Brothers, its production plants were based on even more efficient American technology. After Chance had ceased tableware production in 1954, the United Glass Bottle Company became the market leader and dominated the glassware market for a decade. 'Ripple' was a popular design from the early period. It was in production from 1945 to 1948, and had jugs, vases and glasses in its range.

The company was renamed United Glass in 1959, and from this time onward its production was divided between the Sherdley plant and the Ravenhead plant in St Helens. Although the traditional home of pressed glass was the North-east of England, the two big companies Davidson and Sowerby had refused to consider new designs in the postwar period. They had relied instead upon a traditional approach, using old and tested patterns, some of which dated back to the 1800s. Unfortunately, the view of the public at this time was anything but traditional – people wanted something new, and if the tableware did not have a contemporary feel, then it did not sell. Sales of old favourites, such as 'Chippendale' and 'Jacobean', dropped after being in production for almost 50 years. As a result, these companies lost their hold on the market. Contemporary design at United Glass was now in the hands of designer Alexander Hardie Williamson, who was employed as a freelance designer at both production plants from 1944 until 1974.

'Waverley' bowl.

CHANCE BROTHERS

After the war, a huge investment in modern machinery allowed the newly established company Chance Brothers, based in Smethwick, to begin production of huge quantities of modern pressed glass as soon as the restrictions were lifted. R.Y. Gooden was the in-house designer, and his first range of glassware – 'Spiderweb' – owed something to the prewar Art Deco style. It had been designed by Gooden in 1934 and exhibited at the British Art in Industry Exhibition at the Royal Academy in 1935. This range of bowls, pots and vases was made from 1948 to 1953.

Two new patterns were introduced in 1949: 'Britannia', which had visual roots in cut glass; and 'Waverley', which had a lighter, more modern look. Two further ranges, 'Lancer' and 'Gossamer', were launched in 1951. Export trade of the new pressed glass began very successfully at the end of the 1940s. As the 1950s progressed, however, import taxes in other countries that were also trying to rebuild economies after the war reduced demand and forced Chance to discontinue production of traditionally produced tableware in 1954.

In 1951, Chance launched a new range of glassware that was produced in a completely different way. Sheet glass was rolled to the required thickness, then decorated by transfer or texture and finally moulded round a form in the kiln. This method produced very thin glassware that was extremely light and delicate, and which allowed scope for unlimited surface designs. The new range was just right for the outburst of decorative designs which started with the Festival of Britain in 1951. The range was called 'Fiesta', and it was an immediate success, remaining in production until the closure of the factory in 1981.

The first designs in the 'Fiesta' range were called 'Lace' and 'Greco'. These were produced as a series of shallow bowls and dishes in a single colour – usually white with a gold edge on the clear, fine glass. 'Swirl' was the first full tableware set range. It had a modern, linear, pinwheel type of pattern. The set consisted of glasses, a tray, various small dishes and the very tall giraffe-necked jug, which had no handle and an asymmetrical rim.

A large number of designs followed throughout the 1960s and 1970s, encouraged by the simplicity of production methods which designers needed very little understanding of to use. Many designs were by named designers. Some were wildly coloured, and some were textured, but all of them had the contemporary feel of the time. Handkerchief vases, which were a bestseller, were first produced in the 1950s as copies of the Italian Venini fazzoletti vases of the time. These were in production until the factory finally closed in 1981.

'Britannia' divided dish and covered cheese dish, made by Chance Brothers in the late 1940s.

FACING PAGE Chance Brothers glass carafe in an asymmetric shape named 'Giraffe', with assorted matching tableware, all in the 'Swirl' pattern. The fabric is by Marimekko.

1950 ~ 1959
The 'New Look' Decade

'Black and White' vase by Nelson Pottery.

The 1950s saw the birth of a new enthusiasm for life that was full of positive expectation and potential. Britain was in a stage of postwar reconstruction and regeneration, and by the early '50s, with the gradual lifting of rationing, the British people were ready to embrace all things new and forward-looking. New materials that had developed during the war were now adapted to civilian use, and new scientific discoveries were used for design inspiration. Wartime symbols and images were restyled to promote a feeling of safety, rather than threat, in what the author Bevis Hillier describes as 'The Oyster Principle' – the transformation of a piece of grit into a pearl. Pictures of carnival balloons replaced those of bombers, and figures of mermaids made the seas seem friendly rather than threatening. Beaches were cleared of barbed wire and mines, and people flocked to the seaside once again for the great British picnic.

Enjoyment and escapism were wholeheartedly embraced, and this was reflected in the design imagery of the period. Fairground and circus themes, ballet, Surrealist art, Bohemian Paris street scenes, French Poodles, artists' palettes and wild fruit and flowers inspired by the headdresses of the 'Brazilian Bombshell' Carmen Miranda were all translated into textiles, ceramics, wallpapers and household objects. These themes, along with the new science-inspired designs of atomic structures and the space race were the signatures of 1950s design.

America had surged forward in manufacturing in the immediate postwar period, and by the early 1950s Britain was open to the influences and ideas that were already popular in the USA. Britain wanted part of the 'American Dream', and new kitchens, brightly coloured plastic utensils and televisions were in increasing demand in British households.

The coronation inspired a new patriotic optimism, and the crowning of the young queen was an event watched by the entire nation on new TVs. Ideas put on hold during the war began to take off again. At the World's Fair in New York in 1939, 'streamlining' had come into its own as a design concept. Industrial designers were established as the people who would pioneer the idea of 'building the world of tomorrow', encouraging a belief in technology and a faith in the future in the minds of the population. The Festival of Britain stood as a symbol of freedom from wartime restrictions, and new ideas flourished and grew in many directions throughout the 1950s.

Popular design began to diversify from the establishment-controlled ideas of 'good' design, and manufacturers catered to all budgets and levels of taste. Everything was clean, bright and new, and described as 'contemporary'. Christian Dior's 'New Look', launched in 1947, took hold in the fashion world after much controversy over the extravagant use of materials in a Europe that was still under rationing. His sculptural, hourglass shape was echoed in other areas of design such as light fittings and glassware. In men's fashion, the desire for a more carefree existence was echoed in the 'Teddy boy' look, supposedly based on a revival of the flamboyant style of gentlemen's dress in the Edwardian era.

Immediately after the war, Britain had its first truly socialist government of the 20th century, but by 1951 the Conservatives were back in power, and Sir Winston Churchill, hero of the war, became the prime minister. There were rifts in the Labour party over where they fitted into this new, affluent society. The Conservatives remained in office throughout the decade, and in 1957 Harold McMillan was able to say, 'You never had it so good.' Foreign travel once more became an option, and more people began to take their holidays abroad.

The start of the 1950s had been dominated by American influences, but as the decade wore on, a much more European look began to prevail. Scandinavian design, which had been developing along its own course through the early 20th century, now began to increase in popularity throughout the rest of Europe. Its modernist approach had influenced the USA in the 1930s, and was further developed by the American ceramic artists Russell Wright and Eva Zeisel, who in turn strongly influenced British manufacturers, most notably Midwinter, throughout the 1950s. Italian style in fashion, interior design and industrial design was beginning to establish itself as an enormous influence, from the sought-after Vespa and Lambretta motor scooters to stiletto heels and winkle-picker shoes. Coffee bars sprang up everywhere around the country and became the place to be seen in the new, youthful culture, and 'expresso' became the new buzz word. Italian style was cool, as was jazz. If you weren't a Teddy boy, you had to be a beatnik.

Restaurants were increasing in number and variety. Italian, Greek and Middle Eastern restaurants reflected the public's memories of hot summer holidays. Chinese and Indian restaurants brought a taste of the East. The more traditional French and English establishments were now catering to a more knowledgeable and sophisticated clientele with higher expectations. Intimate family TV dinners were part of the new, 'contemporary' way of life, and entertaining at home was more on the level of a cocktail party rather than a full-blown dinner party. As the decade progressed, however, Elizabeth David's books on European cooking encouraged people to try making for themselves the foods they had enjoyed on holiday, and the seeds were sown for the 'dinner party decade' of the 1960s.

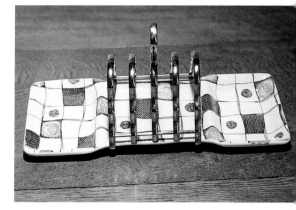

Midwinter 'Homespun' pattern toast rack designed by Jessie Tait.

ABOVE AND BELOW Babbacombe Pottery, Torquay.

The Cocktail Party

Cocktail parties at home were adopted in the 1950s as a stylish way of entertaining large numbers of guests without the need to cook elaborate meals. Everything became a matter of assembly and presentation, so there was an upsurge in recipe books and leaflets that were completely devoted to the party snack and the cocktail hors-d'oeuvre. For the busy hostess without the time to prepare her own canapés, there was always the cocktail sausage, the cheese football and the ubiquitous olive, and the only implement a guest required for these was a cocktail stick. Martinis were popular drinks, and they became even more fashionable when Ian Fleming's fictional hero, the cool and stylish James Bond, first declared that he preferred his Martini 'shaken, not stirred'. Some guests might have preferred a Babycham – 'the genuine champagne perry' – a well-advertised drink for the fashionable young lady.

Cheese rationing ended in the UK in 1954, and the cheese and wine party became another popular way of entertaining at home. Cubes of cheddar cheese were impaled on cocktail sticks with a selection of pickled onions, gherkins and cocktail cherries. Crisps were everywhere. Although Smiths first started producing potato crisps in the 1920s, it was in the 1950s that they became an essential addition to any party and the trend for crisps and dips was firmly established. A 1950s *Good Housekeeping* leaflet devoted to crisps has recipes for everything from snacks to main courses with crunchy crisp topping, and even chocolate-covered biscuits decorated with crushed crisps!

The spotted glass handkerchief vase was a shape peculiar to the 1950s. Jetique glass vases by Bagley of Knottingley. Black plate with red edge by Seguso of Italy. Curtain fabric by David Whitehead.

Cocktail Hour. The woven plastic bucket chair, the Formica®-topped, boomerang-shaped table and 'contemporary style' textiles were all part of the exuberant and fanciful new optimism and celebratory spirit of the early '50s.

KIR FELIX

This drink is named after Abbe Felix Kir, the wartime Mayor of Dijon and Resistance hero, which probably places its origin to sometime after 1945. The original recipe was from Burgundy and called for 1 tsp. crème de cassis in a wine glass topped up with chilled white Burgundy, but any dry white wine will suffice. Kir Royale uses champagne and should be served in a champagne flute.

SINGAPORE SLING

This cocktail was reputedly invented at Raffles Hotel in Singapore. Other recipes have fewer ingredients but still have plenty of kick! This recipe is one of the simpler versions.

Shake together 2 oz. gin, 1 oz. cherry brandy, 1 oz. lemon juice and ¼ oz. grenadine and pour into a large goblet. Add soda water to taste.

Spotted Chance glasses on a tray printed with cocktail recipes.
BELOW A coaster from the Raffles Hotel in Singapore, where the barman Ngiam Tong Boon invented the Singapore Sling in 1915.

DRY MARTINI

Opinions vary as to how 'dry' a dry Martini should be. Apparently, the Martini was first made with equal measures of gin and dry vermouth, but this evolved generally to about four parts gin to one part vermouth. Some people prefer a mixture of six parts gin to one part vermouth, and connoisseurs of the very dry Martini would add only a spot of vermouth to the gin. Sir Winston Churchill recommended only glancing at a vermouth bottle across the room! In any event, all of the ingredients and implements used for a Martini should be very well chilled. The drink may be served with a twist of lemon or an olive if desired.

ADVOCAAT

This is an old family recipe for advocaat, found written on the back of an envelope. Its origin is uncertain, but it was a popular Christmas gift, bottled in old White & McKay whisky bottles that gave an added dimension to the flavour. You could also enjoy it with lemonade – a concoction known as a Snowball.

3 eggs
3 lemons
1 gill brandy
1 gill cream
½ lb. demerara sugar

Break eggs and shells into a bowl. Pour lemon juice over. Leave for 48 hours. Strain into a jug. Add cream, brandy and sugar. Stir and bottle and drink!

I had the Original
SINGAPORE SLING
at **RAFFLES HOTEL**
It was created by barman
Ngiam Tong Boon in 1915
at the **LONG BAR**
It is made with Beefeater Gin,
Peter Heering, D.O.M., Cointreau,
Pineapple and Lime Juice,
Angostura

Fabric cushion designed by Robert Stewart and embroidered by Kath White.

Festival of Britain glass made by the United Glass Bottle Company.

THE FESTIVAL OF BRITAIN

The initial concept for the Festival of Britain began with a letter from Gerald Barry, the Editor of the *News Chronicle*, to the President of the Board of Trade, Sir Stafford Cripps, on 14 September 1945 suggesting the staging of an exhibition to mark the centenary of the 1851 International Exhibition. The event that he envisioned would promote British industry, encourage overseas trade and attract foreign tourists. Cripps replied, 'Perhaps it might be a good idea.' Shortly afterward, Gerald Barry became the Director General of the Festival of Britain. Gordon Russell was appointed Director of the Council of Industrial Design in 1947, and he played a very significant role in all aspects of the organisation and visual identity of the Festival of Britain. Hugh Casson became the Director of Architecture.

The festival was a herald of the future as much as it was a celebration of the past and present. The first meeting of the Council of the Festival of Britain was held on 31 May 1948. It was addressed by Princess Elizabeth, who encouraged the council to set the highest standards in everything they planned and to make the festival 'a beginning of many good things'. Publicity before the show involved a promotional tour of Europe by four red double-decker buses from London, fitted out with models and plans, which were seen by more than 122,000 people.

The Festival Pattern Group, which included 28 companies, was formed to promote a new approach to pattern making, inspired by science and the formation of crystals. Technical diagrams of blood cells, hormones, minerals, chemicals and synthetic compounds, depicted using either 'dot and line' or 'Patterson map' methods, were commissioned from scientists and circulated to members of the Festival Pattern Group for reference. Many products were illustrated in *The Souvenir Book of Crystal Designs* that was published for the festival.

The main event was in London's South Bank, but there were also major sites in Glasgow and Ulster. Manufacturers had been invited to submit goods for a selection process. Chance Brothers, a successful entrant, produced sheets of figured and rolled glass for screens and shelves in one of the pavilions. The festival was very popular as a 'feel good' event for the public, and it attracted approximately 8 million visitors. In the early 1950s, Gordon Russell and the Council of Industrial Design liaised with a new generation of designers and architects who came to dominate ideology and practice in the 1950s and 1960s. Many of them went on to teach in art and design colleges. The Royal College of Art pioneered for Britain a new profession in 'industrial design', a concept born in the USA and established at the New York World's Fair.

When the Design Council Showroom opened in Haymarket in 1956, its stock list of approved designs – started for the 'Britain Can Make It' Exhibition of 1946 and extended in 1951 for the Festival of Britain – became the basis for the Design Index, a photographic record of approved designs available to professionals and public alike.

HAWKHEAD *EDINBURGH*

These tankards are extremely ornate, each design being printed in four colours and designed to hold one pint. In the Crinan design the colours are mainly blue or red, and in the Kintyre design blue or lilac both with black overprinting.

PRICE 21'6 each ex works plus purchase tax.

In a more humorous vein these tankards are printed in three colours, these being lilac and dark grey, or tangerine and pale grey, both with black overprinting.

ROBERT STEWART

Robert Stewart studied during the 1940s at the Glasgow School of Art, where he later became an inspiring and influential teacher. He was appointed as Head of the Department of Printed Textiles in 1949, and he held this position until 1978, when he was appointed as Head of Design. Three years later, he became the Deputy Director of the school, and remained in this position until his retirement in 1984.

During the late 1940s and '50s, Stewart also worked as a painter and a freelance designer of textiles, graphics and ceramics. His work for Liberty of London included textiles in the contemporary style, silk scarves and even wastepaper baskets. He also made ceramic tiles and designed table-mats, greetings cards, wrapping papers and posters for the Edinburgh Tapestry Company. He also designed tapestries and murals, one of which hangs today in the departure lounge of Prestwick Airport. The ceramics were produced in Stewart's own workshop. Some were marketed under his own name through Liberty and Primavera. His storage jars were a popular item throughout the 1960s.

CLOCKWISE FROM TOP Brochure for Robert Stewart ceramic tankards. Fabric designed by Robert Stewart. A ceramic tankard by Robert Stewart.

CORONATION CHICKEN

Opinion varies on the exact origins of the dish known as Coronation Chicken. According to some sources, it was created by Rosemary Hume and Constance Spry for a lunch served in the Great Hall at Westminster School to over 300 overseas dignitaries after the coronation ceremony in Westminster Abbey in 1953.

The dish became instantly popular and was made for many coronation celebrations by people throughout Britain. It was an ideal buffet dish, as it could be prepared in advance and eaten cold, leaving people free to enjoy the festivities. There are many adaptations of the dish, as individual cooks have created their own versions, although the basic method remains the same as in 1953.

The chicken was simmered in water with herbs and vegetables until tender and left to cool. It was then cut into small pieces and dressed with a creamy mayonnaise flavoured with curry powder and lemon juice. Cooked dried apricots were added to the dressing, which was then sprinkled with chopped walnuts. A more interesting flavour can be achieved with the addition of fresh mango and mango chutney in place of the apricots.

Margaret Stewart fabric with Coronation Chicken on an 'Oakwood' pattern plate by Washington Pottery of Hanley.

Jacob & Co. advertisement featuring a commemorative coronation biscuit tin.

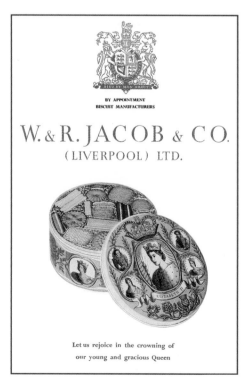

LEMON MERINGUE PIE

This pie requires fresh eggs and fresh lemons, and so it became a favourite in the 1950s when these foods again became more widely available after the rationing and shortages of the '40s.

Filling
*Grated zest and juice of 1 large
    lemon
Water
³⁄₄ oz. cornflour
1 oz. plain flour
3 oz. caster sugar
1 oz. butter
2 egg yolks*

Combine the lemon juice with enough water to make up ¹⁄₂ pint. Blend in the flour and cornflour, and pour the mixture into a saucepan. Add the lemon zest, butter and sugar.

Stir over a low heat until it thickens. Remove from the heat and whisk in the egg yolks. Return to the heat and cook slowly for 2 minutes. Put the filling into a pastry case.

Meringue
*2 egg whites
3 oz. caster sugar*

Whisk the egg whites until they form soft peaks. Gradually beat the sugar into the egg white, then spread this over the lemon filling, making sure that the meringue covers the filling completely. Bake for 1 hour. Allow to cool and chill in the fridge until required.

MIDWINTER POTTERY IN THE 1950S

The Midwinter pottery was founded in 1910 by W.R. Midwinter, and by the 1930s it was one of the largest potteries in the country. Production was cut back during the war, but the factory was then modernised and expanded. By 1951, it had achieved record sales, although these were for classic and 'Utility' shapes.

Roy Midwinter, the son of the founder, was responsible for revitalising the company when he rejoined it in 1952 after five years of service in the RAF. During a sales trip to Canada, where response to the company's new ranges was disappointing, he was advised to look at the new design styles being produced in the USA. Looking at American design, he was inspired by the 'organic modernism' of Russell Wright and Eva Zeisel. On returning to the UK, he promoted this innovative look, and Midwinter designed and produced a completely new range in a remarkably short space of time.

In February 1953, the company launched 'Stylecraft', which was timed to coincide with the end of the government restrictions and the 'Utility' period. The range was streamlined and modern, and designed to appeal to a new, young, forward-looking market both at home and overseas. Within 12 months, 60% of the company's total sales were for the new styles, which comprised 40 new shapes and 36 contemporary patterns, most of which were designed by the in-house designer Jessie Tait. Her spotted 'Domino' pattern was produced in red, blue, green and black. Much of Tait's inspiration came from textiles, including patterns such as the plaid 'homeweave' – another look much produced throughout the '50s by various companies.

Artists and designers were also commissioned. The wildlife artist Peter Scott produced a 'Wild Geese' range. Eva Zeisel's 'Tomorrow's Classic' range was the inspiration for Midwinter's 'Fashion shape', launched in 1954, and Terence Conran's 'Nature Study' was produced in this shape. Hugh Casson's 'Riviera' was one of the most popular designs of the era. It was later reworked as a 'Fashion shape' range named 'Cannes'. One of the most striking patterns was Jessie Tait's much-imitated black and white 'Zambesi' design, which was based on an earlier version in the 'Stylecraft' range named 'Cloudline'. John Russell produced a number of designs for the 'Fashion shape' in more traditional, naturalistic and illustrative patterns. 'Riverside', a transfer print of bulrushes, cow parsley, leaves and grasses on dark green holloware, sold in very large quantities and remained in production for more than ten years.

In the 1950s, plastics were gaining a degree of acceptance in the British market, and W.R. Midwinter launched its range of melamine around 1958. It was based on the 'Fashion shape' and made by the Streetly Manufacturing Company, using a powder called 'Melmex'. It was available in eight colours – four 'modern' and four pastel – and initially one pattern, a blue and white floral named 'Meadow Flowers'. It carried a 12-month guarantee against breakage, chipping and cracking, but this proved to be a little overambitious. Its most obvious use was as picnic ware, but even for this purpose it did not overtake ceramics in popularity, as it was equally expensive.

Midwinter 'Fashion shape' tableware.

Midwinter 'Mink Rose' casserole.

Hugh Casson 'Riviera' tea ware.

Italian-style Dinner

Magazine features and product advertisements of the mid-1950s encouraged readers to plan dinners with a 'Continental' theme to entertain their friends. Simply-cooked French and Italian dishes could be accompanied by appropriate wines to give the correct ambience and style whilst remaining within the means of those on a low budget. The meal might be served on one of Midwinter's new 'Fashion shape' dinner services, which had the latest contemporary look.

Our dinner party has an Italian theme. Spaghetti and Meatballs are accompanied by Grilled Aubergines with a Garlic and Herb Crust. The dinnerware is the 'Carmen' pattern in Midwinter's 'Fashion shape'.

SPAGHETTI AND QUICK ITALIAN MEATBALLS

Olive oil for frying
1 large onion, finely chopped
2-3 cloves garlic, finely chopped
4-6 Italian sausages, skins removed and each cut into 4 pieces
1 chopped red chilli
1 large tin of chopped tomatoes, with 1 teaspoon sugar
1 glass red wine
Salt and freshly-ground black pepper
Parmesan cheese
Long spaghetti

Fry the onion for several minutes until soft, add the garlic and sausage and brown. Add chilli, tomatoes, red wine and seasoning, and cook for about 30 minutes. If possible, leave to cool and reheat just before serving with spaghetti, which has been freshly cooked in boiling salted water. Top with freshly grated Parmesan cheese.

Spaghetti and Quick Italian Meatballs on a 'Carmen' plate by Midwinter.

GRILLED AUBERGINE SLICES WITH A GARLIC AND HERB CRUST

1 small aubergine
Olive oil
2 oz. melted butter
Crumbs made from 2 medium
  slices of bread
1 clove of garlic, crushed
2 tablespoons of finely chopped
  parsley

Cut a small aubergine diagonally into ¼ slices. Brush with olive oil and grill on both sides for several minutes until gently browning. Combine the other ingredients with the melted butter and spread this mixture over the aubergine slices. Grill for several minutes until the crumb coating becomes slightly crisp.

Dinner of Spaghetti and Quick Italian Meatballs, with Grilled Aubergines with a Garlic and Herb Crust, served on Midwinter's 'Carmen' dinner service, designed by John Russell in the 'Fashion shape'.

The 1950s Picnic

Car ownership rose from 2,000,000 to 5,500,000 during the '50s, and led to the first motorways and the first traffic jams. Trips to the country and the seaside were popular family outings, and picnic baskets became necessary purchases for stylish outdoor eating. Sandwiches, crisps and cups of tea were consumed in all weathers. British beach barbecues began in a modest way with the frying of sausages in a small pan over a driftwood fire; sausages never tasted as good when eaten at home, even if they had been prepared in a Sunbeam electric frying pan.

Sandwiches were the basic mainstay of the picnic, with fillings of all types to suit all tastes. Potted sandwich pastes were available in a variety of flavours,

mostly involving meat or fish. Fillings might be sweet as well as savoury; banana or date sandwiches were sometimes included in the picnic basket. Scotch eggs and individual pork pies were often eaten with tomatoes or even coleslaw, if using a picnic set that included knives and forks. Not only tea and coffee but also soup could be kept hot in thermos flasks for the cold-weather picnics that were a common occurrence in the British climate. Desserts such as fruit set in jelly could be transported in individual covered plastic containers. Fresh fruit was popular served with chunks of cheese.

QUICHE LORRAINE (OR HAM AND EGG PIE)

The name *quiche* was practically unknown in Britain in the early '50s, although Elizabeth David included a recipe for Quiche Lorraine in her book *French Country Cooking* in 1951. The idea began to catch on, and it became a popular picnic option, as it was relatively easy to handle in an outdoor setting. Quiche has the potential for a huge variety of fillings, but this was the first option to become widely accepted.

This recipe includes cheese, which was not one of Elizabeth David's original ingredients, but which was often included in other contemporary recipes. The base can be made with homemade or frozen shortcrust pastry. Most recipes suggest that the pastry be baked blind for about 15 to 20 minutes before the filling is added, but others recommend that everything be baked in one operation.

Filling
6 rashers of grilled or fried
   bacon,
   cut into small pieces
6 oz. grated cheese
2 eggs and 2 egg yolks
½ pint of single cream
Black pepper and salt to taste

Preheat the oven to 200ºC. Spread the bacon and cheese onto the shortcrust pastry base. Combine the other ingredients and pour over the bacon and cheese. Return to the oven and bake for a further 25 to 30 minutes, until the filling has just set. Serve hot or cold.

Any meal a square meal

and thank Hovis for that

An advertisement for Hovis from the 1950s.

FACING PAGE: TOP Frying sausages on the beach.
FACING PAGE: BELOW Picnic hamper filled with melaware.

ABOVE Quiche Lorraine, a sandwich and crisps.

RIGHT A Schweppes advertisement from the 1950s.
FAR RIGHT: TOP Glass lemonade set with gold spot transfers.
FAR RIGHT: BELOW Blue lemonade set with gold stripes.

HOMEMADE LEMONADE

The fabulous new Kenwood Chef could perform a myriad of kitchen tasks. The juice extractor and liquidiser attachments were very useful in the production of home-made lemonade. Here is our recipe, adapted from the Kenwood Chef recipe booklet which accompanied all purchases of the new miracle machines.

1 lemon
1 ½ lbs sugar
2 pints water
1 oz. citric acid

Liquidise the zest of the lemon with ½ pint of water. Place mixture in a pan with the remaining water and bring to the boil. Extract the juice from the lemon. Add the juice, sugar and citric acid to the pan. Stir well, then remove from heat. Allow to cool completely. When cold, strain through a sieve and bottle. Serve diluted with water for still lemonade or with soda water for the sparkling variety.

GRAPEFRUIT
Schweppes
SQUASH

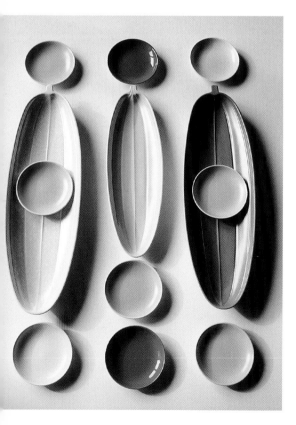

A Poole hors-d'oeuvre plate.

Poole cucumber plates and relish dishes in various 'Twintone' colours.

POOLE POTTERY

The original pottery company in Poole was founded in 1873 by Jesse Carter, whose sons formed Carter & Co. in 1901. They produced architectural ceramics and a variety of candlesticks, vases, dishes and jardinières, including ranges for Liberty of London designed by Archibald Knox. From 1914 onward, the Carters developed a relationship with Roger Fry's Omega Workshops and artists such as Duncan Grant and Vanessa Bell.

After World War One, the demand for decorative vases grew, and the company's first Handcraft Pottery catalogue was issued in 1920, featuring ware by James Radley Young. Harold Stabler, an artist, designer and goldsmith, was invited by Charles and Cyril Carter to become a partner. These partners were joined by the potter John Adams and his wife Truda, who was also an artist and designer and who later became the wife of Cyril Carter.

In 1921, Carter, Stabler and Adams was formed as an independent but wholly owned subsidiary, producing pottery in the modern style by the best traditional methods. The company also employed Dora Batty, Phoebe Stabler (wife of Charles) and Minnie McLeish (sister of Phoebe), and freelance designers such as Edward Bawden and Olive Bourne. Although production of pieces by these artists was small, it established Poole's tradition of working with contemporary artists and designers – a tradition that continued all through the 20th century.

John Adams's 'Streamline' tableware was designed in the mid-1930s, although this style, with its modernist look, two-tone finish and vellum glaze, was very much associated with Poole throughout the '50s and '60s. It became known as 'Twintone' and established Poole as a major tableware producer. In 1950, Lucien Myers took over from John Adams as Managing Director. Alfred Burgess Read, an established industrial designer, was appointed as Head of the Design Unit, which included Design Assistant Ruth Pavely and Senior Thrower Guy Sydenham, who had been with the pottery since 1932. Read and Pavely created a series of abstract patterns inspired by contemporary textiles and Scandinavian style.

In 1953, as a celebration of Coronation Year, Poole Pottery was reopened to the public. In 1955, the Princess Royal visited Poole and was presented with a specially-made vase in the new style. Alfred Read's daughter Ann designed a limited edition of plaques and plates from 1955 to 1956. In the late '50s, Poole began to look in new directions, appointing Robert Jefferson as Resident Designer in 1958. Whilst maintaining the company's modernist association, he developed new styles for the 1960s and '70s, concentrating first on domestic ranges and new oven-to-table wares. 'Contour' became the new contemporary 'Twintone' shape, but it was also produced in printed patterns. The stacking 'Compact' shape of the mid-1960s remained in production in various patterns until 1992, developing from the chestnut and snow-white version of 1965, through the stoneware look of the '70s and on into printed patterns throughout the '80s and into the '90s.

Robert Jefferson continued the Poole tradition of bridging the gap

between studio pottery and commercial production. In January 1961, he worked with Guy Sydenham to produce individual pieces to relaunch the Poole Studios. These were further developed, and the resulting 'Delphis Collection' was launched by Sir Gordon Russell at an exhibition at Heal's in 1963. It was marketed as hand-painted from 1965 onward.

Freeform Poole designed by Alfred Read and Guy Sydenham, painted by Gwen Haskins.

The influence of the ranges produced in the company's Craft Section, officially reopened in 1966, carried through to the tablewares designed by Sydenham and Morris in the late '60s. Although the range was withdrawn in 1980, it is currently being revived and reinvented, and contemporary versions are now on sale. The dark-coloured 'Aegean' range, created with techniques developed by Leslie Elsden, was introduced in 1970.

'Twintone' coffee and tea pots, and blue salt and pepper shakers.

In 1963, the company was bought by Pilkington Tiles and officially renamed Poole Pottery. The 'Beardsley Collection', developed by Ros Sommerfell and introduced in 1979 to meet the upsurge of interest in Art Nouveau, included a variety of small dishes, plant pots, ginger jars and other giftware items. Robert Jefferson's 'Style' range, designed in 1979, was made throughout the '80s. Various printed patterns for 'Style' were produced, all of which were suitable for microwave and freezer use. Throughout the '80s, many freelance designers were employed in addition to the in-house staff. Robert Welch designed the 'Campden' tableware range, introduced in 1989.

The most significant design input from the 1980s came from the Queensberry Hunt partnership, beginning in 1983 with the 'Flair' tableware range. The next year saw the introduction of the 'Calypso' range of decorative ware in pastel colours, which was developed in a variety of finishes including black and white pearlized lustre. The fluted 'Corinthian' range and the marbled 'Cello' range followed. 'Astral' tableware was introduced in 1989. Designs in blue sponge ware, initially created by the partnership Hinchcliff & Barber in 1986, and Alan Clarke's 'Dorset Fruit' pattern formed the basis of Poole's image in the '90s.

A management buy-out in 1992, led by Peter Miles, released the company from Pilkington Tiles's 30-year ownership. David Queensberry was appointed as Design Director in 1992. He acted as Director from 1994 to 1997, and artists Sarah Chalmers, Anita Harris, Nicola Wiehahn and Kate Byrne worked with the new design team.

DENBY POTTERY

Pottery has been produced in Denby since the beginning of the 19th century, when a clay seam of exceptional quality was discovered in the town during the construction of a turnpike road. William Bourne and his son Joseph established their pottery on the site, and production of salt-glazed earthenware jars and bottles began in 1809. Towards the end of the century, as glass became a cheaper and more popular medium for these items, production began to switch to ranges of kitchen ware, developed in richly coloured glazes which became the recognised Denby style.

By the 1920s, pie dishes, jelly moulds, colanders, hot water 'bottles' and other household items formed only part of the range. Giftware was also developed, including decorative vases, bowls and tobacco jars, and the 'Danesby Ware' stamp was introduced. The 'Danesby Ware' ranges were acclaimed for their innovative and expert use of glaze effects, which were usually difficult to achieve on stoneware. Albert Colledge, who had joined the pottery in 1904 at the age of 13, became the first in-house designer in 1923.

In the 1930s, high quality ornamental ware was the focus of production. 'Electric Blue' and 'Orient Ware' were the classic giftware colourings, and a range of animal novelties was also produced at this time. 'Manor Green', a range named after the colour of its new glaze, was based on rounded oven-to-table ware shapes designed by Donald Gilbert in 1938 and 1939. Denby was not given permission to export during the war, and production of coloured domestic ware was gradually phased out during these years. 'Utility' articles for the domestic market were mainly glazed in mahogany or plain brown. 'Manor Green' and 'Cottage Blue' resumed production after the war, and the new 'Homestead Brown' colourway was added in 1953. All three remained popular until the 1980s.

Glyn Colledge left school in 1938 at the age of 16 and joined his father at the Denby pottery as a trainee modeller. Later that year he became a full-time student at the Burslem School of Art in Stoke-on-Trent. The school was run by Gordon Forsyth, who had trained Susie Cooper, Clarice Cliff, Charlotte Rhead and Mabel Leigh. After a period of wartime service in the RAF, Colledge returned to Denby as a trainee designer. He continued his education on a part-time basis over the next 10 years, and eventually became a part-time lecturer at Derby College of Art and Ilkeston College of Further Education. As a trainee designer, he worked and developed several ranges with his father. Gradually he was given more independence, and was allowed to develop a range of studio pottery, each piece of which was signed by hand. In order to avoid purchase tax, each item of the decorative 'Glyn Ware' range was given a functional description.

The factory reconstruction planned during the war was completed in 1951 – just in time for the Festival of Britain. Prestigious new showrooms were built at Denby in a contemporary Scandinavian style, with modern, 'Utility'-style furniture and fittings designed to complement the Denby products. The influence of modern American 'streamlined' shapes was

---

STEAK AND ALE CASSEROLE

2 pounds rump or braising steak
Seasoning and flour
1 large onion
1 carrot, chopped
2 red peppers
A pint of ale

Cut the steak into cubes and toss in the flour and the seasoning. Fry a finely chopped onion in some butter and oil until soft and add the steak. Brown quickly and add the chopped carrot and then enough beer to cover the meat. Transfer to an ovenproof dish if not using oven-to-table cookware. Cook in a medium oven for about 2 hours, adding more beer if necessary. Add 2 finely chopped peppers and cook for another hour, or until the meat is soft.

ABOVE Steak & Ale Casserole.

OPPOSITE PAGE, FROM TOP
'New Glyn Ware' hand-painted dish by Glyn Colledge.
Denby 'Peasant Ware' gravy boat.
Selection of 'Glyn Ware' tableware on a printed table-mat.

apparent in some of the new dinner and tableware ranges. One such range was designed specifically for Eaton's of Canada at the direction of Fred Cooper, the manager of Langley Pottery. It was a great success.

'Peasant Ware', introduced in 1954, combined modern, two-tone influences with the rustic style of hand-decorated patterns used in French pottery. 'Dovedale', which followed in 1955, was dark grey with a bright yellow interior. Albert Colledge's 'Greenwheat' pattern, inspired by the decorative brush strokes of Japanese potters, was introduced in 1956 and it remained one of Denby's bestselling lines for over 20 years.

Tibor Reich, a distinguished and innovative textile designer, set up a small studio pottery to produce black and white ceramics that would complement his bold and colourful fabrics. The studio did not have sufficient capacity to provide for his expanding business, however, and in 1953 he asked Denby to produce his original designs. Denby readily agreed, and the 'Tigo Ware' range became a distinctive part of Denby's production in the 1950s, alongside Glyn Colledge's 'Cheviot' wares. Kenneth Clark was commissioned to update the oven-to-table ware ranges in 1956, and his 'Gourmet', introduced in 1957, was described as 'a classic design for the sophisticated table'. He also designed three series of vases called 'Cotswold', 'Asphodel' and 'Classic', which was not marketed until 1960.

In 1959, Denby took over the Langley Mill pottery, which at first continued to trade under its own name. Then, in 1976 Joseph Bourne and Son Ltd. and Langley Pottery Ltd. were united to form Denby Tableware Ltd.

The 'Dream Kitchen'

All types of plastics were used in the construction and equipping of the most desirable, up-to-the-minute, gadget-filled 'Dream Kitchen' of the 1950s advertisements. Formica®, first invented in 1913, became the most popular of the new, tough, laminated plastics. It was used for tables, work surfaces and cupboards. These new, labour-saving, wipe-clean surfaces came in a range of colours and patterns. Lightweight plastic storage containers, bowls, basins, rubbish bins and all manner of objects were produced in vast quantities in a range of modern, bright colours to complement every kitchen. Even tablecloths and doilies were made from reusable, wipe-clean plastic. The modern housewife never had it so good!

One of the most popular gadgets was the Kenwood Chef mixer, which had multiple attachments for mincing, slicing, juicing, chopping and blending. The Sunbeam electric frying pan was the perfect way to prepare a full English breakfast, and of course the Cona coffee maker was a must for that fresh coffee taste. Traditional items like the Tala kitchen measure were still popular.

Electrical goods accounted for a large proportion of consumer spending, and gas and electric cookers were both popular. Sales of fridges rose enormously from the mid-1950s onward. Those who did not have a separate freezer had to make do with the ice-making compartment of a refrigerator to store the new frozen food products which began to appear on the market. Clarence Birdseye had opened his fast-freezing plant in New York in 1923, but it was not until the 1950s that this type of 'convenience' food started to become popular in the UK. Fish fingers and frozen peas were the most popular items.

The Kenwood Chef food mixer.

BELOW The Sunbeam electric frying pan. A Tala kitchen measure. The Cona coffee maker.

BELOW LEFT A 'Dream Kitchen' from a contemporary advertising leaflet.

Pyrex® dinnerware with spotty tablecloth printed with bowls of salad and knives and forks.

CHILDREN'S TEATIME

'Convenience foods' became the new description of ready-prepared and pre-packaged dishes during the 1950s. This term covered everything from the new frozen dishes to tinned goods which had been available for many decades. Recipe leaflets promoted all sorts of ideas for using tinned and condensed soups as a crucial ingredient of main courses, from curried egg tarts to fish pies and lamb stews, but staples such as tomato soup remained popular in their basic form. Busy mothers could quickly and easily produce a simple three-course meal.

Tomato soup from a tin, frozen fish fingers and peas, followed by tinned fruit and custard made a feast which was a universal favourite with children of all ages.

PYREX®

This new, heat-resistant glass was developed by the American company Corning from the initial pioneering work of Dr Otto Schott and Dr W.C. Taylor. Corning registered the name Pyrex between 1915 and 1917, and patented the invention in 1919. Early Pyrex® casseroles came with pierced metal stands.

New shapes developed throughout the early part of the century, but these were all produced in colourless glass. In 1936, a range of red casseroles was introduced, but the colouring agent was discovered to be poisonous and the range was quickly withdrawn. The opal glass variety with sprayed colour exteriors first appeared in the USA in 1947. Blue, red, green and yellow were the first colours, followed by flamingo pink, turquoise and lime green in the 1950s. Screen-printed patterns were used as decoration from 1956 onwards. 'Snowflake' is perhaps the most familiar one.

In 1921, the Sunderland glass works James A. Jobling acquired the patent rights to produce Corning's Pyrex® in Britain and the British Empire, excluding Canada. This move was a great success for the company, which expanded its factory in order to meet the demand for production. In 1954, Corning acquired 40% of the James A. Jobling company and it took full control of the company in 1973. Then in 1994, Corning sold the factory and the Pyrex® manufacturing rights to the Newell Company, which also owned Anchor Hocking, another major producer of this type of ware.

Throughout the '50s there was an increasing demand for Pyrex®. The first UK line of Pyrex® 'Colourware' was introduced in 1952 in the colours blue, red, yellow and green. The first UK 'Opal ware' version was created for the canteen trade in 1954 and released to the domestic market in 1957. It was decorated in a variety of patterns; the 'Gaiety' range was one of the most popular. The '50s was undoubtedly the era of coloured and decorated Pyrex®, and although patterned ware continued into the 1960s and '70s, today's market has returned mainly to clear glass production.

Assorted Pyrex® with Formica®-topped table and plastic-covered chairs.

A blue Pyrex® bowl with lemons.

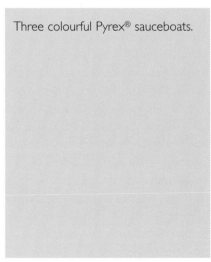

Three colourful Pyrex® sauceboats.

ELIZABETH DAVID

Elizabeth David was the most influential English writer on food of the 20th century. Born in England in 1913 as one of four daughters of Conservative MP Rupert Gwynne and the Hon. Stella Gwynne, she spent time living with a French family while studying French history and literature at the Sorbonne in Paris. She left for the Mediterranean before the Second World War with Charles Gibson Cowan, met and befriended the writer Norman Douglas, and lived for several months on a Greek island. She was then evacuated to Egypt, where she worked for the Admiralty and the Ministry of Information. She married in Egypt and then moved to India, returning to England in 1946.

Elizabeth David began her writing career in postwar Britain. She brought a new passion for sunlight and simply cooked, fresh food to a country that was still in the grip of rationing. Her book *Mediterranean Food* was first published in 1950, followed in 1951 by *French Country Cooking*. David's *Italian Food* was published in 1954, *Summer Cooking* in 1955 and *French Provincial Cooking* in 1960. Auberon Waugh said of her, 'She has brought about a greater change in English life than any other woman this

Mushrooms, garlic, eggs and other fresh ingredients, with Camembert and Denby 'Peasant Ware'.

A kitchen in the French country style.

Moules Mariniere in classic French soup bowls with a copy of Elizabeth David's *French Country Cooking*.

century'. Her friend Lawrence Durrell wrote to her that a French devotee had told him she was the Jane Austen of cookery writers.

David's kitchen shop opened in Pimlico in 1965, providing her readers with the essential *batterie de cuisine* in which she so firmly believed. Most of her books included a chapter devoted to this subject. There was no need for unnecessary clutter, but she encouraged her readers not to 'hamper your cooking and waste time and materials through lack of the right tools for the job'. At the shop, assistants gave detailed advice on various types and sizes of knives, saucepans, casseroles, terrines, fish kettles and gratin dishes. Highly recommended were French *mouli* food mills for puréeing, a *mandoline* for finely slicing vegetables and a *hachoire* or *mezzaluna* – the half-moon-shaped curved blade so useful for the fine chopping of herbs. A good pair of scales, a measuring jug and a pliable palette knife were considered necessities, along with a selection of wooden spoons, kitchen scissors, various sizes of strainers, a large selection of mixing bowls, airtight plastic boxes and a clock.

Elizabeth David established in Britain the idea of the kitchen as a place to eat and entertain as well as to cook. She promoted the belief that the kitchen should be the most comforting and comfortable room in the house, and that as much time and effort as possible should be devoted to making it so.

MOULES MARINIERE

The best tasting mussels are those you have gathered yourself, and the preparation is all part of the experience!

Allow about 1 pint of mussels per person plus a few extra, in case some have to be discarded. Clean them by placing them in a bowl of cold water, covered with a damp cloth, for 2 to 3 hours. Throw away any that are opened or broken. Preferably under running cold water, scrape and beard the mussels and place them in a fresh basin of cold water. They should be rinsed several times, as it is important to get rid of any grit or sand.

For Moules Mariniere, the mussels are cooked in white wine infused with parsley and several shallots. Place the mussels in a wide pan with a small amount of wine and the chopped shallots and parsley. Put the pan on a moderate heat, moving the mussels around gently to ensure even cooking. When they start to open, they are ready to eat. This should take only about 10 minutes. Overcooking spoils them. Discard any which do not open.

The liquor can be strained through muslin cloth to remove any last traces of grit and used as a stock for soup or risotto. Serve the mussels in individual bowls and provide extra bowls for the debris!

SCANDINAVIAN DESIGN

The roots of the success of Scandinavian design in the 20th century lay partly in the Svenska Slojdforeningen, the Society for Industrial Design. It was founded in 1845 to bring about improvements in Swedish handicrafts and industry through cooperation between artists. In this way, it aimed to bring about a change in society's taste levels by developing culture within the home.

In 1899, Ellen Kay published a book called *Beauty for All*, which promoted the work of Carl Larsson. Larsson's paintings and photographs of his home in Sindborn in Sweden were very popular, and sold widely throughout Europe at this time. The simplicity of these interiors was refreshing and new, after the heavy, superficial decoration of the 19th century, and it related closely to the Arts and Crafts movement led by William Morris in Britain after the Victorian era.

In 1914, the Swedish Society of Craft and Design (SSCD) opened an agency promoting contact between artists and craftsmen who were interested in working in industry. This was another move to highlight the importance of combining craft tradition with industrial manufacture and social reform. To promote this idealism in modern design, the SSCD sponsored an exhibition in 1917 called the 'Home Exhibition' in an effort to bring these elements into focus. The exhibition included 23 furnished interiors intended for model homes for the Swedish working class. The Scandinavians took little part in the decorative style in Europe that was embodied by the Exhibition of Decorative Arts in Paris in 1925, but the work of Simon Gate and Edvard Hald on the Orrefors Glass stand was widely admired for its own individual style.

Another exhibition in 1930, organised by the Society for Industrial Design, marked a breakthrough in functional design, The Stockholm Exhibition illustrated the concept of modernism in Sweden by showing proposals for modern homes, public housing and cheap, mass-produced furniture, combining progressive design with social reform. Scandinavian Modern was born – a light, simple style in glass, ceramics and silver. The style was easy to use and cherish, and free from heavy decoration. It was exhibited and admired at world events and fairs throughout the 1930s. These ideas, conceived in the 1930s, took another 20 years to become established as concepts for 'good design for the mass of the population'. In the wake of the Second World War, a new energy had emerged within modern design which at last would take the Scandinavian ideals to the rest of the world.

The 1950s saw a boom in consumerism which appreciated the simple, gentle but still very contemporary style that was being promoted in Scandinavia. Finland was at the heart of this movement, with a strong wave of design activity which quickly spread throughout Europe and the USA. The deceptive simplicity of the work of Tapio Wirkkala and Timo Sarpaneva symbolised a movement which was based on natural, organic forms that were exaggerated and decontextualised. A return to natural

Three polished rim Stromberg vases.

Rorstrand ice bucket designed by Marianne Westmann.

sources for design, combined with the skill of the craftsman or manufacturer, had at last produced a style that was available to everyone and that would enhance the consumer's quality of life.

The work of the Scandinavian designers continued to be synonymous with good design for the rest of the century. In America, companies such as Dansk were set up to import only Scandinavian goods and distribute them throughout the USA. Eventually, these companies commissioned work that would sell particularly well in the American market. Towards the end of the century, the giant company IKEA, under the guidance of Ingvar Kamprad, dominated the world of inexpensive home-making, building up from its humble roots in rural Sweden in 1946.

Good design was always profitable in Scandinavia throughout the 20th century, thanks to well-financed government support policies and the subsequent rises in living standards. Designers in Scandinavia have always received more recognition for their achievements than in any other European country. Often, designers are treated with the kind of fame reserved for footballers or pop stars in other places.

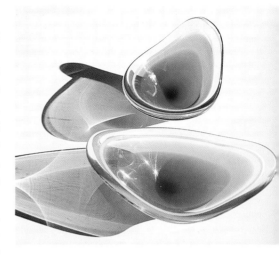

Two pieces of Flygsfors 'Coquille' design by Paul Kedelv.

RORSTRAND

The ceramics company of Rorstrand was founded in Stockholm in 1726. Its earliest managers used imported workmen to produce cobalt blue faïence ware only. The company steadily expanded, and set up the Arabia factory in Finland in 1873 to take advantage of the Russian market. By the end of the 19th century, the company was producing designs in the Art Nouveau style.

In 1917, Edvard Hald joined the company. He worked as a freelance designer for Rorstrand until 1929, producing highly acclaimed work in earthenware ceramic production. In 1926, Rorstrand moved to Gothenburg. It expanded to Lidkoping in 1939, under the art direction of Gunnar Nylund. Rorstrand established a tradition of employing new, young designers of stoneware and porcelain, and thus maintained a contemporary look in some of its ceramics collections, alongside the more traditional ranges.

A Rorstrand fruit bowl.

Marianne Westman was employed by the company in 1956 to design a range of kitchen ceramics under the direction of Nylund. She produced a range called 'Picknick', which consisted of stylised fruit and vegetables drawn in line with bright hand colouring and coordinating self-coloured lids and handles. This range was high quality and very popular, and fitted in well with the bright kitchen and dining rooms during the late 1950s and early '60s. Westman remained with Rorstrand from 1950 until 1971. In 1988, Rorstrand became Rorstrand Gustavsberg in a merger with Gustavsberg, and in 1990 this company was taken over by the Finnish Hackman Group.

Smorgasbord

The smorgasbord luncheon is unique to Scandinavia, and to Sweden in particular. It consists of a decorative and luxurious feast which is unparalleled by other types of meals in quantity and quality. The smorgasbord had humble beginnings. It began over 200 years ago as the introduction to a formal dinner that was similar to Spanish tapas. A table was set in a corner of the dining room or an adjoining room to offer pickles, cheeses and smoked fish delicacies for guests to nibble as they chatted with aquavit and other drinks. As time passed, greater numbers of speciality herring dishes found their way to the table and it became known as the *sillbord* or herring table. Gradually during the 19th century, as more and more dishes were added, what was once a simple buffet had grown to a gargantuan feast of up to 200 different appetisers and a traditional urn or barrel filled with six or seven varieties of schnapps. This was still of course an appetiser – a large meal followed! Despite a completely different lifestyle in modern times, Sweden remains loyal to the smorgasbord. Although the quality is sustained, the quantity remains very much in the pocket of the party giver.

In Sweden it is more or less obligatory to start with one or two salt herring dishes, accompanied by either bread and butter or boiled potatoes. After this, frequent return visits to the table are encouraged, as is collecting a clean plate, knife and fork at each visit. Dishes include: more herring or mackerel; egg and cheese specialities; luxuries such as smoked eel, smoked salmon or seafood; cold meats, pâtés and brawns; hot dishes from a side table; and, finally, some fruit or fruit salad.

A Scandinavian buffet table.

SMØRREBRØD

Danish *smørrebrød*, or open sandwiches, are very close to the heart of every Dane. In the 1960s Oskar Davidson's Restaurant in Copenhagen boasted 600 different varieties for sale, printed on a menu over one and a half metres long!

Here are a few options:

Choose a bread which is firm enough to hold the toppings; rye or wholemeal are the best options. Butter the bread thickly to act as insulation and stop the bread from going soggy.

Toppings can include slices of cold meats and salamis, hard-boiled eggs, pâté, fish, chicken or sliced game.

Garnishes can be as simple or elaborate as you want. They include shellfish such as shelled or dressed prawns, potato salads, eggs, chopped salads, olives, anchovies, caviar, chopped herbs, sliced fruit, chutneys and nuts. Become a smørrebrød artist and create your own Danish delights!

PICKLED SALT HERRING

Clean a large salt herring, remove the head and soak for 12 to 14 hours to remove excess salt. Fillet and cut into diagonal slices about 1 cm thick.

In a saucepan place the marinade ingredients:
6 tablespoonfuls mild vinegar
2 tablespoonfuls water
2 oz. sugar
1 small onion, peeled and finely chopped
6 white peppercorns and 8 whole allspice, coarsely crushed

Bring to the boil slowly. Pour over the fish and refrigerate for at least 4 hours until fully chilled. Garnish with dill and fresh, chopped onion.

SWEDISH MEATBALLS

2 oz. fresh breadcrumbs
½ pint pouring cream
1 lb. mixed minced meats
1 onion, finely chopped
1 beaten egg
Salt, allspice and pepper to taste
3 oz. butter and oil for frying

Soak the breadcrumbs in the cream for 30 minutes until swollen. Mix meats with egg, onion and seasoning and add to the crumb mixture. Form into small balls. Fry in oil and butter until cooked through – about 10 to 15 minutes. Serve hot with lingonberry or cranberry sauce.

There is still a culinary etiquette to eating a smorgasbord and the food should be eaten in the correct order. It is also considered impolite and greedy to pile up one's plate with food, to mix hot and cold foods or to take too much of any one dish. There should be no shortage of clean dishes and cutlery for each return visit to the table. Refilling the dishes from reserves in the kitchen until the meal is over could present quantity problems for a meal in the home, where the smorgasbord is therefore a smaller affair than it is in a restaurant. At home, the meal may start with a few herring dishes, hot potatoes, crispbread, butter and cheese. When a few hot dishes and a dessert are included, the smorgasbord becomes the casual kind of serve-yourself meal which the Scandinavians believe encourages enjoyment, with each person able without pressure to eat as much or as little as they wish. It is certainly a relaxed way to entertain in the modern world, even if it is a rather less lavish affair than in the past.

JANSSON'S TEMPTATION

In the 19th century, a religious zealot named Erik Jansson, who had sworn to give up earthly pleasures, gave into temptation when he smelled this dish!

6 raw potatoes
3 medium onions
1 oz. butter
1 can anchovy fillets in oil
½ pint pouring cream
2 level tablespoons breadcrumbs

Peel and wash the potatoes and slice thinly. Cut the slices into matchstick-sized strips. Wrap in a tea towel. Peel and chop the onions. Slowly fry them, covered by the lid of the pan, in half the butter until very pale gold in colour and soft. Butter a casserole dish and fill with the potatoes, fried onions and anchovy fillets. Pour the oil from the fish and half of the cream over the mix, and bake in a hot oven for 15 minutes. Pour the rest of the cream over the dish and top with the breadcrumbs. Bake for a further 25 to 30 minutes, until the top is golden and crusty.

STAVANGER FLINT AND FIGGIO FLINT

Stavanger Flint was founded in Stavanger, Norway in 1949. The company quickly established a creative design department and began producing dinnerware ranges as well as highly decorative items. Kari Nyquist was employed as a freelance designer from 1956 onward, and her name appears on the backstamp of most of the pieces she designed. Kaare Fjeldsaa was Chief Designer and Art Director, a post which he held until the final closure of the company. In a merger with Figgio Fajanse in 1968, the company became Figgio Flint. The combined works closed in 1979.

These changes are reflected by the backstamps on the base of the pieces, which are clearly marked with the various combined names of the companies. The patterns used by both companies are well-drawn, with figures surrounded by decorative flowers and foliage, and they have a strong Scandinavian feel. The earthenware shapes are elegant and well-fired, which gives the pieces a high quality finish.

TOP Figgio Flint dinnerware.

RIGHT Scandinavian cheeses and crispbread wheels.

FACING PAGE: TOP Smorgasbord table.

FACING PAGE: BELOW Open sandwiches with coffee on Figgio Flint china.

Decorative tableware designed by Bjorn Wiinblad for Nymolle, including two from a set of twelve calendar plaques depicting the story of a romance, from courtship to marriage, children and abandonment! Wiinblad made several series of this type.

BELOW Detail of a Wiinblad plate.

BJORN WIINBLAD

Bjorn Wiinblad was born in Denmark in 1918. He was educated in Copenhagen and has worked in various media, including furniture, textiles, glass, metals, graphics and stage design. He is best known, however, for his work in decorative ceramics with the Danish company Nymolle and the German company Rosenthal.

Wiinblad began work with Nymolle in 1946, establishing the single-colour, imaginatively drawn patterns and forms that became his trademark. He drew his inspiration from Danish folk tales. Some were magical, with strange creatures and mythical scenes, while others were stories of romance and even infidelity. One of his most popular designs was a series of breakfast wall plaques depicting the months of the year. Together, they illustrate the full story of a romance, from the first meeting to the birth of the first baby!

Wiinblad also produced a range of hand-modelled items and some one-off studio pieces, now highly prized for their quality and rarity. In 1956, he left Nymolle and went to the giant ceramics company Rosenthal, where his output has been prolific. As well as single-colour ranges, he has designed highly patterned, coloured plate series, fancy wares in porcelain and simple tea and coffee ranges. He has even produced some designs on glass. There have been few figurative designers of the 20th century who have produced such a wide range of individual, high quality products.

DANSK

The distribution company of Dansk was founded in America in 1954 by Martha and Ted Neirenberg. The couple had made a trip to Denmark in 1950 and had been so inspired by the work of the Scandinavian designers of the time that they decided to open a business selling quality, contemporary goods in the USA.

The business operated out of Mount Kisco in New York, and at first it bought generally made goods by well-established designers, but soon the couple began to develop new products with the designers that could be distributed solely through their company. In this way, Dansk acted as a market researcher for Scandinavian products. Many new designs were made in stainless steel cutlery, cookware, glass and pottery, particularly for the American market. Popular designs included 'Fjord' flatware in 1957, and the ceramics ranges 'Flamestone' and 'Generation', which were still in production at the end of the 20th century.

Dansk was popular and successful from its beginning, pulling together the best of European designers for the huge North American market at a time when Scandinavia was leading the world in modern design. Between 1954 and 1970, the volume of sales rose from one million to ten million dollars, and Dansk showrooms were opened in parts of the world outside the USA. In 1968, Dansk opened one of the first outlet stores in America in Kittery, Maine, and in 1984 the Neirenbergs sold the company at a considerable profit.

Dansk was a ground-breaking company for many reasons during the 1960s. It took on the role of distributor rather than retailer, and as such it was able to control the quality of contemporary goods being imported under its name. It recognised the size of the American market and capitalised on an enthusiasm for simplicity in form and design by capturing Scandinavian design at the time when it was leading the world.

Royal Copenhagen 'Aluminia' vase by Kari Cristianson.

BELOW LEFT 'Arabia' coffee ware and 'Whitefriars' textured vase.

BELOW littala glass service plate with avocado plate.

HOLMEGAARD

In 1825, Countess Henriette Danneskiold-Samsoe, the owner of the Holmegaard Marsh on the Danish island of Zealand decided to build a glassworks which would be fuelled by the local peat. Throughout the 19th century, the company developed from bottle making to employing Bohemian glassmakers and producing high quality cut glass.

Then in 1905 the freelance ceramic designer Svend Hammershoi was invited to produce two ranges for the company. They were cut glass and the first, 'Margarethe', was so popular it was in continuous production until 1959. Holmegaard did not employ a permanent designer until 1923, when the company signed a short-lived contract with the porcelain company Royal Copenhagen to design some glass to complement its ceramic tableware.

The first important designer was the architect Jacob Bang. In the years between the two world wars, Bang transformed the company into one of the most innovative in Europe by designing functional glass tableware in the modern style. Bang worked at Holmegaard until 1941, introducing such ranges as 'Primula' and 'Viola', which were international successes. In 1937, the exhibition 'Ten Years of Danish Art Glassware' confirmed his contribution to the company's position in the glass world.

After the departure of Bang, the company appointed Per Lutken as resident designer in 1942. Lutken was to remain with the company for the rest of his life. His first work was rather showy and extravagant, but by 1950 he was beginning to refine his glass designs into the fluid, organic forms for which he is so well-known today. He designed the elegant 'Beak' vase, the heart-shaped 'Minuet' range of vases and many other 20th century classic pieces of glass design.

Almost unbelievably, Lutken never actually blew glass; he worked constantly alongside the glassblowers until he understood every technique and trick of the trade. Lutken died in 1998, after 56 years of designing glass at Holmegaard.

The most notable glass designer in these years, apart from Lutken, was Otto Brauer, who designed a striking series of elongated bottle vases with a flat rim in 1962. The 'Gul Vase' was produced for about 20 years in all colours and sizes, both cased and clear, and became one of the company's most popular designs.

In 1968, Jacob Bang's son Michael was appointed to Holmegaard to produce cased glass tableware and lighting designs, and he remains with the company today. In 1985, the company became part of the Royal Copenhagen Group along with Georg Jensen. More amalgamations took place in the 1990s, but the company is in production today, still producing domestic and ornamental glass.

Per Lutken 'Beak' vase by Holmegaard.

ORREFORS

'Sand, water, fire – man's basic elements. Then it needs to be blown by an expert and it swells like a bubble at the end of a stick, except that it doesn't vanish into nothing. There it stands – splendid in its fragility. It is an Orrefors object.' – ORREFORS IN CASA VOGUE, *1977*

The glass factory of Orrefors grew up on the site of an old steel factory which gave its name to the town of Orrefors in Sweden. The factory converted to glass when steel production dwindled, and it began producing industrial sheet glass for windows and small items such as inkstands.

The modern company of Orrefors began in earnest with the arrival of Simon Gate and Edvard Hald in 1915 and 1917. They had already been working on the design of porcelain tableware, and they began to apply their industrial experience to designing new modern forms of glassware. Gate and Hald were pioneers in Swedish design, and the new shapes they created gave the production of glass at Orrefors a completely new look. In 1917, they introduced a technique to the factory which involved holding the colour and decoration within the glass itself, creating an illusion of suspending the colour in air. The technique was called *graal*, and it was developed from 19th century French glass-making. Graal became one of the specialities of the factory and the technique is still being used today. A high degree of expertise and control in the blowing of the glass was involved in making these pieces. As time went on, and the pieces became more and more complex, they became some of the most valuable 20th century works in glass.

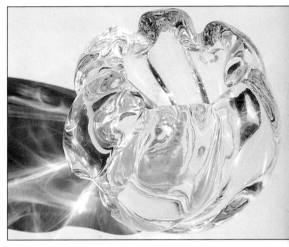

The company attracted many other great names in 20th century glass; Nils Landberg, Sven Palmquist, Vicke Lindstrom and Edvin Ohrstrom were all designers at Orrefors. There are still young, contemporary designers taking up the next design challenge. It is this approach to design that has kept Orrefors at the forefront of glass design for almost a century. The factory in the village of Orrefors has sponsored a school where young trainees are taught all the skills of glass-blowing for two years. This means that the skills are being handed down in a positive way, and there is always a new labour force waiting in the wings.

TOP RIGHT Simon Gate bowl, circa 1930.

CENTRE RIGHT Orrefors globe vase by Sven Palmquist.

RIGHT Nils Landberg vase, circa 1950.

1960 ~ 1969
Popular Revolution

The 1960s was a period of free development in almost all aspects of design and style. The '50s had moved design towards an abstraction of form and imagery, allied to a new freedom of colour, and these foundations permitted the designers of the '60s to allow anything to happen! This freedom produced some of the best and worst designs and artefacts of the 20th century.

Scandinavia was still promoting a deceptive simplicity of design in the applied arts. Scandinavian designers reached a standard of quality in craft and beauty that was never bettered but often diluted and echoed for the next 30 years. Taking their inspiration from nature, the Finnish designers Tapio Wirkkala and Timo Sarpaneva at the Iittala Glassworks revolutionised glassware by casting vessels in tree bark moulds. Royal Copenhagen in Denmark was producing studio and moulded ceramics with hand-drawn and textured images abstracted from the natural world. The giant German company Rosenthal was commissioning the best of the European designers, including Wirkkala and Sarpaneva, to produce ceramic collections for them under the Studio Linie label.

Orrefors, the great Swedish glassworks, was producing a new form in cased glass. The *graal* vases, started in the 1940s, trapped textures, lines and images in the transparent walls of the vessels. The Finnish company Arabia led the European market in top-quality household tableware, from simply decorated, high-gloss porcelain to mass-produced stoneware which had the appearance of hand-thrown studio pieces.

In Britain, the best companies followed the Scandinavian lead in their own way. The British taste was slightly more decorative, but Denby stoneware successfully hit the market with many well-designed ceramics such as 'Arabesque' and 'Chevron'. The ceramic company Midwinter had similar success with its 'Sun' and 'Moon' designs. Geoffrey Baxter at Whitefriars led the Scandinavian look in British textured glass, followed by the glass companies Ravenhead and Dartington.

At the same time, the decade was veering in an entirely different and almost opposite direction. The rise of popular culture was making its first big mark on people's lifestyles. The postwar babies, now grown to adulthood, had more money to spend on their homes and their recreational lives, and they were determined to influence the choices available to them. The mass market rose to fill this demand for variety by producing more consumer goods than ever before for every area of the home. In tableware, bad design followed good until discrimination was no longer possible. Fashion, for good and bad, was taking over!

The Beatles were leading a cultural revolution in popular music, and Mary Quant and the funky clothes of Carnaby Street led Britain and the rest of the world away from the French *haute couture* domination of fashion. London became the centre for popular culture, and the youth of the rest of the world followed. Class barriers of the past were disappearing; most of the youth of the day ignored them. Nearly everyone had a job and expectations of the good life if they worked for it. Entertaining in the home became the focus for after-work socialising. Everyone now held simple dinner parties, and people met over food to discuss politics, religion, culture and fashion.

Holidays abroad, now a common item on many people's calendars, encouraged the use of foreign foods in cooking. Supermarkets began to rise to the demand for these goods, and the high street saw its first delis. These were small shops specialising in all types of Continental and Asian foodstuffs, often run by local Italians, Greeks or Indians. Elizabeth David's series of paperbacks for Penguin Books on Mediterranean cooking was written in a relaxed, conversational style and suggested a new attitude toward cooking. Robert Carrier's *Great Dishes of the World* encouraged people to try to recreate the holiday atmosphere at home.

Cordon Bleu Cooking became the first weekly publication that concentrated solely on home cookery. The magazine was offered with a binder which could turn it into a large reference library. It was designed to take much of the mystery out of home cooking and encourage people to be more adventurous with all food, even in everyday cookery. Other weekly editions followed *Cordon Bleu*. There was a Robert Carrier weekly and much later, in the 1970s, *Supercook* became a bestseller. Journalists were also introducing new ideas in newspaper cookery columns which challenged the rules of the past. Katherine Whitehorn wrote several cookery volumes telling us that *Cooking In A Bedsit* was easy. Len Deighton, the popular spy writer, wrote a food column and a how-to cookbook which stated that cooking was easy. With the right instructions, even a man could master it!

The 1960s undoubtedly produced the widest range of styles in the 20th century, including some of the strongest influences and some of the best pieces of design in the applied arts. In the same decade, however, a cultural division sent art and design in two different directions. Minimalism and simplicity was one direction, and the unpredictable influence of popular culture and the media was the other. These two directions have continued along their own tracks to the present day.

CLOCKWISE FROM TOP LEFT Langley vase and Denby 'Chevron' dish. Beatles Fan Club Christmas record. Carltonware candle holder and Australian pattern dish. Pak-a-Pic picnic set. Saltoun coffee grinder and Hornsea storage jar. Royal Copenhagen 'Aluminia' dishes.

TOMATO RING

1200 ml tomato juice
Salt, pepper and a good pinch of
  brown sugar
1 packet of gelatine
3 garlic cloves
Dash of balsamic vinegar

Melt gelatine in ¾ pint hot water
and whisk into tomato juice.
Add whole garlic cloves and all
seasoning. Stir over a gentle heat
until nearly boiling, then discard
garlic cloves. Pour into ring
mould and when cool
refrigerate until set. Turn out
and decorate with chopped
vegetables.

HADDOCK ROULADE

½ lb. smoked haddock, weighed
  when cooked and flaked
4 eggs
½ gill double cream
1 or 2 tablespoonfuls grated
  Parmesan cheese

Filling
3 or 4 hard-boiled eggs
½ pint béchamel sauce, made
  with 1 ½ oz. butter, 1 oz. flour,
  ½ pint seasoned milk and
  chopped parsley

First prepare the filling. Make
the sauce, chop the eggs coarsely
and add a good spoonful of
chopped parsley. Keep warm.
Purée haddock. Separate the eggs
and work the yolks and cream
into the fish. Season and add
two-thirds of the cheese. Whip
the egg whites until stiff and fold
into the mixture. Line a Swiss
roll tin with greaseproof paper
and fill with the mixture.
Smooth over and sprinkle with
the remaining cheese. Bake in a
hot oven (200ºC) for 10 to 15
minutes. Turn over onto another
sheet of greaseproof paper,
dusted with Parmesan. Peel off
the paper and spread thickly
with the sauce. Roll up, long
sides together, and tilt onto the
serving dish. Serve at once.

BANANA CHARTREUSE

3 bananas
1 package of lemon jelly
1 packet boudoir biscuits
½ pint cream
1 teaspoon lemon juice

Make the jelly with ¾ pint of
water. Pour a thin layer into the
base of a deep soufflé dish and
arrange a sliced banana on top
of the jelly. Dip each biscuit into
the jelly and use them to line the
soufflé dish. Leave in the fridge
until set. Whip cream into soft
peaks and mash remaining
bananas with a fork. Blend
together with remaining jelly
and fill the soufflé dish. Leave
for several hours in the fridge
until set.

Dinner in the 1960s

Our Scandinavian-inspired 1960s dinner party was set on a Habitat table and chairs with a mixture of Habitat glass, Arabia 'Ruska' and Denby 'Arabesque' tableware. The cutlery was by Arne Jacobson and the candle holder by Dansk. Orange linen table-mats and napkins added some essential '60s colour. The menu was inspired by the many all-colour cookery books that were available at the time. It consisted of a Tomato Ring with vegetable crudites, Cream of Carrot Soup and Haddock Roulade, with Banana Chatreuse to end the meal. Coffee from the iconic giant 'Arabesque' coffeepot concluded the meal with 1960s style!

FACING PAGE: LEFT Tomato Ring surrounded by freshly-cut vegetables.

FACING PAGE: RIGHT Banana Chartreuse at the dinner table.

BELOW The 1960s dinner party.

ARABIA

Arabia started the 20th century as the leading ceramic producer in Finland, and it remained in that position until the end of the century. Originally founded by the Swedish company Rorstrand to capitalise on the Russian market in 1874, the company separated from Rorstrand in 1916. During the 1920s, the factory produced well-designed conventional and inexpensive porcelain. In 1932, however, with the founding of the Arabia art studio under the direction of Kurt Ekholm, the company started to lead in design innovation. Ekholm had been trained in Sweden and he joined the company at the age of 25, full of energetic ideas and youthful enthusiasm for the art studio. He encouraged artists to come to the studio to work within the company. Very soon, the factory became the Finnish centre for mass-produced and studio ceramics. A gold medal at the 1933 Milan Triennale confirmed the factory as being one of the leading companies in Europe.

During the next few decades, Kaj Franck led a stream of Finnish designers working in the Arabia factory. It exemplified the Scandinavian ideal of producing beautifully crafted, well-designed, utilitarian tableware which was mass-produced and priced within the affordable range of most of the market. Over the years, Arabia established close links with other Finnish companies, including the glassworks Nuutajarvi and the ceramic companies Rorstrand, Gustavsberg and Hacksfors Porcelain Company. Throughout the company's amalgamations, the emphasis has been on maintaining the individuality of each company within the group while taking advantage of the promotion and advertising strengths that acting as a group can bring.

'Cylinda' line coffeepot by Arne Jacobson.

Arabia 'Ruska' coffeepots and Iittala platter.

ARNE JACOBSON

Arne Jacobson was born in 1902 and educated in the Department of Architecture at the Copenhagen Academy of Arts, from which he graduated in 1927. He later became an Emeritus Professor there in 1956. Jacobson became an architect influenced by the work of Corbusier and Van der Rohe. He opened his own practice in Hellerup, and this became his base until his death in 1971.

During the 1950s, Jacobson decided to work with other companies to allow his modernist approach to design to expand into a broader field. The flatware he designed in 1957 for the Danish company A. Michelson embodied the look of the 1950s, and it is still being made by the Danish company Georg Jensen. His 'Cylinda' line of stainless steel tableware was designed for Stelton in 1966. Jacobson's work encompassed a wide range of materials, and it was his understanding of the materials and his knowledge of manufacturing processes which allowed him to see his designs realised in mass production as some of the most significant household items of the 20th century.

MIDWINTER IN THE 1960s

In 1962, Roy Midwinter launched a new shape in collaboration with the Marquis of Queensberry. The new shape was designed to break with the successful but now old-fashioned look of the designs of the 1950s. Although the 'Fashion shape' was still popular, the patterns were becoming rather chocolate-boxy, and a new style was needed. The clean lines of the 'Fine shape' had its roots in 18th-century English cream ware, and many other companies echoed the cylindrical form during the 1960s. The clean lines of the 'Fine shape' and the later, amended 'MQ1 shape' allowed for easier transfer decoration and more scope for elaborate, free designs.

Design for fashion and textiles had a strong influence on all aspects of the decorative arts during the 1960s. Mary Quant and the boutiques of Carnaby Street epitomised the 'Swinging Sixties' and 'the Look', which at this time appeared to lead the world in a new, youthful approach to style. The ceramic manufacturer Midwinter used textile designers Barbara Brown, Nigel Wilde and Joti Bhowmik to decorate its 'Fine shape' and later its 'MQ1 shape' ranges with patterns such as 'Focus' in 1964, 'Cherry Tree' in 1966, and 'Kismet' and 'Bengal' in 1968.

Jessie Tait was still the principal in-house designer for this shape. 'Mexicana', 'Graphic', 'Contrast' and 'Oakley' (for Boots) were some of her designs, as well as the bestselling design of all – 'Spanish Garden'. The designs echoed the contrasts in the influences of the decade. On the one hand, they reflected the popular abstract art movements of the time, and on the other they presented the highly decorative, colourful, Eastern-inspired florals, with their travel references from such popular destinations as Morocco and India. The designs were almost psychedelic in style, and so they became popular with the new, young generation of consumers in the '60s.

Despite the success of the 'Fine shape', another range launched in 1966 called 'MQ2' was not a success, and the company was financially strained. In 1968, it was taken over by J.G. Meakin and some of its designs were transferred over to Meakin shapes. In 1970, there was another takeover, this time by Wedgwood. The company continued under its own name, with the line 'member of the Wedgwood group' being added to the backstamp.

Following the general ceramic direction of the time, the 'Stonehenge' range was introduced in the 1970s under the direction of Roy Midwinter's wife Eve. The three designs were 'Sun', 'Moon' and 'Stars', and they consisted of heavy stoneware in geometric-shaped bodies with fluid handles. Despite the success of this 'Creation' series, Midwinter sank under the pressure of competition, and in 1987 the company finally closed its doors.

The Midwinter collection, circa 1965.

BELOW 'Bengal' trio.
BOTTOM 'Sienna' plates.

TV Dinners

In 1953, many families in Britain sat down in front of their first television sets to watch the Coronation of Queen Elizabeth. No other item of 20th-century technology was so quickly accepted into the hearts of people's lives. Although the first TV sets had only been on sale since 1946, by 1960 75% of the population had them at home, with an average viewing time of 12 hours per person. By the end of the decade, close to 100% of British homes had TVs.

Furniture had to be reorganised to accommodate these monsters as they became the focal points of many rooms. Evening meals began to be dominated by watching the 'telly', and this was a good reason for families to avoid the inevitable mealtime argument. If relationships were a bit strained, then the television offered an easy alternative to discussion. Social dining and family dinners were now under threat!

TV trays and tables soon began to hit the market, and a wealth of easy meals began to appear on shopping shelves. Convenience foods were sold in packets, or bags in which you could boil the food. Vesta Chow Mein and Vesta Curry meals were reconstituted with water, and Fray Bentos steak and kidney pies were cooked straight from the can. Frozen meals called 'TV dinners' became very popular. In America, the favourite TV dinner was Swanson & Sons Turkey Dinner, and in Britain it was Bird's Eye Fish Fingers. Everyday china was required for TV watching, and the perfect answer was the brightly patterned, cheap and cheerful pottery which Kathie Winkle designed for Broadhurst.

GOURDON'S SARDINE PÂTÉ

4 oz. fresh breadcrumbs
2 tins of sardines
Juice and grated rind of a lemon
2 oz. melted butter
Fresh parsley
Salt and black pepper to taste

Mash sardines in oil and beat with all of the other ingredients. Put into a dish or individual ramekins and chill until firm. Serve on toast as a snack or as a starter.

Fray Bentos steak and kidney pie dinner.

LEFT Ingredients for a TV dinner.

Cups and saucers by Kathie Winkle.

KATHIE WINKLE AND BROADHURST POTTERY

After the war, the lifting of restrictions during the 1950s had created a demand for new, colourful china to be available for all levels of society. New shapes and patterned designs were required, and these needed to be produced in the style of the times, suitable for an unconventional, young market.

Kathie Winkle had joined the firm of James Broadhurst as a paintress in 1950, but it was not until 1958 that she started to design the geometric patterns which eventually bore her name on the backstamp. Broadhurst had started using a new method of printing designs on tableware. Rubber stamps were used to apply the mainly black outline of the design, which was then filled in by paintresses using as many as five colours. The technique was called 'stamp and fill', and it was the method of production used for almost all of Kathie Winkle's designs. Her designs were mainly geometric in style, although some had a floral look to them, and the colour used was bold but always with some black. The names of the designs often had an exotic air about them – 'Monte Carlo', 'Acapulco' and 'Palma', for instance – which was probably more the result of a marketing exercise than by design, to interest a public that travelled often.

Many of the designs were sold abroad, mainly in Canada, Australia and South Africa, where there was disbelief that the designer's name could be Kathie Winkle! Broadhurst then produced the backstamp with her signature on it, rather like the Clarice Cliff signature on the 'Bizarre' china of the 1930s. This seemed to add to the selling potential of the designs, so it was used on all the wares designed by Winkle until 1978, when the patterns began to be discontinued. The output from the factory was prolific for more than 10 years, with one design alone – 'Rushtone' – selling more than 50 million pieces. In 1984, Broadhurst was renamed Churchill Tableware, and the company is still in existence as Churchill China today.

Ritz® Crackers and Kraft® Cheese Slices.

GIL PEMBERTON AND DENBY

After she had completed four years at the Birmingham School of Art and three at the Royal College of Art, Gil Pemberton was invited to join Denby Potteries in 1960 as a part-time designer. Her ability to design catering ware had been obvious at her end-of-year degree show, and for the first year she was put to work on the hotel ware end of the business. It was the beginning of a career with Denby which was to last for 21 years and produce some of the most innovative designs in British tableware. In 1962, Pemberton visited the Scandinavian countries and Russia with her husband Neil Harding, and on her return from this trip she finalised the designs for the 'Chevron' range and designed the new range 'Arabesque'.

'Chevron' tableware was an outstanding success both in Britain and the USA. In America, it was named 'Camelot' to avoid confusion with a chain of Chevron gas stations, and it was marketed in a personal, countrywide promotion by one of the directors in 1969. It was a whistle-stop tour, but by the end of it the Denby company was established as a name in the USA. Even the wife of the President was said to have put 'Camelot' on her wedding list. 'Chevron' was accepted as a Design Centre product and was put forward for a Duke of Edinburgh Award for Industry.

The form and colour of the decoration on Pemberton's 'Arabesque' range were inspired by her visit to Russia in 1962, and her designs for a full range of tableware were completed in 1963. The rich red and gold circular pattern was originally designed to be hand-painted over the brown glaze before firing, but this became technically difficult. Eventually, the pattern was produced using a painted transfer, although some of the quality of the design was lost. 'Arabesque' was a very popular design, and remains so today, with collectors still paying high prices for special pieces.

From 1964 onwards, the contemporary tableware shapes at Denby were designed by Gil Pemberton and produced with hand-painted patterns at the Langley Pottery. Other contemporary potteries tried to follow the trend set by Denby, but they were unable to find the necessary artistry within mechanised production. Other designs by Gil Pemberton in the 1960s included 'Mayflower', 'Bokhara' and a white and brown design using 'Arabesque' shapes called 'Summit'. In the 1970s, Pemberton created 'Gypsy', 'Troubadour', the 'Artisan' range of stackable tableware and the highly successful 'Renaissance'. There were many other designs, some of which were the product of collaborations with Glyn Colledge and others.

The success of Denby tableware lay in the fact that it was designer-led during the '60s and '70s. Subsequently, the company suffered from too much control over production being in the hands of management. It was not until a takeover by Coloroll Tableware Ltd, and a fairly ruthless appraisal of the company in 1987, that Denby returned to its original, design-conscious roots. Other takeovers changed the company again, but at the start of the 21st century, the key figure of the designer is still vital to the production of its successful tableware.

Breakfast with Old Hall stainless steel and Gil Pemberton's Denby 'Chevron'.

BELOW Denby 'Arabesque' jugs.

OLD HALL STAINLESS STEEL

J. & J. Wiggin was founded in 1893 as a father-and-son company that made buckles for the saddler trade. The business was successful, and it soon expanded beyond the size of its premises. By 1901, the Wiggins had moved into an old Salvation Army Mission Hall which had been lying empty for some years; they called it Old Hall. During World War One, general development was suspended as the company was assigned to make munitions for the war. After the war, various different products were tried with varying degrees of success: motor car parts, roller skates and, finally, chromium-plated bathroom fittings which were marketed under the company's original trademark Old Hall.

In 1913 Harry Brearley, a metallurgist working at the steel company Thomas Firth, discovered a 'rustless' steel that contained 12% chromium. A patent was taken out on this steel under the name of 'Staybrite'. In the mid-1920s, William Wiggin decided to make his products at Old Hall from 'Staybrite' steel, and these new bathroom accessories were marketed successfully with the 'Staybrite' stamp. The first item of tableware to be made in 'Staybrite' was an experimental toast rack made in 1928. This was the beginning of Old Hall tableware, and by 1930 the first stainless steel teapot in the world had been manufactured. Marketing these products started seriously in 1934 at the *Daily Mail* 'Ideal Home' Exhibition at Olympia. There was an area in the show called 'Staybrite City', and Old Hall exhibited products within this area that were a big success.

The Second World War again stopped development from 1939 onward, as the company went back into munitions. At the end of the war, however, the company had a strong direction and grew rapidly. The emphasis was always on good, modern design, a high quality of workmanship and a wide range of well-conceived products.

In 1955, an excellent partnership began when Robert Welch the silversmith was appointed Consultant Designer to the company. He won three separate Design Centre Awards for his work with Old Hall. The first, in 1958, was for the 'Campden' toast rack. The second, in 1962, was for a range of twenty-two dishes, and the third was in 1965 for the cutlery range 'Alveston'. Several tea and coffee services, such as the bestselling 'Connaught' tea set and the majestic 'Super Avon' coffeepot, were produced, and so were smaller items such as glass beaker holders and single rose vases.

During the whole postwar period there were never less than 500 people working at the Old Hall Works, and stainless steel was marketed as the 'Wedding Present of the Sixties'. Indeed many valued collections of Old Hall started as one wedding gift. In 1970, Old Hall became part of the Prestige group, the largest houseware manufacturers outside the USA. It came to play a large part in developing stainless steel products within that group. In 1982, the company was sold to the Japanese company Oneida, but in June 1984 the Old Hall at Bloxwich closed its doors for the last time.

'Alveston' cutlery by Robert Welch for Old Hall.

SHOPPING IN THE '60S

During the 1960s, the possibilities for shopping expanded beyond all expectation. On one hand, many city centres were 'regenerated', with large, concrete shopping centres beginning to appear, complete with car parks for easy access. Credit cards were available for the first time, and there was no lack of spending power. Electrical kitchen gadgets such as blenders, egg boilers, even bottle openers filled the marketplace, only to be discarded when it was found to be quicker to do it the traditional way.

In the kitchen, paper towels, tinfoil and plastic food wrap made their first appearances, and the throwaway society even had paper dresses and undies. The self-service supermarket now began to provide everything required for the family in a 'weekly shop.' The decline of the corner shop had begun. At the other end of the market, consumers were realising that they had more choice in goods than ever before and they could now choose goods to their personal tastes rather than follow the masses. Small, specialist shops or 'boutiques' appeared, often off the beaten track. Some were started by designers and craftspeople who filled their shops with handmade items of fashionable clothing, handmade bags and jewellery or decorative items for the home. The famous Carnaby Street in London was originally a back street which filled up with this type of boutique. It eventually became a pilgrimage centre for the most fashionable celebrities of the day.

Habitat brought a new dimension to the kitchen, selling Continental pots, pans and utensils, and creating a frenzy of buying when it first opened in 1964. Shops sponsored by Scandinavia and selling only imported goods from the

Wedgwood 'Sheringham' and 'Brancaster' candle holders.

Marimekko paper napkins.

FACING PAGE: LEFT Casa Pupo pottery lemons.

FACING PAGE: RIGHT Avocado dishes for avocados!
'The thrill of the avocado had just reached Britain.' — JENNIFER PATERSON

Scandinavian countries were also popular. As well as 'The Scandinavian Shop', there were also Danasco and Dansk shops in many large towns. They sold good designs in a modern setting, from Georg Jensen silver cutlery and jewellery to prize-winning glass objects made by Iittala and Orrefors. Arabia stoneware and Rorstrand china dinnerware could be bought for a price. These shops also sold traditional items, such as reindeer boots and beaten pewter fashion and kitchen items. There were Danish Food Centres in some cities, selling Danish products and serving traditional Danish meals. It was even possible to enjoy a Danish smørrebrød for a buffet lunch while out shopping.

Casa Pupo was a Portuguese company which opened many small shops in Britain as well as franchised space in some of the large city centre stores. They specialised in a wide range of Spanish and Portuguese goods, from traditional cooking pots and earthenware dishes to the highly decorative majolica-like china table centres of stacked fruit. The Casa Pupo woven reversible rug was a 'must have' item of the '60s, as was the avocado dish shaped like an avocado. There was no other way to serve this popular starter.

Another 'must have' item for the kitchen was the storage jar. Most of the big companies sold them to coordinate with their dinnerwares. Every possible item for storage was named on the front of a jar, from bay leaves to barley. Other, smaller companies and designers also made them and sold them as gift items in stores such as Liberty or in smaller boutiques. Gift shops and boutiques held a wonderful selection of beautiful but often unnecessary treasures. Scandinavian glassware stood beside candlesticks by Wedgwood, stainless steel cutlery and Carlton coffee sets – it was an 'Aladdin's cave' of shopping!

Carlton ware coffee set.

THE HABITAT PHENOMENON

In 1956, Terence Conran and John Stephenson founded the Conran Design Group to design and market contemporary furniture and interiors. Conran then opened the first Habitat store in May 1964 at 77 Fulham Road in London, combining the modern style of the Conran Design Group with the more traditional 'French Provincial' style in an eclectic mix which covered all aspects of the modern home. In a contemporary magazine article, the company director of the shop, Mrs Pagan Taylor, said, 'We don't claim to have a monopoly of goods which cannot be found elsewhere, but we hope to be able to stock what we consider to be the very best of everything under one roof.' The marketing was incredibly successful, with Habitat fast becoming a watchword for good, affordable design as well as a place to buy almost anything for the 1960s lifestyle.

The shop was designed by the Conran Design Group. Yellow floor tiles lined the windows and grey sisal matting covered the floors in the main shop areas. The walls were grey engineering brick and the ceiling and some walls were painted white with simple, wooden slatting, providing semi-open partitions between areas. The ground floor contained furniture that included wide-ranging European pieces as well as Conran's own, with such classics as a Bertoias birdcage chair and a rare Corbusier dining chair which, according to an account of the time, was sold to an architect who was 'feverishly mouthing his order through the window before the shop was even open'.

The basement was 'a sophisticated warehouse' with diffused lighting showing off a range of some of the best in fabrics, lighting, glass, pottery and kitchen equipment. Spode's 'Blue Italian' pottery rubbed shoulders with brown and green Arabia stoneware and Le Creuset cooking pots. Fabrics had the same kind of mix, with modern Conran and Boussac designs sitting next to tiny, traditional florals by J.P. Baker. Products catering to a wide range of tastes were available, and their cost was everything from a sofa at seventy guineas to a meat skewer at one penny!

The shop was instantly successful, and within a few years Conran had built up a chain of stores within Britain, France and the USA. Later expansionist moves during the 1980s, including a merger with Mothercare and the furniture firm of Heal's, created an organisation which owned 1,000 outlets selling well-designed, affordable goods by 1990, the year of Conran's retirement from his position as Chairman. The success of the shop had a lot to do with its comprehensive marketing policy. The quality of the staff also contributed to the company's unprecedented success. Conran achieved with Habitat something which had been tried several times earlier in the century – making modern design affordable and available to all of the British public.

A collection of the type of goods stocked by Habitat: Blue Denmark china, a Mouli cheese grater and Liekki stoneware oven-to-table ware.

MARIMEKKO

Marimekko was created in Finland out of the new movement of modernism that was central to Scandinavian design in the middle of the 20th century. It was a company built around new concepts of equality, freedom of ideas and optimism in a country which was beginning to lead the world in modern design.

In 1952, Armi Ratia started the company with a group of friends who were interested in graphics, art and textiles. She used her husband's oilskin production factory to make a range of huge graphic textiles that were turned into adults' and children's clothes and furnishings. The scale of the fabrics was enormous. The designs were totally different from everything else which was already on the market, and the colours were vibrant and bold, using a wonderful, contemporary range of brights as well as black, brown and white.

The main designer during the peak period of the late 1950s to the mid-1960s was Maija Isola, and her designs were the hallmark of the company. With their roots in the abstract art of the period, these designs have stood the test of time. Indeed, the bold patterns have the same impact as a painting when used within a room, and they are equally appropriate in a domestic as well as a modern office or hotel situation. Not all of the fabrics were used for interiors; some were made into very striking garments which were seen on the covers of *Vogue* and *Harpers Bazaar* magazines in the 1960s.

The company had a Utopian approach to business which, as for many businesses in the 1960s, became unrealistic. By the late 1970s, Marimekko was in financial difficulty. Ratia died in 1979, and although her son continued the business, it was not until 1991 that the company was re-established by supplying mainly archive designs to a limited number of worldwide stockists. The fact that they still look so fresh and modern 50 years after their creation makes one feel that they will still be around in another 50!

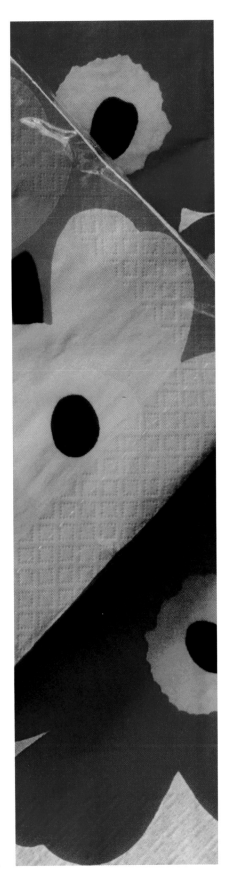

A Marimekko napkin design.

COFFEE AND DANISH PASTRIES

The 1960s was perhaps the decade in which more coffeepots were made than in any other (though many remained unused). The shape had moved on from the organic, amorphous shapes of the 1950s to the classic cylinder form that dominated the new era. The taller and thinner the pot, the better it looked, and the 'Totem' pot pictured below was about as tall and thin as you could get.

All that was required to complete the '60s coffee setting was a fine Danish pastry. Danish pastries are notoriously difficult to make at home, but in the 1960s a good alternative could be found in the freezer. Various companies made frozen cardboard tubes filled with dough, which when defrosted needed only to be cut in premarked sections and baked in the oven. Full instructions were given on every pack, and the range included very acceptable freshly baked croissants as well.

BELOW Blue Portmeirion 'Totem' coffee service, Finnish coffee table, Casa Pupo rug, 'Swivel' chair and painting by Donald Paterson.

ABOVE The Susie Cooper 'Heraldry' pattern for Wedgwood.

'Tivoli' cups and saucers.

PORTMEIRION AND SUSAN WILLIAMS-ELLIS

Susan Williams-Ellis was the daughter of the architect Sir Clough Williams-Ellis, the creator of the famous village of Portmeirion in Wales. Susan Williams-Ellis bought the pottery decorating business of A.E.Grays & Co. in 1960 with her husband, Euan Cooper-Willis. The company had previously made items for the Portmeirion shop and hotel.

The company's first designs in 1960 were black and white copperplate reproductions and 'Portmeirion Dolphin' storage jars with labels designed by Williams-Ellis. In 1961, Williams-Ellis and Cooper-Willis bought the pottery firm of Kirkham, and this allowed them to produce their first range of tableware as Portmeirion Potteries.

'Totem', their first pattern, was launched in 1963 and was based on cylindrical moulds found in the Kirkham factory. This design fitted very well with the simple forms that were popular in the early '60s. The design was single-coloured, with a complicated, embossed design, and it was produced eventually as a full dinnerware range including casseroles, rolling pins, and the important kitchen accessory of the 1960s – the storage jar. It was produced in green, brown, pale grey, blue and matt white, with the blue and white being the rarest. The tall coffeepots and storage jars were an immediate success, and they paved the way for a number of other designs based on the decorated cylinder. Williams-Ellis designed printed patterns such as 'Magic City' and 'Magic Garden', 'Tivoli', 'Talisman' and 'Greek Key'.

The bestselling pattern of all for Portmeirion, 'Botanic Garden', was based on botanical drawings of plants, complete with Latin names. This design was launched in 1972 and is still in production in the 21st century. It has almost become a trademark collection for the company, with new flower patterns being added every year.

'Totem' and 'Cipher' coffee cups and saucers.

'Totem' storage jar and rolling pin.

In the 1960s, the 'look' had to be as good as the food. In this designer-inspired dinner party, the table is a very fashionable Arkana white melamine circle with a column base. The places are set with thick, hessian table-mats and stainless steel cutlery.

THE CORDON BLEU COOKERY COURSE

A new concept for food in Britain was introduced in 1968 through a weekly cookery magazine that celebrated the principles of the Cordon Bleu Cookery School. The magazine's co-authors were Muriel Downes and Rosemary Hume, and their aim was to provide instruction in a very clear way, using accessible words and pictures without compromising the quality of the traditional recipes.

As the weeks passed, readers were encouraged to experiment with new foreign foods and recipes, create menus, write letters for question-and-answer sessions and take advantage of readers' offers for kitchen equipment. The magazines were very popular, and they were reprinted over the years several times.

The authors went on to write many more books on cooking that still have a place on many cookery book shelves. Other serialised cookery books followed during the next 20 years, including various cookery card collections, *Robert Carrier* magazines and the *Supercook* series in the 1980s.

A table set with a Cordon Bleu main course.

A Cordon Bleu dinner

Enthusiasm for shopping and the choice available in all kinds of dinnerware inevitably gave rise to some rather smart dinner parties. French cooking still had its place, and the *Cordon Bleu* and other weekly magazines gave clear directions for preparing quality food at home.

Barbara Brown was the designer of the Midwinter dinner service. Better-known for her large-scale geometric textile designs for Heal's, she also designed some ceramics in the 1960s for Midwinter and Johnston Brothers. The glassware is by Caithness Glass, a company which started in 1961 as a youth employment scheme in the north of Scotland at John O'Groats. Paul Ysart, who had been a major part of Monart Glass in Perth, was in charge of the glassworks, and the designer was Domhnall O'Brion from Ireland. He designed a range of glass which was Scandinavian-inspired, simple and very modern. The candlestick, called 'Sheringham', was one of several ranges of candlesticks designed by Ronald Stennet Wilson under the Wedgwood label.

The menu of Cream of Asparagus Soup and Coq au Vin, followed by black coffee, is inspired by the Cordon Bleu Cookery Course. The wine is the essential Mateus Rosé, which no self-respecting dinner party would have been without in the 1960s.

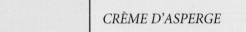

CRÈME D'ASPERGE

Cook 1 chopped onion and 1 chopped leek in a pan with 12 oz. of fresh, chopped asparagus and 2 pints of stock for about 15 minutes.

In another pan, make a sauce with:
1 oz. butter
1 oz. flour
¼ pint milk
¼ pint cream

Bring to the boil and cook for a few minutes, stirring all the time. Add the asparagus mixture and process or sieve until smooth.

COQ AU VIN

1 chicken, cut into pieces
Salt and pepper
1 oz. butter
6 small onions
¼ lb. salt pork, cut into strips
4 carrots, diced
6 shallots
1 clove of garlic
2 tablespoonfuls brandy
1 bottle of red Burgundy
Bouquet garni

Season the chicken. Melt the butter in a pan and brown the onions and the salt pork. Remove them and set aside. Brown the chicken gently for about 15 minutes and add the diced carrots, the shallots and the garlic. Pour in the brandy and set alight. Pour in a bottle of red Burgundy and cook for about 30 minutes over a low flame. Add the pork and the onions and simmer until the chicken is fully cooked. Taste and season as required.

Coq au Vin on a Midwinter dinner plate by Barbara Brown.

After dinner coffee.

THE CONTENTED SOLE

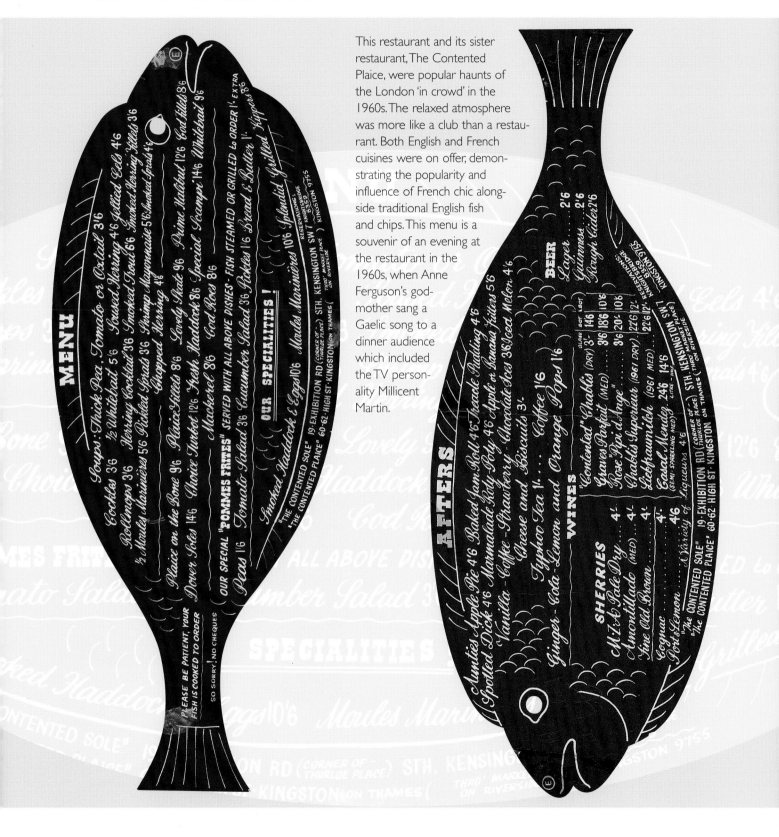

This restaurant and its sister restaurant, The Contented Plaice, were popular haunts of the London 'in crowd' in the 1960s. The relaxed atmosphere was more like a club than a restaurant. Both English and French cuisines were on offer, demonstrating the popularity and influence of French chic alongside traditional English fish and chips. This menu is a souvenir of an evening at the restaurant in the 1960s, when Anne Ferguson's godmother sang a Gaelic song to a dinner audience which included the TV personality Millicent Martin.

CURRIES AND MADHUR JAFFREY

Curries rose to popularity during the 1960s, with a sudden increase in the number of Indian and Pakistani restaurants in the ethnic areas of city centres such as Glasgow, Manchester and London. Over the next 20 years, Indian restaurants became commonplace in every town in Britain, particularly as great places to soak up an evening's beer drinking!

Madhur Jaffrey was the first cookery writer and presenter to demystify the skills of Indian cookery, and her seminal work on the subject, *Madhur Jaffrey's Indian Cookery*, has sold close to a million copies since its publication in 1982. Jaffrey was born in Delhi and came to Britain to study acting at the Royal Academy of Dramatic Arts at the age of 19. Until she came to Britain, she had no need for cooking skills, but she missed her home-cooked food so much that she asked her mother to send her some recipes. With regular correspondence from her mother, she gradually became a good cook, and when she moved to New York City after a few years of acting in Britain, she supplemented her income by writing articles about Indian and Oriental food. This was the start of her very successful career as a cookery writer and presenter. Jaffrey has a very easy, straightforward way of presenting food, and because she herself came to cooking relatively late, she knows how to make processes simple to understand.

A curry dinner party.

Chicken Muglai and Saag Aloo Potato and Spinach Curry.

CHICKEN MUGLAI

Mix together:

1 ¹/₂ teaspoons salt
2 teaspoons cumin
1 ¹/₂ teaspoons ground coriander
¹/₂ teaspoon ground turmeric
¹/₂ teaspoon cayenne pepper
Freshly ground black pepper

Spread half of the mixture over 3 lbs. chicken pieces and set aside for at least 3 hours. For the sauce, you will need:

6–7 cloves garlic
1-inch cube of finely chopped
  fresh ginger
6 tablespoons oil
1 medium onion, finely chopped
6 oz. tomatoes, peeled and
  chopped

4 tablespoons creamed coconut
1 teaspoon garam masala
6 tablespoons double cream

Blend or pound together the garlic and the ginger with 4 oz. water. Brown all of the chicken pieces in some oil in a frying pan. Remove and set aside.

Brown the onions in the remaining oil and add the ginger paste. Stir until the water from the paste evaporates and then add the rest of the spices. Fry for a few minutes. Slowly add the tomatoes and the coconut cream. Put the chicken pieces into the pan with 7 oz. water and salt. Cook for 20 minutes. Add the garam masala and the cream and mix gently. Cook until the sauce is reduced to the desired consistency and serve.

SAAG ALOO POTATO AND SPINACH CURRY

2 packets of frozen spinach
10 oz. water
1 large onion, finely chopped
5 tablespoons olive oil
2 teaspoonfuls mustard seeds
2 cloves garlic
1 lb. peeled potatoes
1 hot green chilli pepper
1 teaspoon finely grated fresh
  ginger
¹/₄ teaspoon cayenne pepper
1 teaspoon salt

Bring the water to the boil and cook the spinach until cooked. Drain and squeeze out most of the moisture, then chop coarsely. Cut the onions into very thin slices and cook in the oil with the popped mustard seeds and chopped garlic. Stir and fry for 2 minutes. Put in the potatoes and the cayenne pepper, and stir and fry for 1 minute. Put in the spinach, salt and a little water. Bring to the boil, then cover and cook for about 30 minutes or until the potatoes are cooked. Check that the pan does not dry out during cooking.

1970 ~ 1979
Self-sufficiency

The 1970s witnessed the true birth of the home electronics era, as calculators, pocket televisions, hi-fi equipment, digital watches and Sony Walkman®s became everyday necessities. It was the disco decade, when the film 'Saturday Night Fever' gave us flared trousers and glam rock. It was also the decade of ultimate electrical gadgets, such as freezers, microwave ovens, slow cookers, yoghurt makers and the mighty Magimix. Designed to free the housewife from time-consuming chores, these gadgets often took more time to use than the original task did!

Paradoxically, it was suddenly important to worry about what we were eating. Countless books appeared on the market about vegetarianism and whole food, including John Seymour's *The Complete Book of Self-Sufficiency*. In Britain, Delia Smith encouraged a no-nonsense approach to cookery. 'The Good Life' on television promoted an alternative lifestyle in fictional Surbiton, and vegetarian restaurants such as Cranks opened and prospered in London. Rose Elliot, one of the best of a number of vegetarian cookery writers during the '70s, wrote a book called *Not Just a Load of Old Lentils* and was overwhelmed by the number of readers who wrote to her claiming that her book had changed their lives. Of course, there was a school of traditional, meat-eating opponents who defended the 'good old ways'.

Brown was the colour of the decade, from lentils to hessian wallpapers, fitted shag pile carpets and cork tiles on the floors and walls. Vinyl wallpapers covered the bathrooms and kitchens with wild, flowery patterns and more than a touch of 1970s 'Art Deco' replaced the 'Space Age' style of the '60s.

Tableware turned to stoneware. Eve Midwinter produced her 'Sun' and 'Moon' dinnerware for Midwinter, and the softer 'Gypsy' and 'Potter's Wheel' patterns came from Denby.

There were many craft potters living the self-sufficiency dream, producing hand-thrown tableware from country potteries inspired by Hans Coper or Bernard Leach at St Ives. Hand decorating was also a major part of production in the larger companies, as everyone wanted a handmade look. Poole Pottery produced its 'Delphis' range from 1963 to 1980. This was a highly coloured, hand-painted range which had strong links to the abstract art of the time and used painters in a similar way to the production of Clarice Cliff works in the 1930s.

'Oven-to-table ware' appeared on the market from all the major tableware companies, from Wedgwood to Marks & Spencer. By the end of the '70s it was possible to buy all of your dinnerware, cook ware, tablecloths, table-mats and even knife handles in a matching pattern. The dining room, next to the open kitchen, was the favourite place to eat, where guests could examine the kitchen ware and hosts could show off their latest purchases.

Genuine Oriental food was now being prepared at home with the help of cookery books by such experts as Kenneth Lo and Madhur Jaffrey. Ingredients could be bought at specialist delicatessen shops or, if you really wanted authenticity, at the ethnic food shops which were springing up in the Asian communities all over Britain. Other options were available for the stylish or novel dinner party; fondue sets were 'must have' items, as a fondue party left the hostess free to enjoy the cooking while socialising next to her guests. During the 1970s, the kitchen was the centre of the home. The nuclear family was still important and most preschool children were still being looked after at home.

CLOCKWISE FROM OPPOSITE PAGE TOP Danish candelabra. Teak bowl with a Whitefriars 'Hedgehog' vase by Geoffrey Baxter. Three red 'Spear' plates from Poole. Myott coffeepot. Three Hornsea 'Saffron' storage jars. OPPOSITE FAR LEFT Poole 'Delphis' bowl.

BREAKFAST IN A HORNSEA KITCHEN

Hornsea Pottery was founded in 1949 by brothers Desmond and Colin Rawson. The Rawsons had no experience in the production of ceramics, but they were good businessmen. Very quickly, the company was successfully making a range of cheap but rather uninspired pots. In 1958, the Rawsons appointed John Clappison to the post of Head Designer, and under his guidance the company was able to experiment with modern ceramics to produce some innovative, stylish ranges. John Clappison was born in 1937. He was educated in Hull before going to the Royal College of Art to study ceramics from 1957 to 1958. After joining Hornsea in 1958, he produced some memorable designs which pushed the company into producing some of the most technically advanced, sculptural pottery of the 1960s.

Clappison's first contemporary range of tableware was called 'Elegance'. It was Scandinavian in influence, but during the early 1960s Clappison went on to produce ranges such as 'Home Décor' and 'Studiocraft', as well as the tableware range 'Summit', which showed a more original, self-motivated style. During the 1970s, Clappison produced a wide range of high-quality tableware designs, one of which – the highly successful, resist-patterned 'Saffron' – won a Design Centre Award. A number of very successful ranges followed, including 'Heirloom' and 'Tapestry', which remained in production until well into the 1980s. Clappison was elected a Director of Hornsea in 1970, and he rejoined his team as House Designer from 1976 until 1984. He also designed for Ravenhead Glass and he produced ceramics ranges for Marks & Spencer from 1984 through 1986. In 1987, he joined Royal Doulton as Head of Shape Design.

At the end of the 1970s, Hornsea linked with the successful David Queensberry / Martin Hunt Partnership to produce three beautiful, modernist tableware ranges for the 1980s: 'Contrast', 'Concept' and 'Concorde'. 'Contrast' was very popular in Britain, with its simple but elegant matt / shiny finish and its dark brown colourway. 'Concept', which was nicknamed 'Swan Lake' for the swan on the top of all of its lids, was presented to Princess Diana and Prince Charles as a wedding gift. Both 'Concept' and 'Concorde' were produced mainly for the export market, particularly for the USA and Canada. Although the Hornsea company has continued in production, it found its greatest success in the 1960s and '70s.

ABOVE Hornsea breakfast set.

BELOW LEFT 'Saffron' spice rack and egg cups and kitchen textile.

BELOW 'Saffron' coffeepot with Design Centre label.

Self-sufficient Entertaining

During the 1970s, a significant number of middle-class idealists gave up well-paid jobs in the cities to move to the farthest ends of Britain, hoping to escape from the rat race. They wanted to live more simply, raising their children in an environment that was free from all of the pressures of pollution, nuclear war and stress which were becoming daily more apparent. This was a generation of people who thought that their parents had lost their souls to materialism and money. They wanted to decide what length of hair to wear without being told off for wearing it too long. They wanted their children to grow up with a different set of values, appreciating everything for its quality and beauty, rather than for its cost.

John Seymour and his wife Sally had been living on smallholdings for 18 years when he wrote his first book in 1973. *Self-Sufficiency, the Science and Art of Producing Your Own Food* was a manual on how to live, not a vegetarian recipe book, and its first edition sold out within three months of publication. Nine further editions followed, as well as other similar volumes that showed the real concern being felt in society about conservation and the values which were being encouraged by the establishment. In his book *Bring Me My Bow* in 1997, Seymour urged us to live lightly on the planet Earth. He felt that it is important to understand the roots of our food and who it has come from. In his opinion, it was just as important to know the name of the farmer who grew the wheat and the miller who made the flour from the wheat as it was to know the baker who baked and sold the bread.

There were other books on every aspect of the alternative lifestyle during the 1970s: how to grow your own food, how to cook what you grew, how to use alternative sources of power and how to feed your family cheaply but well. The ideals behind the self-sufficient family also supported the goal of educating children in true values and protesting against the threats of the nuclear age. Many women during the '70s were committed to these ideals of

Hazelnut Roast.

HAZELNUT ROAST

This particular nut roast recipe is simple and easy to prepare. It uses only hazelnuts, but different combinations of nuts can be substituted as preferred.
It is best served with a green salad and a tomato sauce. It serves 4 to 6 people.

10 oz. hazelnuts, coarsely
    chopped
8 oz. wholemeal breadcrumbs
8 oz. chopped onion
8 oz. grated carrot
Sea salt
Freshly milled black pepper
1 teaspoon dried mixed herbs
    or 1 tablespoon fresh chopped
    parsley or coriander
2 egg yolks, beaten
A little milk

Preheat the oven to 190ºC. Mix together the nuts, breadcrumbs, onion and carrot, adding the herbs and salt and pepper to taste. Add the beaten egg yolks and a little milk to bind the mixture. Place in a well-greased loaf tin and bake for 45 minutes.

the home, rather than those of the wider community, and they lost interest in many of the traditional grassroots organisations which had been a source of influence for generations. New feminist groups, child-orientated play-groups and young mothers' groups were locally formed. These were more self-centred, self-promoting groups that did not have the same sense of community values and mutual support that the old Townswomen's Guilds or the Women's Institutes once had, and they had the effect of compart-mentalising different elements of society.

The increasing number of food worries gave society another good reason for an 'eat healthy' regime. Already in the 1970s, battery farming was causing concern, and protests were being held over the use of pesticides in farming. As the number of food scares continued to rise throughout the '80s and esca-lated almost out of control in the '90s, it became difficult to find any foods that had not been tampered with or that did not have health warnings attached to them. In 1994, A.A. Gill wrote in his 'Eating Out' column in the *Sunday Times* that good food no longer meant food which tasted good. Good food meant the ever-decreasing list of foods which would not kill us!

Wholefoods were certainly the order of the day in the 1970s. There were lots of cookery books that advocated brown rice and vegetables, including ones that promoted 'the best possible diet', which was a macrobiotic, raw menu from which living nutrients would literally 'revitalise the body'. This diet also had the advantage of being very cheap, especially if you grew your own vegetables — healthy food was also cheap food.

During the 1970s, parties for larger numbers would have been serve-yourself. This table includes a Nut Roast, Potatoes Dauphinoise, Roasted Corn on the Cob and a large salad to satisfy the vegetarians, but also includes Chilli with Beans and Chicken Paprikash for the carnivores in the company. The Lemon Cheesecake for dessert was an important part of 1970s cooking.

CHICKEN PAPRIKASH

1 jointed chicken
2 oz. lard or fat
2 medium onions
2 tablespoons paprika
2 or 3 teaspoons salt
1 green pepper, seeded and cut
   into fine strips
3 chopped tomatoes or a tin of
   plum tomatoes
¼ pint chicken stock
1 oz. cornflour
Cold water
¼ pint pouring cream
¼ pint sour cream

Fry the chicken pieces in the lard until lightly browned. Remove and cook onions very slowly, with a cover on the pan, for about 15 minutes until soft. Return the chicken to the pan and add paprika, salt, stock and tomatoes. Make sure that the liquid half-covers the chicken. Cover and cook either on top of the stove or in the oven until the chicken is tender. When cooked, remove the chicken and keep it warm. Mix the cornflour with water and add to thicken sauce. Bring to the boil before adding the creams. Continue to heat thoroughly with the chicken pieces but do not boil again. Adjust seasoning and serve with flat noodles and a green salad.

LEFT Chicken Paprikash.

OPPOSITE Chilli Con Carne. Grilled sweet corn. Chilled Lemon Cheesecake.

CHILLI CON CARNE

1 lb. lean beef mince
12 oz. dried or two large tins red
   kidney beans
2 onions
2 tablespoons olive oil
1 tablespoon tomato purée
Large tin of tomatoes
2 level teaspoons hot chilli
   powder
½ teaspoon ground ginger
2 squares dark chocolate
Salt

If using dried kidney beans, soak
overnight and boil hard until
soft. Heat the oil and cook the
thinly sliced onions until golden.
Add the chilli and the ginger,
then fry the meat, stirring until
it is browned and coated with
the spices. Add the tomato purée
and continue cooking. Then add
the tin of tomatoes with their
juice. Finally, add the drained
beans and the chocolate and
season to taste. Cover the pan
and simmer for about an hour.
Serve with rice or crusty bread
and a green salad.

POTATOES DAUPHINOISE

1 lb. waxy potatoes
Milk
1 clove crushed garlic
5 fluid oz. double cream
Parmesan cheese, finely grated
Salt and freshly ground black
   pepper

Peel the waxy potatoes and slice
thinly. Place in a heavy-bottomed
pan and just cover with milk.
Bring to the boil and allow the
wax to slightly thicken the milk.
Add a clove of crushed garlic, salt
and freshly ground black pepper
and the double cream. Bring back
to the boil, remove from heat and
transfer to an oven-to-table ware
dish. Cook for about 40 minutes,
add more cream if necessary and
cover with finely grated
Parmesan. Return to the oven
and cook until the potatoes are
soft.

QUICK LEMON CHEESECAKE

For the crust:
6 oz. digestive biscuits
3 oz. butter
2 oz. sugar

For the filling:
½ of a 1-pint jelly tablet
8 oz. soft cream cheese
2 oz. caster sugar
Grated rind of a large lemon

For the topping:
3 tablespoons lemon juice
1 ½ teaspoons arrowroot
1 oz. caster sugar
Butter

Crush the biscuits and melt the
butter. Mix together with the
sugar and press into a loose-bot-
tomed tin. Chill for 2 hours.
Make up the jelly with ¼ pint
water and chill until just starting to set. Beat the cream cheese
with the sugar and the lemon
rind and gradually beat in the
jelly. Spoon the smooth filling
into the biscuit crust and chill
until the filling has set. Make the
lemon juice up to ¼ pint with
water. Blend the arrowroot with
a little of this to a smooth paste,
and then add back to the rest of
the liquid with the sugar. Bring
to the boil, stirring all the time,
and keep boiling until the
mixture is clear. Remove from
the heat and add a knob of
butter. Cool and spoon topping
over the filling.

NATURAL FOOD IN THE USA

America was also in the middle of a food revolution during the 1970s, and many people in the USA saw the role of homemakers as preserving the natural resources of the world. Frances Moore Lappe wrote a bestselling book on vegetarian nutrition called *Diet for a Small Planet* at the start of the decade. The companion volume by Ellen Ewald, called *Recipes for a Small Planet*, was published in 1973 and by 1980 it was in its 20th edition.

In her introduction to the recipes, Ewald stated how liberating eating natural foods could be. Despite the food industry creating new 'plastic' food products every day, the experience of eating really fresh produce straight from the ground was a truly new and exciting one. If time was taken to read the artificial foods' labels, where one could find mostly sugar, starch and flavourings, a change to natural foods would be like deciding to eat food instead of chemicals. Ewald claimed that her cookbook was for everyday use, and that time and effort would be required to prepare the food. She made no apology for the fact that this was not a book about 'instant food', but that was certainly no obstacle to its sales.

Another popular volume from 1976, which had sold more than 80,000 copies and was in its sixth printing by 1978, was *Laurel's Kitchen* by Laurel Robertson, Carole Flinders and Bronwen Godfrey. The authors were young, well-educated women with growing families in California who had embraced the new ideas about ecology and living and eating in a natural way. They advocated a return to the woman of the house being the 'keeper of the keys'. They felt that the responsibilities of holding the 'keys' of the household stores, attics and cupboards was a position of honour. The role of women in times of poverty was to ration and allocate supplies in such a way that would see them through shortages. In times of plenty, a woman would think ahead and provide for the future. These three Californian women felt that this worthwhile tradition seemed to have been lost in only a couple of generations, and the world was suffering for this mistake. It was no longer only individual households that were suffering from the squandering of natural resources and lack of frugality. Women needed to be trustees not just for families, but for the entire planet.

Books such as *Laurel's Kitchen* were also an unsuccessful attempt to stop the takeover of consumerism in the latter part of the 20th century. As more women went out to work, their positions as homemakers became threatened. Far from 'releasing women from the drudgery of the home to pursue a more meaningful existence', women found that reliance upon child minders, instant meals and household gadgets often cost them more than they were earning.

During the 1970s, many educated women realised that the ideal life which centred around self-sufficiency and home building was not enough for them. No matter how much talk about feminist ideals was had around mugs of Nescafé, there was still a standard of 'men at work - women in the kitchen'. For some women it was great, but for many it was not enough.

Homemade yoghurt and Krups Yoghurt Maker.

WEDGWOOD OVEN-TO-TABLE WARE

Wedgwood oven-to-table ware led the field in Britain when it was introduced in the 1970s. It set the scene for versatility at the table. It combined style with practicality, and made possible an elegant mode of living for even the busiest of modern women. The demand for this new tableware soared. New patterns were introduced and the range grew with its increasing popularity. Apart from kitchen wares, there were matching items for the table, including cups, saucers, plates, salt and pepper pots. There was no need for a jumble of unsightly dishes at the table. Instead, a precooked meal could be brought straight from the oven to the table.

Wedgwood oven-to-table ware was hardy and tough, despite its attractive appearance. Extreme tests and experiments went into perfecting the superlative glaze so that it would be safe in dishwashers and microwave ovens, as well as resistant to damage caused by high temperatures and everyday rigours. Even though it was a quality product, it required no special treatment other than sensible use. Everything could be bought separately so that a set could be built up to meet individual family and lifestyle requirements. Oven-to-table ware could grow with the consumer's lifestyle needs, and the quality was unsurpassed.

Wedgewood 'Blue Pacific' oven-to-table ware.

Fondue Party

One of the favourite ways of entertaining during the 1970s was the fondue party or 'dip in dinner', which originated in France and returned to Britain via the USA. There was a variety of different types of fondue. Swiss Fondue used Swiss cheese as a dipping base for cubes of bread, a Fondue Bourguignonne involved cooked, marinated chunks of beef in hot oil, served with a dipping sauce, and there was even a Chocolate Fondue for dessert. Fondue sets were supplied with a heavy iron pot which sat over a spirit burner on the table. Each guest used a fork with an identifiable mark or colour on the handle to avoid confusion, which could spear different items from the selection on serving dishes. The guests then dipped their forks into the hot fondue pot to cook their food to their personal tastes.

With a Fondue Bourguignonne, some crusty French bread, a green salad and a glass of red wine were served. A Swiss Fondue would have been served as a communal supper, ideally beside a roaring fire in the middle of winter with a glass of dry white wine. It was very easy to lose your bread in the cheese pot. Swiss tradition says that if a man drops his bread into the pot, he has to pay for the meal; if a woman drops hers in, she has to kiss each man at the table. Chocolate Fondue, which can be white or dark, relies on the very best chocolate being used. It is self-explanatory and absolutely delicious!

A fondue table.

FONDUE AU FROMAGE NEUCHATEL

No two recipes for fondue are alike, but certain rules must be followed if the fondue made at home is to taste like the real thing from Switzerland. The cheese should be a mix of Emmenthal and Gruyère. Other hard cheeses can be used, but the flavour will be different.

Rub the inside of the fondue pot with a clove of garlic, and then discard the clove. Put into the pot:
2 lb. grated cheese
³/₄ pint white wine, maybe a Moselle
¹/₄ teaspoon pepper and nutmeg
A shake of cayenne pepper
Juice of a small lemon
6 teaspoons cornflour

Stirring continuously, bring to the boil and cook carefully until smooth. Gradually stir in 2 liqueur glasses of kirsch and transfer the fondue pot to the spirit burner. Spear bread with a fork, dip it into the fondue, swirl and eat. If the fondue is too thick at the table, add a few pinches of bicarbonate of soda. If it's too thin, add some cornflour mixed to a smooth cream with a little wine.

FONDUE BOURGUIGNONNE

A Fondue Bourguignonne is a luxurious version of a fondue for which small cubes of steak are speared and cooked in hot oil, accompanied by a selection of mayonnaise-based sauces and pickles.

Make a minimum of 3 sauces and a maximum of 8. Choose from the following examples or make your own. To ¹/₄ pint of good quality or homemade mayonnaise, add:

Chopped parsley, garlic and onions
Tomato purée with paprika, Tabasco, and Worcester sauce
Curry paste and garlic
Chopped gherkins, capers and hard-boiled eggs
French mustard and lemon juice
Anchovies, onions and gherkins
Mint and finely chopped cucumber
Watercress, celery and whipped cream

For 6 people, cut 2 to 3 lb. of rump or fillet steak into cubes and pile onto a large plate. Spoon sauces onto small dishes. Arrange this on a dining table with 6 dinner plates, 6 fondue forks and 6 dining forks. When the guests arrive, heat the oil and place it in the fondue pot. Each guest then helps himself to sauces before spearing a cube of meat and cooking it in the oil to his own taste. He can then transfer it to his plate and eat it with the dinner fork and the sauces.

CHOCOLATE FONDUE

Fill the fondue set with melted Swiss chocolate, either all dark chocolate or with a swirl of white chocolate at the last minute. Toblerone melted down with a little milk makes another genuine and unusual Swiss alternative. Lots of fruit pieces (such as strawberries, etc.) should be made ready to dip, and plenty of serviettes should be to hand for cleaning up!

'AUTUMN LEAVES'

'Autumn Leaves' was a range of kitchenware designed in 1979 and marketed as an exclusive range for Marks & Spencer in the United Kingdom. The range was so popular that each year it was extended as new manufacturers were added to the production. General tableware was made by Johnson Brothers, while some of the serving dishes were produced by T.G. Green. Cloverleaf made melamine chopping boards, trays and cutlery. Pyrex® produced glass, Hornsea produced ceramic storage jars, Brabantia made bread bins and metal storage containers, Swan Moulinex made electrical goods, Dorma created textiles and H & R Johnson made ceramic tiles. All of the goods were produced by the best companies in their fields. Some pieces were added to or eliminated from the range over a period of 10 years, but 'Autumn Leaves' was still being sold in Marks & Spencer's stores until 1994.

'Autumn Leaves' is a good example of the way in which a very large retail chain would commission a wide variety of manufacturers to produce a range exclusively for them. Marks & Spencer used one pattern and adapted it to many products to give a completely coordinated look to a room, in this case a kitchen. For the consumers, the items were all available to purchase in one store, and the coordinated kitchen was a strong fashion look for the '70s and '80s. For the manufacturers, a link with Marks & Spencer gave a huge boost to sales and a guarantee of production for a number of years. Unfortunately, there was no guarantee beyond the first contract, and the outcome for some smaller manufacturers who had turned their production over exclusively to one large retailer was a loss of other business. This resulted in the closure of some small companies during the '80s and '90s.

'Autumn Leaves' encompassed a range of more than 200 different items, not including items that were rejected by Marks & Spencer and then sold off by the relevant manufacturers. The range was typical of the middle-of-the-road, highly popular designs that were mass-produced for the popular market at the end of the 1970s.

'Autumn Leaves' cutlery and storage jar.

Various 'Autumn Leaves' items in a 1970s kitchen, with a Villeroy and Boch lookalike casserole.

TEXTURED GLASS AND CERAMICS

During the 1970s, the *only* kind of glass to use was textured. The Scandinavian designers had been working for 20 years with natural inspirations. Tapio Wirkkala and Timo Sarpaneva in Finland had been creating glassware which was sculptural in form and based on the structures of ice, rain and natural growth. Bark moulds had been made, which were used to form individual pieces of glassware. Source and inspiration were clear in the work of these ground-breaking designers.

By the 1970s, most of the large companies had followed their lead. In Britain Whitefriars, under the leadership of Geoffrey Baxter, had already introduced a range of textured glassware, and during the 1970s this was expanded in form and colour to include several ranges of table glass. Ravenhead Glass was mass producing a very similar range under the banner of United Glass Ltd. This range was called 'Siesta', and production started in 1973. Alexander Hardie Williamson had originally designed this range, but the Hornsea designer John Clappison expanded it later in the decade. Clappison also designed another textured range called 'White Fire', and both 'Siesta' and 'White Fire' were very successful and were produced and marketed in huge numbers until the 1980s. Textured glass was produced in Europe and in the USA, and for 10 years it dominated the fashion in glassware.

The same development was taking place in ceramics. All over Britain, ceramics departments in art colleges were training studio potters to produce pottery. Following the success of the St Ives Pottery, Troika, Winchcome and many other studio ceramics business, many young potters were keen to start up their own business. Often these were set in country premises where a simple, self-sufficient lifestyle could be supported by a small pottery. Chunky, slip-decorated earthenware or stoneware was popular, and the handmade quality only added to its appeal.

The big names in British ceramics were following the heavy, handmade look – pots had certainly turned into stone! Denby used the studio pottery influence to produce 'Potter's Wheel' and 'Rondo' in the early '70s. Eve Midwinter designed the 'Stonehenge' range, which included the popular 'Sun' and 'Moon' ranges of stoneware. Even the old, traditional china companies like Myott and Wedgwood had their stoneware coffee pots and oven-to-table ware. Textured designs had a heavy, durable appeal which suited the lifestyle of the period. They are now some of the most collectible items of tableware of the 20th century.

A Ravenhead 'Siesta' glass, cooling in a river.

A Midwinter 'Sun' coffeepot.

TAPIO WIRKKALA

Studio 'Bark' vase.

Born in 1915 and educated in Finland, Tapio Wirkkala studied at the Central School of Industrial Design from 1933 to 1936. He then worked with the Karhula Iittala glassworks from 1946 until his death in 1985. The name Tapio means a spirit which inhabits a forest. Tapio Wirkkala spent much of his life working and living in the great wilderness of Finland and being directly influenced by nature in its wildest forms. He had a home in Tapiola, a Finnish garden city which was built in the 1950s outside Helsinki. The city was a textbook example of town planning – it was an ideal place, where it was possible to live within reach of the city but not be overwhelmed by it. Wirkkala also owned a home in Lapponia; he built a small house at Ljarvi on a narrow peninsula which was lost under a mountain of snow and ice in winter, but which stood proudly between two lakes in the summer. It was contact with nature and silent communication with the natural elements that gave inspiration to Wirkkala's work.

Wirkkala was a multitalented artist. He worked on paper, wood, ceramics, exhibition design and glass. He was inspired by communion with the processes of nature, the suspended qualities of ice and snow, which he captured graphically in his glass and wood forms.

Wirkkala and his colleague Timo Sarpaneva were responsible for moving the Finnish glassware industry from the creation of utilitarian objects to the creation of an art form. They created pieces which allowed the medium to exist in its simplest form, with or without a function. In 1946, Wirkkala designed the 'Kanterelli' range of vases — graceful, mushroomlike glass forms which swept the board with awards at the 1951 Milan Triennale. Wirkkala and his wife Rut Bryk, who worked with Arabia, also designed the complete Finnish exhibit. Finnish designers won six awards at the exhibition; three went to Wirkkala himself, and Finnish design was given a prominent place within industrial design for the following two decades.

'Suomi' table ware designed by Timo Sarpaneva for Rosenthal.

The glassware produced by Finnish designers won prizes at all of the European exhibitions during the '50s and '60s, and established Iittala as a major leader in contemporary design. Over the years, Wirkkala's work has covered the full range of glass design, from one-off exhibition pieces to 'Ultima Thule', the range of glassware originally designed for the beginning of commercial transatlantic airline flights in 1967. This range went on to be commercially produced and expanded, and some pieces are still in production today.

Wirkkala designed on a freelance basis for many other companies all over the world: Raymond Loewy in New York; A.G. in West Germany from 1956 onward; Venini in Italy from 1959 onward; and ceramics for Rosenthal in Germany from 1955 until his death in 1985. He designed the Finlandia vodka bottle in 1968, the Rihimaki Glass Museum in 1981 and even the Finnish currency notes.

Tapio Wirkkala stands as one of the leading figures in 20th century design. By following a path that was true to his ideals, he produced ground-breaking work that influenced design all over the rest of the world. In all of his work, he retained a balance between industrial techniques and craftsmanship. His work embodied the Finnish love of nature; the leaves, seashells, ice, movement of water and birds that he observed were integral to his final designs, and for this he will be remembered as one of the outstanding names in modern industrial design.

TIMO SARPANEVA

Timo Sarpaneva was born in Finland in 1926 and was educated in Helsinki. He joined the Graphics Department of the Central School of Applied Arts from 1941 to 1948. In 1950, he was invited to join the Iittala-Karhula glassworks as a Product Designer and Head of the Exhibition Section. At first he worked mainly in sculptural forms, not utility glass. His orchid vases from 1953 are his best-known pieces from this period; they have become design icons of the time. Sarpaneva soon began to consider the challenges and possibilities of working on utility glass. His simple, clean-cut lines were ideal for manufacturing timeless objects for everyday use.

Unlike the designs of many forward-thinking designers, few of Sarpaneva's designs remained in prototype form. Because his design process was so closely allied to the production methods, manufacture was never a problem and he became sought-after to design in fields of industry other than glass. He designed cast-iron pots for W. Rosenlew from 1959 to 1963, textiles for Villayhtyma Oy from 1960 to 1962, glassware for Iittala, Corning in New York and Venini in Italy, and 'Studio Linie' ceramics for Rosenthal in Germany. Many of his works have entered museums of industrial art as classic pieces of 20th century design.

In 1964 and 1965, Sarpaneva developed a new technique for part-blowing and part-moulding glass. The glass was encased in a mould made of wood, part of which was burnt away at every firing. The process

PLUMS WITH BRANDY

3 lb. of plums
½ lb. butter
4 oz. sugar
Brandy to taste

This recipe can be made in larger quantities for the freezer, and should only be made in the autumn when plums are at their best. Freeze in individual plastic freezer bags for instant desserts all winter. Victoria plums have a wonderful flavour, but black plums, which are sweet and strong, can also be used.

Wash, stone and quarter about 3 lb. of plums. In a large, heavy-based pan, melt about ½ lb. butter and place the plums in the butter with about 4 oz. of sugar or to taste. Cover and cook slowly until soft but not a purée. Add some brandy to taste. Place in a large serving dish and chill overnight. These plums must be very cold, although they can also be used to effect as a base for plum crumble.

Plums for autumn in an Iittala dessert set.

produced a unique, colourless, glass sculptural form which changed each time the mould was used. This technique was widely copied by many of his close contemporaries. Geoffrey Baxter, the principal designer at the British company of Whitefriars, produced a similar coloured range very soon after the launch of Sarpaneva's work with Litalla. In 1967, Sarpaneva designed the 'Festivo' range of glassware, candlesticks and vases based on his initial work with textural forms. The candlesticks came in ten sizes that stood out like ice sculptures of different heights on a table. They are still in production almost half a century later.

Sarpaneva continued designing throughout his life, travelling across the world to take part in new projects. He received worldwide recognition for his contribution to 20th century industrial art in many fields, and he was made an Honorary Royal Designer for Industry in Britain in 1963. He later received an Honorary Doctorate from the Royal College of Art in London for his services to industry.

LEFT Apple Trifle – perfect for a summer wedding in an 'Ultima Thule' dessert set.

BELOW Rosenthal's 'Suomi' coffee service designed by Timo Sarpaneva.

APPLE TRIFLE

2 lb. Bramley cooking apples
4 oz. sugar
1 packet trifle sponges or some
　　plain cake
Brandy or calvados or, for a
　　different taste, sherry
1 pint cream

Peel and chop the apples and cook with a little water and butter until soft. Mash or purée through a sieve and leave to cool. Crumble sponge or cake in the bottom of a trifle bowl. Mix brandy with about ¼ pint cream and pour carefully over the sponge. Leave to soak in for 20 minutes. Whip the cream to soft peaks and fold into the apple purée. Cover the base and chill for a few hours or overnight.

Textured 'Bark' vases and 'Kingfisher' TV vase.

GEOFFREY BAXTER

In 1954 William Wilson, the Head Designer at Whitefriars glassworks decided to appoint another designer and he found Geoffrey Baxter, a designer fresh from his degree at the Royal College of Art under R.Y. Gooden. Geoffrey Baxter was an outstanding student who was greatly influenced by Scandinavian glass, but his first work within the company was influenced by the responsibility of maintaining the 'Whitefriars look'. Contemporary styling with lopsided, bio-morphic forms and heavy, cased glass in colours such as forest green and ruby were the fashion of the 1950s, and Whitefriars had its own brand of these.

Baxter had a special feel for cut glass in the modern style, and he produced some interesting pieces between 1954 and 1957. Heavy-based vases inspired by Scandinavian design appeared at the same time, but by the beginning of the '60s Baxter was designing glass forms in strong colours and shapes which were moving into a more self-motivated style. By 1966, he had started producing the range of textured vases for which he is best known. Log-shaped vases with heavy, barklike textures were followed by other shapes: the 'Banjo' vase; the 'Hooped' vases; the geometric 'Shouldered' vase; and the well-known 'Drunken Bricklayer' design and others were made during the 1960s, followed by a host of other shapes in the 1970s. Although there was a strong link between Baxter's designs and the work of the Scandinavian designers Sarpaneva and Wirkkala, Baxter relied on a range of strong colours and his shapes were more controlled and less organic in form.

During the '70s, he also designed a range of studio vases in strong colours with random strapping in contrasting colours, as well as a streaky range which had links to the streaky ranges of the 1930s. By the end of the '70s, Whitefriars was struggling to gain new orders and a decision was taken to finally close the works in 1980.

ABOVE 'Kingfisher Volcano' vase.

BELOW Lemonade and wine glasses.

CHEESE AND WINE PARTY

One of the most fashionable and easy ways to feed a large number of people in the 1970s was a cheese and wine party. It was also a good way of mixing people who didn't know each other very well. According to writers of the time, the quantity of wine required was roughly about ¾ of a bottle per head and the quality was whatever suited your pocket. Small, cheap glasses were recommended so that guests could keep score of their drinks and breakages were not a worry.

Various different types of party food were recommended for a cheese and wine party. Creamy dips and savoury biscuits spread with butter and garnished with different cheeses and pickles, cheese and fruit or pickles and olives spiked onto cocktail sticks were all possible. Cheese straws and savoury flans and pastries could be augmented with crisps, nuts or prepackaged savouries.

Some of the food was prepared in advance. Savoury flans, dips and pastries were kept in a fridge and reheated before serving, but garnished biscuits went soft after an hour or two, so they needed to be prepared fresh. A large centrepiece was often made with a cheese board containing a wide range of cheeses, along with grapes and apple wedges. Orange wedges added a splash of colour.

TOP RIGHT Dartington decanter. RIGHT Ravenhead 'Siesta' glasses, designed by Alexander Hardie Williamson in 1973, cooling in a river.
BELOW Assorted Ravenhead glasses lining up for a cheese and wine party.

GOVANCROFT POTTERY

The Govancroft Pottery was started in Glasgow at Tollcross producing industrial stoneware. Jars and pots of every shape and size to hold everything from bleach, acid and whisky to hot water for foot warmers were produced at the factory. Govancroft exported its wares throughout the world through the London agent G.W. Neale and an agent in South Africa.

From the 1920s onward, Govancroft started to produce some glazed articles for the domestic market. The company sold a simple stoneware jug and bowl which were decorated with many different types of glaze, from simple matt pastel shades to strongly coloured spongeware lustre finishes. Soon the design of the jug developed into several different forms, with an Art Deco inspired ewer being the most extreme. During the 1930s and '40s, the company sold all its wares all over Britain, with F.W. Woolworth's being a principal retailer. The hot water bottles were still very popular.

A Govancraft coffee set with cookies.

By the end of the 1960s, a craze for stoneware table ceramics had hit the market, and every company was now producing heavy, chunky, natural-coloured pottery. Govancroft seized its chance, and in a swansong produced a very stylish tableware range of its own. The colours were muted and natural – brown, yellow, ochre and oatmeal – and the shapes were simple and modern. Govancraft had some successes with this new range, but unfortunately it was short-lived and the company, the last pottery in Glasgow, closed at the end of the 1970s.

MILLIONAIRE'S SHORTBREAD

This chocolate-covered caramel short-bread gained recognition in the 1970s and continues to be very popular – it is extremely rich and indulgent, and very delicious. This recipe is courtesy of our good friend Janet.

Grease a 7" x 11" Swiss roll tin. Preheat oven to 180ºC.

Shortbread
5 oz. butter
2.5 oz. caster sugar
6.25 oz. self-raising flour

Cream together the butter and sugar and seive in the flour. Beat the mixture until well combined. Spread evenly into the tin and bake in the centre of the oven for 15 to 20 minutes, taking care not to burn. Allow to cool in the tin.

Caramel
4 oz. butter
4 oz. caster sugar
2 generous tablespoons of golden syrup
7 oz. (200 grams) condensed milk

Combine all of the ingredients in a saucepan and cook gently over a fairly low heat, stirring constantly. Continue cooking and stirring until the mixture comes away from the edges of the pan and is beginning to caramelise slightly. Pour the mixture over the shortbread and allow to cool completely before covering with the chocolate.

Chocolate Topping
2 oz. plain chocolate
2 oz. milk chocolate

Plain, milk or white chocolate may be used, or a combination of these. Whichever you choose, heat the 4 oz. of chocolate in a heatproof bowl over a pan of simmering water until it is completely melted. Spread this over the caramel mixture, which must be completely cool and set or the chocolate will not spread properly, and allow the chocolate to harden. Cut into squares and serve with coffee or your choice of beverage.

STUDIO POTTERY

BERNARD LEACH

Bernard Leach was born in Hong Kong in 1887. His parents were English, but his early life was spent with his grandparents in Japan, who sent him home to be educated at school in England at the age of ten. After school, he studied drawing and etching at the Slade School of Art in London under Frank Brangwyn and his contemporaries. He returned to Japan in 1909 with the intention of starting a career as an artist and printmaker.

Leach became interested in pottery when a friend took him to a raku party in Japan, where he decorated his first pot for fun. He fell in love with the craft and studied every aspect of it under the sixth Kenzan, from the clay to the glaze, in the same manner as a traditional Japanese pottery student.

ABOVE LEFT A selection of St Ives and other studio pottery made circa 1970.
ABOVE Denby 'Cascade' bowl.

BELOW Two pieces of Scottish studio pottery by Mo Fraser and John Draffan, illustrating the rise of the craft potter during the 1970s.

Bornholm bowl.

Eventually, he was awarded the title of seventh Kenzan; he was the only for-eigner ever to achieve this honour. For eleven years, he remained in Japan to study ceramics. Then he returned to England to establish the Leach Pottery in St Ives in Cornwall with his Japanese friend Shoji Hamada. These two potters had been brought up to respect the traditions of their country and their craft, and the work that they produced in the prewar days was a wonderful mixture of early English slipware and Oriental ceramics.

Leach believed that a potter should understand and be in sympathy with every aspect of ceramics at all stages of production. He spent most of his time before the Second World War setting up kilns and experimenting with different glazes and firing techniques. Consequently, times were financially hard and he appeared to have little success. After the war, however, things were very different. He took part in various exhibitions, started teaching and lecturing and began to produce the kind of ceramics which were to inspire the following generations of studio potters. He worked continuously, took on assistants and was finally recognised in Britain as a Master Potter.

He continued to write, teach and run the pottery while travelling con-stantly until 1972. In 1977, the Victoria and Albert Museum honoured Bernard Leach by holding a retrospective of his work. He died in 1979, but his children Janet and David have carried on his pottery tradition. He will undoubtedly be remembered as the best-known of all of the British studio potters of the 20th century.

'St Ives' teapot by Bernard Leach.

Cinque Ports vase.

CINQUE PORTS POTTERY

David Sharp, the founder of the Cinque Ports Pottery, was born in London in 1932. He showed an early artistic talent and was eventually enrolled in a foundation art course in Maidstone College of Art. During a summer holiday, he visited the town of Rye in Sussex, where he saw the Rye Pottery and met with the founders John and Walter Cole. He was so impressed with the company that in 1947 he returned to the town and became Rye Pottery's first apprentice. He was with the pottery for six years, learning all of the skills of the studio potter before doing national service in 1953.

When Sharp returned to Rye after his national service, he found that the aims of the pottery had become more commercial and less artistic in his eyes. He also wanted to work for himself, so in 1956 he left to form the Rye Art Pottery with his friend George Gray. Rye Pottery threatened legal action because of the similarity in name, and consequently the name of the new pottery was changed to Cinque Ports Pottery.

At first, the combination of Gray the businessman and Sharp the artist was a successful one. Together, they had a thriving business which, at the start of the 1960s, was employing 15 workers and using four kilns. The pottery became a limited company and they changed its name to Cinque Ports Pottery Ltd. The work of Cinque Ports Pottery Ltd. was creative and new. Its pots retained the decorative elements that Sharp had learnt at Rye, but they

were also more contemporary in concept, shape and colour. The company was a commercial success, but when Gray wanted to develop this, Sharp's artistic temperament made him disagree. In 1964, the two men decided to go their separate ways, although they remained friends for the rest of their lives.

Sharp remained at the original pottery, while Gray, who retained the Cinque Ports name, moved into a new premises at the local monastery. Gray's business went from strength to strength during the '70s, but by this time Gray was older and had other business interests. He finally sold the name without the 'Ltd.' in the mid-1980s.

Cinque Ports cruet.

TROIKA

In 1963 Lesley Illsley, Jan Thompson and Benny Sirota jointly bought the Wells Pottery in St Ives for £3000 and the Troika Pottery was born. Sirota was the only member of the group to have any previous experience as a potter, having worked with Douglas Zadek at Cobham. Illsley was a sculptor and Thompson was an architect, but the type of pottery that they decided to produce was made by a simple slab process which did not require high levels of traditional ceramic skills. At first, they produced a range of easily made, small items, mainly for the tourist market in St Ives. Small teapots, wall plaques and perfume bottles were made, mainly because of the limitations of their small kiln. These ceramics proved to be very popular.

At first, the artists were derided by the pottery establishment because their shapes were simple and rather crudely made. They worked basically on two ranges. The style of the first was smooth, white, geometric forms, often with square bases rather than the traditional, wheel-thrown pot shapes. They were marked on the surface rather like the work of the sculptress Barbara Hepworth, who had lived at St Ives with her partner, the painter Ben Nicholson. The second range was again simple in form, but it was very textured on the surface, with scratched marks and colour applied in a natural way. The surfaces of these pieces had a feeling of worn stone.

The members of this group were very different from the wealth of studio potters who had grown up in the wake of figures like Bernard Leach, whose pottery was still based in St Ives, but this would finally prove to be their strength. They appeared to have a wider appeal than the studio potters of the day, and they were willing to market their products in a more aggressive way. They expanded their range, and produced some very large lamp bases and vases which combined function with a strong sculptural form. They wanted to sell their pots, and were happy to travel to London to market their work to a larger public.

They moved to a bigger premises in 1970, and throughout the 1970s they expanded steadily, selling as far afield as New York City. By 1980, however, the dream was beginning to fade. Thompson had moved to Scandinavia and the two remaining partners lost momentum. Sadly, the banks foreclosed on the company in 1983.

'Coffin' vase and small 'Square' vase by Troika.

1980 ~ 1989
The Consumer Lifestyle

Queensberry Hunt 'Concept' teapot.

The 1980s was a decade of economic affluence, optimism and rampant consumerism. The American photographer Barbara Kruger captured the mood of the decade with her image of a hand holding a card bearing the slogan 'I shop therefore I am.' The marketing strategies of the '80s were aimed at promoting lifestyles. Warehouses and docklands were converted into smart dwellings and enormous shopping malls. The 'yuppie' generation aspired to possess everything with a designer label. Only the best would do. High-powered business suits with enormous shoulder pads were de rigueur for both men and women.

A recognisable brand was essential. This trend was capitalised on in the High Street by the reinvention of the chain store, pioneered by George Davies. Davies regenerated the Hepworth chain into the enormously successful NEXT brand of stores, beginning with women's wear in 1982 and expanding throughout the decade to include menswear, children's wear, jewellery, mail order and interiors. Interior decoration was now firmly in a fashion context and NEXT, like Habitat in the 1960s, offered the customer the complete package.

The return to Victorian values preached by the Conservatives and Margaret Thatcher led to a revival of 19th century-inspired chintz for interior textiles and wallpapers. Decorative paint finishes were everywhere. The vogue for country house style was engendered by the television adaptation of Evelyn Waugh's *Brideshead Revisited*, which was broadcast in 1981. The magazine *World of Interiors* was launched in the same year, showing people how to achieve this look. In contrast to this hankering for the conservative past and the style of stately homes, the influence of early 20th century 'modern' artists such as Matisse and Picasso could be seen in many textiles of the '80s. A sharp, graphic look emerged as a prevalent design direction that used simple, geometric shapes and bold black and white or strong colour on a large scale. The textile designers Sue Timney and Graham Fowler started their business in 1980, combining these influences by producing neoclassical furnishing textile prints featuring urns, statues and Roman emperors' profiles in bold black and white.

Irony, wit and provocativeness were the tenets of the new postmodern design movement, which was defined in the '80s by the Italian design group Memphis. The group was founded by Ettore Sottsass in 1981, emerging from the Studio Alchimia started by Alessandro Guerriero and Alessandro Mendini in 1976. The name came from a Bob Dylan song. Memphis combined rich

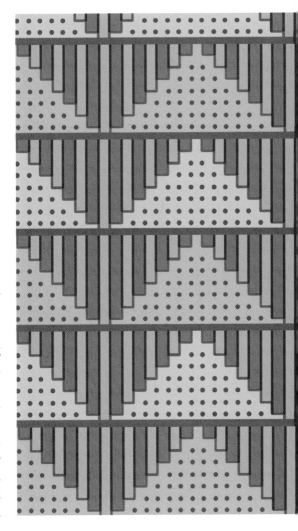

ornamentation with minimalist form, and expensive materials with kitsch. Plastic laminate was the new material, and patterns were inspired by commonplace urban surroundings, such as wire fencing and mosaic floors. Products and furniture were simple in structure, bright in colour and suitable for mass production. The ideas were extreme and humorous.

This frivolous side to the direction of design was apparent in many household accessories in the '80s, which saw the emergence of teapots, mugs, egg cups and other products in the shapes of animals, cars and aeroplanes. Some, like the Carlton 'Walking Ware' range, even had legs and feet. 'Walking Ware' was designed by Roger Mitchell and Danka Napiorkowska and was launched as early as 1973. It gradually gained in popularity, which reached its height in the 1980s. Fluck and Law, the creators of the satirical television comedy show 'Spitting Image', designed a series of caricatural Margaret Thatcher egg cups, mugs and teapots in the '80s which are now highly collectible. Fitted kitchens were popular in the '80s, and people spent a great deal of money having everything tailor-made to match. Agas® were produced in new models and became extremely popular status symbols.

Close-up of sideboard featuring a Poole vase.

Delia Smith rose to ever-greater acclaim as the decade progressed. TV cookery programmes featured authentic dishes from China, Japan and India. Ken Hom and Madhur Jaffrey were the TV chefs of the moment. Thai restaurants began to appear, woks became a 'must-have' item and people began stir-frying at home. Keith Floyd combined cookery with travel and a very laid-back approach to TV programme presentation.

Government health warnings about diet and foods were issued, urging people to cut down on animal fat, as high cholesterol levels could lead to heart trouble in this high-powered, fast-living decade. Sales of fish, chicken and turkey increased as people began to take note of these edicts. Low-fat spreads and semi-skimmed milk appeared on the supermarket shelves. More books on healthy eating and regimes such as food combining appeared on the market, and vegetarianism increased. Food scares surfaced, such as the 1988 announcement about salmonella in eggs, which led to a reduction in egg purchasing and subsequent suffering for poultry farmers. Imported fresh fruit and vegetables were available all year round. Mange-tout peas became an indispensable accompaniment to almost every dish. Fresh herbs were sold in packs and growing pots. Basil, coriander and flat-leaf parsley were essential ingredients in stylish cooking, and sun-dried tomatoes appeared on the long list of ingredients which characterised every trendy restaurant menu.

In many restaurants, the description was larger than the dish, as the 1970s trend for *nouvelle cuisine* was still in vogue in some circles. Mineral water was a phenomenon which began in this decade and was ordered in all smart restaurants along with the wine. It was in vogue to drink champagne. High-powered meetings took place over breakfasts, and a brunch party was the thing to have at weekends to entertain your friends.

The '80s was a time of excessive consumerism, and by the end of the decade there was a distinct move towards minimalism and individuality, which developed further during the '90s.

QUEENSBERRY HUNT

The Queensberry Hunt Partnership was started by David Queensberry and Martin Hunt in 1966, when design consultancies were a fairly new phenomenon. Today, it continues successfully to combine excellent design and style with wide commercial appeal. The partnership began when Queensberry and Hunt were both teaching at the Royal College of Art and it later expanded to recruit two more partners, Robin Levien and John Horler.

The partnership worked at first for several UK companies who were committed to manufacturing good contemporary design, but over the years the team worked increasingly for European and Far Eastern companies. Their 'Trend' range of tableware for Thomas in Germany in 1983 became the bestselling contemporary tableware in Europe. The 'Tea-for-One' design for Bing and Grondahl in Denmark sold extremely successfully in Europe and the USA, although not in the UK.

Both David Queensberry and Martin Hunt studied originally as studio potters, and their designs for mass production have come from a hands-on approach to the craft involved in making the objects they have designed. Their excellent model-making skills have been a crucial element of the process. Martin Hunt became a student at the Royal College of Art in 1963. He graduated in 1966 and was taken on as a tutor. Eventually, he became Head of the Glass Department.

David Queensberry's first major project was with Crown Staffordshire China in 1955. His design came second in the 1959 Council of Industry Awards for Elegant Design. In the same year, Queensberry became a Professor of Ceramics at the Royal College of Art, at the age of 29. He met Terence Conran in the mid-1950s, and it was Conran who introduced Queensberry to Roy Midwinter, who also became an important business contact and friend. The 'Fine shape' designed by David Queensberry for Midwinter in 1962 became a huge success, setting a much-copied style that was popular throughout the 1960s. Queensberry also designed cut crystal for Webb Corbett, which later became part of Royal Doulton. His range won the Design Council's Duke of Edinburgh Award for Elegant Design in 1963.

Hornsea, a company with a forward-looking attitude to design, was the main British company that commissioned work from Queensberry Hunt in the 1970s. The 'Contrast' range, produced in 1974, was Hornsea's bestselling range for over 12 years and won a Design Council Award. Its distinctive use of vitrified, unglazed surfaces made it different from anything else on the market. The next Queensberry Hunt shape was 'Concept' in 1976, which also used the special polishing technique. It featured a distinctive, swan-shaped knob on the lid of the teapots and coffeepots. It too won a Design Council Award and was particularly popular in the USA and Scandinavia. 'Concord' was produced in 1980 and it also won an award. The company gifted a set of 'Concord' china to Charles and Diana on their wedding day in 1981.

'Concord' tableware by Queensberry Hunt, produced in 1980.

CONRAN DINING

Terence Conran was born in London in 1931 and he studied at the Central School of Art and Design. In 1952, he started a small furniture and interior design business in Bethnal Green in London called the Conran Design Group. His business was varied and included work in all fields of interior design, including textiles for David Whitehead and ceramic designs for Roy Midwinter. The company was not an immediate success, and in part to support it, Conran made his first venture into the catering world by opening The Soup Kitchen in London in 1955. It filled a gap in the market, and soon two more Soup Kitchens in London followed, then another in Cambridge, and after a few years Conran sold out to his business partner. This financed the opening of his first restaurant, the Orrery in the Kings Road in 1956. The two sides of Conran's business were running parallel until 1964, when he opened Habitat and became a household name in the world of design. Habitat was a unique concept for its time, and it very quickly influenced the way of life of the '60s generation. It sold everything for the modern home, from timeless classics like the Breuer Wassily chair to a modest terra-cotta chicken brick made in the South of France.

The first Conran Shop opened in 1973 on the original site of the first Habitat, which had now expanded into several new stores and a new London site. Conran opened this shop to sell products which were too expensive for Habitat or too extreme in design. In the Conran Shop, he could also sell small runs of individually designed products that were commissioned from young designers or handmade by craftsmen.

In 1985, the old Art Deco Michelin Building across the road from the Conran Shop became vacant, and Conran seized the opportunity to move to a premises which was three times larger than the original shop and into a building which he had always admired. Stock for the new shop came from British designers, but also from craftspeople around the world. Items were carefully chosen to give the shop a contemporary but eclectic mix of cultures and crafts – very much the look of the best interiors during the 1980s. By the end of the century, there were four more Conran Shops in Marylebone, Paris, New York City and Tokyo. With the acquisition of the Michelin Building, Conran was able to combine his two loves by opening the restaurant Bibendum on the top floor of the shop building. In the 21st century, it is still one of London's best eating places.

Conran's commitment to British design was still evident when he started the charitable Conran Foundation in the Boilerhouse Project with the Victoria and Albert Museum in 1981. From this successful concept of promoting design through exhibitions, discussions and events, the idea of a design museum was born. In 1987, the Design Museum was opened within the development at Butlers Wharf at Tower Bridge. It is still the most important showcase for design in London. Butlers Wharf allowed Conran to expand his other interest in food to several new restaurants. Le Pont de la Tour and The Chophouse opened, as well as related specialist food stores

Conran 'Choti' fabric.

Black dining room furniture, table and glassware, all from Habitat.

and wine shops. These were in an area of well-designed riverside apartments, which provided an immediate clientele which was ready to appreciate Conran's commitment to quality at every level of the market.

In the heart of the recession of the early '90s, and against most advice, Conran opened his huge restaurant Quaglino's in 1993. It seated over 400 people, and was followed by Mezzo in 1995. Both restaurants still receive critical acclaim and they have been followed by a stream of eateries across the world.

To the children of the '60s, Conran changed their lives by changing their homes. To their children, he was the creator of huge eating places at every market level for their entertainment. Terence Conran was knighted for his services to British industry in 1983, and he continues to be a voice and a champion for good design all over the world. His ambition in 1964 to 'provide everyone with a good salad bowl' has almost certainly come true!

WEDGWOOD IN THE 1980s

Wedgwood is an example of a well-established firm of worldwide reputation that was involved in the 1980s business trend of mergers. In 1986, Waterford Crystal merged with Wedgwood, and by 1998 the company had acquired an 85% share in Rosenthal AG of Selb, Germany, which increased in 2001 to 89.9%. The Waterford Wedgwood Group was joined in May 1999 by All-Clad of Cannonsberg, Pennsylvania and in 2001 by W-C Designs of Anaheim, California.

The Wedgwood 1988 *Fine Bone China Collection* catalogue featured an extensive range of over 80 patterns, divided into three collections. The 'Classic' collection was for traditional patterns. The 'Fine White' collection was self-coloured with embossed decoration, produced to meet the demand for mixing and matching, and the 'Country' collection featured mainly floral designs. The most innovative range was 'Shape 225', which had been commissioned from the American designer Jerome Gould and his associate Tom Kellogg. This new 'contemporary classic' shape had a streamlined look, and its solar and lunar patterns featured a play of matt and shiny glazed effects on self-coloured black or white. The 'Apollo' pattern had very fine black lines in a 1950s-inspired pattern. 'Aurora' was plain white with gold edging, while 'Crescent' had a delicate, traditional Wedgwood floral pattern.

Waterford Wedgwood described itself as The Luxury Lifestyle Group, having a combined history of over 600 years of heritage, tradition and craftsmanship. The companies in the group complemented each other in the production of luxury tableware. They have continued the tradition of working with well-known artists and designers. Wedgwood has collaborated on the design of tableware ranges with fashion designers such as Bulgari, Jasper Conran, Paul Costelloe, John Rocha and Versace, leading the 1990s concept of the fashion designer presenting a complete lifestyle image.

The Wedgwood 'Shape 225' catalogue.

TIMNEY FOWLER

The design company Timney Fowler was founded in 1980 by Susan Timney and Graham Fowler. Theirs was a small, independent venture that produced printed textiles for fashion. They developed business in the UK, Europe and the USA and formed links with several Japanese companies. They offered specialist design services and consultancies in everything from textiles and fashion to stationery and graphics.

Timney Fowler has successfully continued to produce traditional and contemporary looks, and its designs feature in the permanent collections of museums such as the Victoria & Albert Museum, the Cooper Hewitt Museum in New York City and the Art Institute of Chicago as important examples of 20th century design.

Timney Fowler fabric with Wedgwood 'Queen's Plain' ware.

BRITISH POTTERIES IN THE 1980s

In the 1980s, independent manufacturing companies were prey to being swallowed up by giant conglomerates, and takeovers and mergers abounded. Smaller companies had to fight hard to find a place in this highly competitive world, where big may not have been beautiful but it was certainly powerful.

Federated Potteries was founded in 1982 as the result of a merger between W.H. Grindley, Cartwright and Edwards, and Weymek in an attempt to pool collective resources and work together for survival. The company set up a design studio directed by Roy Midwinter, who employed young designers including Dave Harper. They produced strongly coloured, abstract, coordinated patterns which could be mixed and matched. These designs met the market demand for fashionable, informal dining ware. Unfortunately, the Federated Potteries experiment was ahead of its time. It did not survive beyond 1992, but it did herald the move toward casual dinnerware, which formed a large section of the British pottery industry's production in the late '90s.

Churchills was founded in 1984 as a result of the merger of Wessex ceramics, Sampson Bridgwood and James Broadhurst. It became Churchill China in 1992, and now it also incorporates Crownford bone china and Wren giftware. The company is one of the biggest suppliers to IKEA, producing exclusive designs for its worldwide home furnishings stores.

Roy Midwinter 'Safari' plate for Federated Potteries.

KEITH FLOYD

Keith Floyd was born in 1943 and educated at the Wellington School in Somerset. On leaving school, he became a journalist in Bristol and then, reputedly after seeing the film 'Zulu', he decided to join the army. During his time in the army, he experimented with cooking in the officers' mess. He then worked in London and France in a variety of kitchen-related jobs. By 1971, he owned three restaurants in Bristol. He eventually sold these and spent two years cruising the Mediterranean on a boat called 'Flirty'. In France, he became involved in the antiques business and the wine trade, exporting wine from France to Britain and moving antiques in the opposite direction. He also opened a restaurant near Avignon. In 1991, he opened Floyd's Inn in Devon, which he sold in 1996 when he moved to Kinsale in Ireland. He has always enjoyed travel, and has cooked his way round the world in his series of television programmes.

Keith Floyd brought a flamboyant approach to television cooking in the 1980s. His first TV programme apparently came about through a chance meeting with a TV producer in his Bristol Bistro. This led to a seven-part series called 'Floyd on Fish'. His passion for his subject was infectious, and the relaxed manner in which he prepared the food, with a glass of wine for the chef always at hand, made for very entertaining viewing. Since then he has gone on to make many successful TV programmes with accompanying books which combine travel to exotic destinations with practical advice on cooking wonderful dishes. Presentation of his series has involved both the crew and the presenter risking life and limb to give authenticity to the production of the series! Fifteen bestselling books accompanied the TV programmes, including *Floyd on Spain*, *Floyd on Italy*, *Floyd on Africa*, *Floyd on Great Britain* and *Hangovers* (as his programmes always contained more than a few glasses of wine). One of the most charismatic celebrities of the 1980s, Floyd now lives in Andalucia in Spain with his wife Tess, but he can always be persuaded to emerge from retirement to start a new project.

TROUT IN FOIL

Keith Floyd was fairly scathing about trout in his *Floyd on Fish* book, due to the large quantities of farmed trout being offered in restaurants around the country and often cooked, as he saw it, indifferently. He did confess to being impressed when he was served trout in newspaper and saw the potential of embarrassing one's friends by a careful selection of newspaper for each guest. For himself, he uses *The Times*, naturally.

Each fish is stuffed with fresh herbs and a slice of lemon and wrapped in two sheets of news-paper, which is then run under cold water until thoroughly soaked. It is then placed in an oven at 180ºC until the paper dries out completely. This takes about 8 minutes. Open the package with scissors and peel off the paper, which will take the skin off the trout.

If you don't fancy the newspaper technique, trout can be success-fully baked in tinfoil. Our recipe calls for each trout fillet to be stuffed with parsley butter and sprinkled with vodka — a very 1980s touch — before being sealed in a foil parcel and baked at 200ºC for 10 minutes. It can then be served in the foil and garnished with lemon and fresh parsley.

Trout in foil.

The Trend for Eastern Dining

GOSHISOSAMA – Thank you for the meal.

JAPANESE FOOD

Japanese cooking is internationally acclaimed as not only one of the most beautiful cuisines in appearance, but also one of the finest in taste and preparation. All foodstuffs are served either in their natural state or gently cooked using light and subtle seasonings. Special techniques are not required when cooking in the Japanese manner; only care of preparation and a careful choice of presentation are needed. There are many adornments that can be added to the dishes for serving. Flowers in paper or cut from vegetables, food sculptures and whole leaves or flowers are chosen to contrast in colour and texture with the simplicity of the dishes.

Formal Japanese restaurants have special requirements for eating. Low Japanese tables and cushions on the floor are standard, as is the use of chopsticks. Each dish should be emptied to the last grain of rice, and when finished the dishes should be placed as they were at the start of the meal. In Japanese tradition, there are other recognised formalities. Rice should be eaten with the bowl in one hand and the chopsticks in the other. Sushi pieces should be taken in one bite with either the fingers or chopsticks. Sashimi should be dipped in soya and wasabi before eating. Great care should be taken not to use too much sauce, so as not to cause offence to the chef. When eating miso soup, chopsticks should be used for the solid meats, but the soup should be drunk straight from the bowl. Noodles should be eaten with chopsticks with a controlled sucking, slurping sound.

In Japan there are many different types of restaurants which specialise in different types and levels of food, and now specialist Japanese restaurants are appearing in the West.

Sushi bars specialise in sushi, which consists of variations of sticky rice and cooked or raw fish or vegetables, usually made in view of the customer behind the eating and serving counter. Types of sushi include:

Nigiri Small balls of rice with fish, seaweed, etc., on top.
Gunka Small cups made of rice, covered by seaweed and filled with fish eggs and other seafood.
Norimaki Sushi rice and seafood, rolled in sheets of seaweed around fine-cut ingredients such as ginger and spring onion.
Temaki Rolls of nori seaweed filled with seafood and vegetables.

Sushi restaurants called *kaiten-zushi* display sushi dishes on a conveyor belt. Customers can help themselves to as many or as few dishes as they want, and they are charged according to the amounts they eat. *Soba-ya* restaurants specialise in noodle dishes that are served either cool with a dipping sauce or hot in a miso soup which is made from soybeans and brown rice, with toppings of fresh vegetables. *Yakitori-ya* specialise in grilled chicken skewers, which are a form of fast food enjoyed as an after-work snack. *Tempura-ya* serve freshly cooked tempura. *Suki-yaki-ya* specialise in *suki-yaki*, a kind of beef and vegetable casserole.

Beetroot Cured Salmon.

BEETROOT CURED SALMON

½ side salmon
3 cooked beetroot
1 tbsp each of sugar and salt
½ tsp each of nutmeg, cumin, cayenne, paprika, crushed peppercorns
½ dried chilli

Place the salmon on a large sheet of clingfilm. Shake the sugar and salt over the salmon and rub in well. Mix the remaining spices together and rub over the same side of the salmon. Dice the beetroot and rub over the same side. Wrap up the salmon and beetroot in clingfilm and refrigerate for 2 days. Remove from the fridge and wash off the spices. Slice thinly and serve.

There are several other types of Japanese restaurants, but they are mainly found only in Japan and include Japanese tea and coffee stalls and fast food tents that stand by the side of the road. Since the mid-1980s, the taste for Japanese food has expanded in the West, with noodle and sushi bars springing up in many places. However 'fusion food', for which East meets West in a fusion of different flavours, has turned the beauty and formality of traditional Japanese cooking into a rare and creative experience.

A Chinese dinner for two.

ZEN RESTAURANTS

The American-born architect Rick Mather was commissioned to create interiors for Zen restaurants in London, Hong Kong and Montreal between 1985 and 1991. He designed three restaurants in London: ZeNW3 in Hampstead, Zen Central and Now & Zen. The aim of these establishments was to revolutionise Chinese dining and raise it to a new, fashionable status.

ZeNW3, completed in 1985, was the first of the series. Its building was a dramatic glass, stainless steel and white-walled construction with ice-green carpeting and a central water feature inside. The feel was cool, clean, bright and modern, creating a very different atmosphere to the traditional red and gold flocked wallpaper usually seen in Chinese restaurants. Spectacular water features were central to all of the Zen restaurant interiors. In ZeNW3, the water ran down a glass channel which formed the wall of the staircase. Now & Zen in Upper St Martin's Lane, which could seat 200 people, had a huge glass wall façade through which passers-by could view the diners inside,

SOBA NOODLE SOUP

8 oz. soba noodles
8 oz. prawns
1 pint chicken or vegetable stock
3 tablespoons soy sauce
3 tablespoons mirin
1 tablespoon sugar
Dashi stock
2 spring onions, finely chopped

Cook the soba noodles for 5 minutes in boiling water. Drain and leave aside. Bring the stock to the boil and cook the prawns for a few minutes. Then add all of the other ingredients. Place some soba in each bowl, and cover with the prawn and stock mix. Garnish with spring onions.

SEARED CUTTLEFISH WITH SOBA NOODLES IN A SOYA AND MIRIN DRESSING

8 baby cuttlefish
½ lb. soba noodles
Cloud-eared fungus
* (reconstituted)*
A few Chinese dates
Salt and pepper
Oil for frying

Season the cuttlefish and set aside. Boil the soba noodles and set aside. Drizzle the oil in a wok on a medium heat. Add fungus, dates and soba noodles and toss in oil. Add dressing and remove from heat. Oil and heat a griddle pan until smoking and cook cuttlefish for one minute on each side. Place noodle mixture on hot plates, arrange fish on top and serve.

Seared Cuttlefish.

many of whom were there in order to be seen. Tables were on three floors, linked by an open, oval-shaped well, across which passed a flowing water feature with shallow glass bowls.

These restaurants brought a cutting-edge, contemporary style to the experience of eating beautifully prepared Chinese food. They captured the mood of the times and were extremely popular and successful.

Fish Steamed in Banana Leaves.

FISH STEAMED IN BANANA LEAVES

You will need fillets of firm, white fish.

Marinade
1 teaspoon cumin
Turmeric
Chilli powder
Garlic paste
Ginger paste
Lemon juice
1 tablespoon mustard seeds
¼ teaspoon grated nutmeg
2 tablespoons oil
Salt and pepper

Mix the marinade ingredients together to make a smooth paste. Spread over the fish. Leave to marinate for at least ½ hour. Oil the banana leaf and warm slightly to make it more pliable. Place each fillet in a banana leaf fold and tie with string to make an attractive parcel. Cook in a bamboo steamer over boiling water for about 20 minutes, and serve in the parcel with a garnish.

CHINESE COOKERY AND KEN HOM

Ken Hom was brought up in Tucson, Arizona, where his family lived after emigrating to the USA in the 1920s. At school he was the envy of his friends, as his packed lunch consisted of a vacuum flask filled with stir-fried vegetables and rice rather than sandwiches and crisps. Peeling hundreds of prawns, preparing vegetables and generally working in his uncle's Chinese restaurant from the age of 11 gave Hom a sound basic education in the catering world. He gave cookery lessons to help finance his education at the University of California. He finally went on to teach at the California Culinary Academy in San Francisco.

In 1984, a friend recommended him as a presenter to a producer at the BBC, and so 'The Ken Hom Chinese Cookery Course' came to television. The show débuted at the beginning of an avalanche of TV programmes for cooks to hit the small screen. The new breed of TV cook in the 1980s was much more of a personality in the public eye. Particularly in the case of Chinese cookery, the host needed to be able to perform in front of the camera. Ken Hom was a master presenter, and he encouraged many people all over the world to cook in the traditional Chinese manner.

A Chinese-American, Hom made a food pilgrimage back to China with his mother in the late 1980s. He travelled widely throughout the 'real' China and documented many very basic peasant techniques and recipes which were in danger of disappearing in the aftermath of the Cultural Revolution. *The Taste of China* was his account of his 'personal odyssey', written on his return. It became one of his most successful books. It gave a personal insight into a very different way of living and cooking, many miles away from the image of the usual Chinese carry-out. Over the next decade, Hom made four TV series and wrote more than 20 books. He made Chinese cookery accessible to everyone with his easy, conversational style of presenting and writing.

Chinese food is the original fast food, but it is the healthiest fast food in the world. Stir-frying is recognised today as one of the best ways to cook food for good health. Fresh ingredients are used and quickly cooked over a high heat in a wok or frying pan, sealing in nutrients and vitamins. Delicious sauces made from spices, fruits and vegetables are added to enhance the dishes' taste and flavour. Ingredients are carefully balanced in a harmonious combination of yin and yang, spicy and sweet, chewy and crisp.

Chinese meals are sociable occasions and are often taken in large groups. Dishes are brought to the table and shared. If the meal is a family one, then different dishes are often supplied by different members of the family, each of whom will have a speciality. In a restaurant, many dishes will be presented to the company, who will select a small portion of each dish and eat it from a small bowl with some rice.

Four place settings from a boxed set of Chinese dishes from Habitat.

BRUNCH IN THE 1980S KITCHEN

By 1983, Terence Conran's *The House Book* was in its third reprint, having first been published in 1974. This was a DIY book on styling your home. It offered advice on how to organise your home to its best advantage using the eclectic mix of inherited and acquired furnishings which most people find in their possession. Planning was the key. Placement of furniture, wall coverings, flooring and lighting all had to be considered, and then the curtains, blinds, rugs and pictures could follow. Decisions had to be made about 'the look'. Would it be country house, town house, farmhouse, Mediterranean, international or eclectic? Everything had to be carefully considered and pulled together with some well-chosen, contemporary items. The placement of home furnishings had to look intentional, and not just like a haphazard arrangement of random acquisitions. This was long before the days of the TV 'house makeover' programmes.

The Kitchen Book first appeared in 1977, giving specific advice for that important area of the house. It urged readers to plan their kitchens to fit the lives they led, and guided them through the minefield of expensive gadgetry then on offer. During the 1980s, the 'fully-fitted' kitchen became increasingly popular, and kitchen companies provided consultation services and individual plans that offered bespoke tailoring for the home. Everything had its own place and was discreetly concealed to give a uniform look. Fridges, freezers and dishwashers disappeared behind wood-panelled façades that were purpose-built for the equipment they housed. Drawers that pulled out easily on rollers stored pots and pans. Thermostatically-controlled drawers were also available to keep wine instantly accessible at the correct temperature. Even rubbish bins were hidden under sinks, but they obediently flipped up their lids whenever the doors were opened.

All styles were available, from the grand country house to the minimal urban kitchen for the one-room flat, where essential equipment was ingeniously packed into the smallest possible space. Expensive accessories were on offer everywhere, holding the promise of an instant improvement in quality of life. Shelving also served to display collections of kitchen paraphernalia, both useful and decorative, contemporary and vintage. Glass storage jars allowed the cook to assess the current stock of dry ingredients instantly. Often, decoration would be the sole purpose of displaying more exotic types of herbs and spices, which were seldom included in day-to-day cooking.

Brunch was a popular social event in the '80s. It provided an opportunity to show off a newly fitted kitchen to guests, and it also offered an occasion for more casual entertaining. All the table accessories would of course be coordinated, and implements like cafetieres, toasters and citrus juicers were essential to the successful production of the event. Buck's Fizz was the preferred tipple, homemade muesli was on offer for the health-conscious, croissants were a must and dishes like Eggs Benedict or Scrambled Eggs with Smoked Salmon would almost certainly be on the menu.

OPPOSITE A fitted kitchen from Magnet with coordinating blue and white tableware from Habitat.

Eggs Benedict.

EGGS BENEDICT

Eggs Benedict is an ideal dish to serve for brunch. When done well, it combines lightly toasted bread, crispy bacon and the perfectly poached egg with creamy Hollandaise Sauce in a mouth-watering concoction. It demonstrates the skill of the chef in getting all these components just right, and is an excellent way to impress your friends.

To serve the Eggs Benedict, allow the following for each portion:

Half an English muffin. lightly
  toasted and buttered
2 slices crispy bacon
1 lightly poached egg

Assemble the components in this order and top with a tablespoon of Hollandaise Sauce. Pop under a hot grill for no more than 30 seconds and serve immediately on warmed plates. Your guests will be impressed!

Hollandaise Sauce
Yolks of 3 large eggs
15 ml. white wine vinegar
15 ml. lemon juice
6 oz. butter
Salt and freshly milled black pepper

Blend the egg yolks with the seasoning in a food processor for approximately 1 minute. Heat the vinegar and lemon juice to simmering point. Switch on the food processor and pour the hot liquid slowly and steadily onto the egg yolks. Switch off. Carefully melt the butter in the saucepan, and when foaming, pour it into the egg mixture as slowly and steadily as possible, until all of the butter has been absorbed. This should result in a thick, smooth sauce to top off your fabulous dish.

DELIA SMITH

When Delia Smith started her 'Cookery Course' on BBC2 television in 1978, her aim was to provide a set of guidelines and instructions on all aspects of home cooking that would be accessible to absolute beginners, but also of value to the more experienced cook. Her programme was geared to home entertaining in a way that allowed the cook to enjoy dining with the guests and to avoid a state of last-minute panic in the kitchen.

In a *Radio Times* article written by her husband, Michael Wynn-Jones, to promote the new TV show, Smith said, 'And I am certain it's anxiety that is the biggest obstacle to good cooking ... one of the aims of the "Cookery Course" will be to build up people's confidence ... that's what's so good about television – you can see the technique for yourself – once it's been demonstrated you'll never go wrong again.' Smith aimed to cook basic dishes well, and her recipes were tried, tested and always reliable. They could be depended on to work even when tried out for the first time on a dinner party for important guests.

Smith has hosted regular series of cookery programmes over the last thirty years, and her enormous influence on Britain's cooks has made her a national icon, referred to in some circles as 'Saint Delia' or 'The Blessed Delia'. Her recommendation of certain ingredients in a TV demonstration can cause supermarket shelves to be cleared of particular products within 24 hours of the broadcast. Supermarkets are now warned in advance of items they may need to stock up on because Smith will mention them!

Smith's 'How To Cook' series covers everything the total novice needs to know, including what to do when things go wrong and, for example, lumps appear in the white sauce. There is a Delia Smith website that gives online tutorials and step-by-step guides, demonstrating foolproof techniques for poaching eggs, melting chocolate, making mayonnaise ... the list goes on, as Delia's popularity goes from strength to strength.

A car-shaped egg cup.

Essential equipment for the 1980s cook.

DAVID MELLOR

Born in Sheffield in 1930, David Mellor has successfully combined designer craftsmanship with entrepreneurial skills in his major contribution to British design over the last 50 years. Mellor graduated from the Royal College of Art in 1954 with a silver medal, having won travelling scholarships which took him, as a student, to Scandinavia and Germany. He also studied in Rome. Over the following years, Mellor has designed street lighting, traffic signals, pillar boxes, fountains and craft silverware, but his major production has been in cutlery and tableware.

Mellor set up his first workshop in Sheffield in 1954, making one-off pieces. His 'Pride' silver plate cutlery, developed in 1953 whilst he was at the RCA, was manufactured by Walker & Hall in Sheffield. In 1957, 'Pride' cutlery was included in the first Design Centre Awards. The range is now being made in Mellor's own factory. The knife handle, originally made of bone and then Xylonite, is now made in hard nylon to accommodate dishwashers. In 1962, Mellor was elected Royal Designer for Industry. In the same year, his 'Symbol' cutlery for Walker & Hall won a Design Centre Award. Mellor was made a Fellow of the Society of Industrial Artists and Designers in 1964. Design Centre Awards were received in 1965 for his 'Embassy' sterling silver tableware, commissioned for use in British embassies, and in 1966 for his 'Thrift' stainless steel economy cutlery, commissioned for government institutional canteens. Mellor was made an Honorary Fellow of the Royal College of Art in 1966. His 'Chinese Ivory' cutlery won another award in 1977.

In 1969, the first David Mellor shop opened in Sloane Square in London, selling tableware and kitchenware. Shops were later opened in Manchester, Covent Garden and Butler's Wharf. The David Mellor Country Shop was opened in Hathersage in 1992. The main outlets for David Mellor cutlery continue to be his own stores, but it is also available through top design-led shops in the UK, such as Liberty, Heal's and the Conran Shop.

Mellor was made an OBE in 1981. From 1981 to 1983, he was the Chairman of a Design Council committee of inquiry into Standards of Design in Consumer Goods in Britain. From 1982 to 1984, he was Chairman of the Crafts Council, and from 1983 to 1988, he was a Trustee of the Victoria & Albert Museum, and Chairman of the Buildings Committee. In 1990 The Round Building, his purpose-designed cutlery factory by Sir Michael Hopkins & Partners at Hathersage, won several architectural and environmental awards. New ranges of cutlery continue to be developed there, with the 1998 'City' range being one of the most radical.

A flat brass bowl designed by David Mellor and hand-spun in his workshops for the David Mellor Shop, 1970.

POSTMODERN CONSUMERISM

By the 1980s, decorative objects were beginning to become so contradictory that they made people laugh, or at least smile. Modernist ideals were a serious business. The devotion to form and function had allowed only admiration, almost without any enjoyment. In some areas of design, a challenge to the status quo had been started during the 1960s, but it was the 1980s which brought wit and humour into the design market under the name of 'postmodernism.' This movement suited a society which was accustomed to unlimited credit and it challenged the basic requirements of design.

Aggressive humour abounded in all fields. Alessi produced extremes in the design of coffee services. Memphis created chairs and tables with three legs, or if these objects had four legs, then they might all be different legs. 'A table needs four legs but why should they all be the same?' the company asked. Memphis was creating domestic objects which were meant to be stared at. The company offered as expensive, quality items for the home what would once have been called 'bad taste design' as a personal challenge to long-held opinions. Ron Arad in England and Philippe Starck the French architect and industrial designer were part of this movement against time-honoured ways. Starck insisted that his works be labelled with 'Made by Starck' rather than the traditional 'Made in France' mark.

Many postmodern designs were made in limited numbers or were hand-crafted, showing little participation in the mass production of factory items. This represented a triumph for the socially elite section of society, and once again it allowed only the rich to participate in the cutting-edge designs of the time. Postmodernism was a short-lived rebellion. By the end of the 1980s, even the original Memphis designers were returning to their own version of balance without eccentricities or excess. With the start of the 1990s, a reassessment of the roots of design returned designers to a more minimalist form of modernism, which better reflected the coming of a new century.

A fruit bowl and platter with hand-painted and sponged effects.

Habitat dishes with hand-painted effects in checks and spots.

A hand-painted circular plate by Charles Jamieson.

NEXT AND THE REINVENTION OF THE HIGH STREET CHAIN STORE

The Hepworth empire started with the establishment of J. Hepworth & Son, gentlemen's tailors in Leeds in 1864. In 1981, Hepworth bought the chain of Kendalls rainwear shops to develop a group of shops for womenswear called NEXT. George Davies was brought in as an 'ideas man'. Davies is now credited with starting the 1980s 'High Street revolution'. In collaboration with Sir Terence Conran, who at that time was a Director of the Hepworth Group, he introduced a new concept in shops and captured the niche market of 25–35-year-old women who were looking for affordable 'designer' fashion. Davies laid out the interiors of the shops in a modern and customer-friendly way that gave customers the opportunity to purchase a complete look from one shop.

The first NEXT store was opened in February 1982, and by the end of July there were 70 NEXT stores throughout the country. The clothing ranges met with enormous success, and in 1984 NEXT for Men was launched, with 52 shops opened by the end of the year. In 1985, the NEXT interiors range was launched and the first department store selling the complete range of NEXT products opened in Regent Street, London. The idea of launching an interiors range was the real groundbreaking move, as it capitalised on the aspirations of the '80s consumer public to have 'designer-styled' homes.

The NEXT Interiors Division commissioned designers to produce ranges specifically for the company. A notable example of this is the series of vases and bowls produced by the James Kent pottery for the limited-edition NEXT collection between 1985 and 1989. These were designed by artists such as Gail Fox, Carol McNicoll, Janice Tchalenko, Hinchcliff & Barber, Karen Bunting, Sabina Teuteberg, Jane Willingale and Joanne and Andrew Young.

In 1985, J. Hepworth & Son changed its name to NEXT plc. In 1988, the *NEXT Directory* was launched, creating a whole new look for catalogue shopping. By 1994, NEXT was operating from 300 stores in 16 countries worldwide. Online shopping was introduced in 1999, and NEXT continues to thrive in the new millennium.

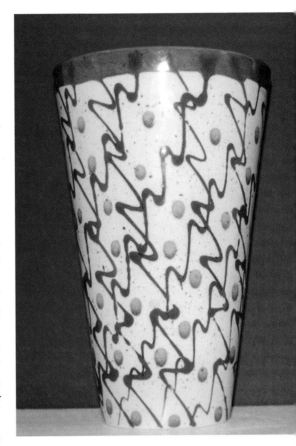

Vase by Janice Tchalenko for the NEXT Interiors collection.

JANICE TCHALENKO

Janice Tchalenko was born in Rugby in 1942. She studied at both Putney School of Art and Harrow School of Art. In the early '70s, Tchalenko taught at Croydon and at Camberwell. In 1981, she became a Tutor at the Royal College of Art, where she is now a Fellow.

In her early career, Tchalenko specialised in stoneware and developed a reputation as a highly competent thrower. In the late '70s, she began to work in a more decorative way, using stencils and slip-trailed glazes on high-fired stoneware. In the early '80s, she began an association with Dartington Pottery, where she is now Principal Designer.

IKEA – RETAIL GIANT

IKEA is one of the home furnishing retail giants of the 20th century. IKEA's phenomenal success has been in bringing desirable design to the mass market at affordable prices. The founder of IKEA, Ingvar Kamprad, was born in Sweden in 1926. He was raised on a farm, but from a very young age he demonstrated good business skills. Kamprad began as a young boy buying matches in bulk and selling them to his neighbours. He further expanded into selling fish, seeds, pencils and Christmas tree decorations. His father gave him a reward for doing well in his studies, and he used this money to set up a business in 1943. For the name, he used his own initials and those of the farm and village where he was brought up, Elmtaryd and Agunnaryd.

IKEA 'Arv' plates, bowls and napkin ring.

IKEA sold such things as pens, wallets, jewellery, watches and picture frames. Kamprad sold whatever was needed by people that could be supplied at a good price. In 1945, he began to advertise in local papers and run a mail-order business. His business was serviced by the local milk van, which delivered goods to the train station. By 1947, locally-made furniture was added to the range. This met with a good response and the range was extended. By 1951, Kamprad made the decision to concentrate solely on low-priced furniture, and he published the first IKEA furniture catalogue.

In 1953, he opened a showroom in Almhult. This allowed IKEA to demonstrate that its products were the best value for money in the market. In 1955, the company began to design its own furniture. This started out of necessity, as fierce competition had led some suppliers to boycott IKEA. Apparently, after an employee removed the legs of a table in order to fit it into a car, IKEA began to explore the possibility of flat-pack furniture, which would reduce costs even further for the customer.

'Rara' champagne glasses by IKEA.

The first IKEA furniture store, the largest in Scandinavia, was opened in Almhult in 1958. By 1963, the first store outside Sweden was opened in Norway. In 1965, a 45,800-square-metre flagship store opened in Stockholm, inspired by New York City's Guggenheim Museum. The store's great success created problems for serving customers quickly enough, and the decision was made to open the warehouse and let people serve themselves. The invention of particle board had a huge impact on IKEA products, and the company launched a new concept with white, lacquered furniture.

Throughout the 1970s, new IKEA stores opened all over the world. By 1983, IKEA had 6,000 employees. IKEA came to Britain in 1987, two years after the first American store had opened. By 1991, there were IKEA stores in China and the United Arab Emirates, and by 1993 the company had 114 stores in 25 countries around the world. In 1997, IKEA launched its first children's range, and two years later it had 53,000 workers in over 150 stores in 29 countries on four continents. In 1992, the company bought Habitat. Kampvar's three sons run the Habitat business, and he is reputed to have stated that whichever of the three is most successful in running his arm of Habitat will inherit IKEA and the family fortune, which at the end of the '90s stood at around £15 billion.

Biscuits and cheese with sloe gin and coffee on Anta tartan stoneware.

ANTA

'Small is Beautiful'

Husband and wife team Lachlan and Annie Stewart started their business in the mid-1980s, selling wild-coloured tartan fabrics and tartan ceramics. They lived in London for several years, but moved back to Scotland in 1991 to rebuild Ballone Castle and make it their home. It took architect Lachlan several years to make the castle properly habitable and to provide the members of his family with a roof over their heads.

The company continues to design different tartans in many innovative colourways, and its ceramics range incorporates flowers and animals as well as the original tartan checks. Anta products are simple but stylish, and offer a traditional look with a modern feel. This has proven a very successful formula, and although the company has remained small and closely controlled, the Stewarts now have shops in Edinburgh's Royal Mile and London's Sloane Square, plus an extensive mail-order and internet business. Anta is a very successful example of the motto 'small is beautiful' and the concept of niche marketing.

SLOE GIN

The location of blackthorn berries is a jealously guarded secret for sloe gin makers! If the berries are not gathered immediately, the birds will eat them first.

About a pound of sloes
(blackthorn berries)
1 bottle of gin
½ lb. sugar
1 teaspoon vanilla

Rinse the sloes under water and prick each one with a fork several times. Place in a preserve jar or bottle, and cover with the other ingredients. Store for 4 to 6 weeks, shaking when you remember. Remove the sloes when the liqueur is deep red, and allow to stand for another month.

SLOE GIN FIZZ

1 ½ oz. sloe gin
1 teaspoon lemon juice
1 teaspoon sugar

Mix all of the ingredients together. Pour over cracked ice and top with soda water to taste.

1990 ~ 1999
Globalisation

Following the rise of international companies and huge conglomerates during the 1980s, smart businesses began to recognise a need to be different from their many competitors in an increasingly saturated market. There was a movement away from giant corporations and toward the idea that 'small is beautiful'. The term 'niche marketing' became the catch phrase for survival in the new decade. Manufacturers tried to convince consumers of the need to buy their products with sleek advertising, celebrity endorsements and product placements in popular films and TV shows.

The move toward simplicity and minimalism led to an upsurge in the popularity of Japanese design. The store group Mujirushi Ryohin, which means 'No Brand Goods', began in Japan in 1980. It arrived in the UK in 1991 with the shortened name of MUJI. MUJI's minimal, industrial look was a key style throughout the decade in everything from furniture to stationery to clothing. Although the MUJI name promised no brands, the company's look was unmistakable and therefore represented the MUJI brand.

The '90s was also the decade of the cult of celebrity and the designer as superstar. From the early '80s onward, certain objects had developed a cult status. Products were selected for the permanent collections of museums as examples of 20th century design and therefore took on the rank of icons. For example, Michael Graves's 'Bird' kettle for Alessi, created in 1985, features in many collections as an archetypal postmodern object. This celebration of design was promoted by an exhibition at the Boilerhouse in the Victoria & Albert Museum in 1982 entitled 'Art and Industry: A Century of Design in the Products We Use'. The exhibition was curated by Stephen Bayley and backed by Sir Terence Conran. In 1989, Stephen Bayley founded the Design Museum at Butler's Wharf in London, which has a permanent collection of 20th-century design icons, as well as temporary exhibitions. Fashion designers dominated the whole lifestyle look in the 1990s, and many had lines of interior and home wares as well as ranges of clothing and accessories.

Many people in the 1990s had a desire to 'get out of the rat race' and find an idyllic country retreat, while somehow retaining the earning potential of a

City job. This aspiration to have the best of both worlds was one that probably created more stress for many people who felt torn in different directions by the idea that they ought to have it all. On the one hand, life was becoming faster, and yet we were urged to avoid stress and 'take it easy'. How was the '90s person expected to balance all of these apparently diverse requirements?

Magazines and newspaper supplements were full of advice on how to achieve this. Celebrity TV presenters told us how to decorate our homes, create wonderful gardens and cook fabulous meals in minutes. We were bombarded with ideas for how to create the style, the flavour and the image – all in half an hour. TV shows like 'Ready, Steady, Cook' and an overwhelming number of cookery books encouraged us to work against the clock to create 'fabulous meals in minutes'. This need to achieve success in the kitchen and impress acquaintances with our culinary skills has led to cooking as a hobby, rather than an everyday habit, in many homes around the country. Pre-packaged and ready-prepared meals are still sold in enormous numbers, as are take-aways and convenience foods.

The Slow Food Society was founded in Paris in 1989 in protest against the rise in consumption of fast foods and convenience foods. It aimed to counteract the trend for everything to be instantly available. The association of ritual with food was not a new one, but its return appealed to a 'multitasking' society that was often eating while doing something else: working, watching TV or even reading about another society that gives due respect to the act of preparing and consuming food.

Cuisine came from all over the world, and 'fusion' was the hot new word in food style. Trendy publications vied with each other to present the most exotic locations for cookery features. The handback of Hong Kong to China in 1997 brought the concept of East meets West into the public consciousness, which encouraged awareness of this meeting of cultures in all areas of design. More unusual ingredients were now available in supermarkets. The *Good Housekeeping New Cook Book*, published in 1999, described itself as the 'ultimate guide to contemporary cooking' and contained over 500 recipes inspired by dishes from all over the world.

Amongst all this, there was also a rediscovery of traditional British dishes. It may have been dismissed as 'nursery food' by some, but when made well it could be delicious. Many restaurants were pleased to put Fish Pie and Bread and Butter Pudding on their new, trendy menus. The new TV cooks on the scene were the 'Two Fat Ladies', Jennifer Paterson and Clarissa Dickson-Wright, who roared around the country on their vintage motorbike and sidecar, cooking up feasts for everyone from nuns to rugby players. They were not afraid to use good, old-fashioned, traditional recipes or to show their contempt for vegetarianism.

A greater public awareness of ecological issues was apparent throughout the '90s. The idea that things which happen millions of miles away could damage the planet and therefore have an impact on everybody's lives began to be taken seriously. This vision of the Earth as a 'global village' influenced many trends in design, lifestyle and eating habits. Eclectic, stylish and innovative were the key words of the decade.

Antonio Carluccio

Priscilla and Antonio Carluccio opened the Neal Street Restaurant in London's Covent Garden in 1972, and were part of the elevation of the Covent Garden shopping experience to cult status. Antonio was passionate about the food of his home country Italy, particularly the regional variations, and Priscilla was the sister of the restauranteur Terence Conran. The restaurant was an immediate success, and was followed by an Italian food shop which sold the huge variety of Italian produce which Antonio loved. A cookbook and TV presentations followed, with Antonio's enthusiastic personality and knowledge of his subject making him a popular household name. At the beginning of the 21st century, the original restaurant is still flourishing and has expanded to about 15 regional cafés or café bars. Here you can eat while enjoying a coffee or prosecco with friends, or just relax. His cafés are usually accompanied by food shops selling everything Italian, from polenta to antipasti to olive oil. Antonio has now written six books, plus smaller related editions, and his cafés also offer these for sale.

The River Café

Ruth Rogers and Rose Gray, inspired by their experiences of living and cooking in Italy, opened The River Café in 1987 in collaboration with the firm of Rogers's husband, the architect Richard Rogers. It gained a well-deserved reputation for excellence by using fresh, homegrown and specially imported Italian ingredients, simply and stylishly prepared. Rogers and Gray's practice of taking Italian home cooking into a restaurant situation has proven to be very successful. It also works well when translated into their books, which allow readers to try their recipes at home.

Bridgewater Pottery

Bridgewater Pottery was founded in London in 1985 by Matthew Rice, a furniture designer, and his partner Emma Bridgewater. The company pioneered the revival of sponge ware, stencilling and other traditional techniques for tableware, bringing a fresh, modern slant to old, established methods of production. Animal, floral and geometric patterns were used on a range of tableware. The company started out small, but it proved successful and moved from London to Hanley in Staffordshire. The 'Toast and Marmalade' lettered ware range, introduced in 1992, was apparently inspired by china made for the suffragette movement at the turn of the century. Bridgewater still produces this and other versions of lettered ware today. There are also many imitations and adaptations of this range, which have remained popular throughout the 1990s and up to today.

MOZZARELLA AND TOMATO SALAD

True mozzarella cheese is made from buffalo milk, and the genuinely fresh item should be eaten when it is no more than three days old.

Slice the mozzarella and fresh tomatoes and arrange them on a plate, sprinkle with lemon zest, drizzle with olive oil, garnish with fresh basil and season with sea salt and freshly ground black pepper.

This dish is simple and delicious, but the ingredients must be fresh and ripe.

ITALIAN MIXED SALAD

This salad is carefully laid out on a large, flat plate. Begin with a selection of salad leaves, including lollo rossa. Slice red and green peppers into thin strips and distribute evenly. Add whole artichoke hearts and decorate with olives, flat leaf parsley and parmesan shavings. Dress with olive oil and balsamic vinegar.

Fusilli pasta on a penne pasta plate.

PASTA, PASTA, PASTA

There was a greater awareness of worldwide food styles in the '90s, and dishes from all over the world became regular favourites in the British kitchen. Italian food had been popular in the United Kingdom for many decades, but more people than ever before were cooking pasta meals at home as a quick way of producing a simple but nutritious meal.

Pasta has been used as a food for thousands of years. It has seen many incarnations in that time, but Italy is generally recognised as the home of pasta as we know it today. Sophia Loren was once quoted as saying, 'Everything you see I owe to pasta'. There are, however, about as many variations in shapes of pasta as there are in the figures of those who consume it.

Different shapes and sizes of pasta are intended to be eaten with specific types of food and sauces. Generally speaking, thinner pasta is for lighter sauces and thicker pasta is for heavier sauces. Certain shapes are designed to hold more sauce. Some pasta recipe books are like design instruction manuals. In 1983, one Italian pasta manufacturer employed industrial designer Giorgio Giugiano to design a new pasta shape. Unfortunately his pasta, called *marille*, did not take off and was discontinued but it did create a lot of publicity for the company and for the designer.

Pasta is also produced in many colours and in novelty shapes such as famous buildings which are sold as souvenirs in cities around the world. There is also a market in 'naughty' shapes, which are also widely available in novelty gift shops. For those who take their pasta seriously, there are hundreds of other types to choose.

TRICOLORE FUSILLI PASTA WITH PUTTANESCA SAUCE

This sauce, which originated in Naples, is traditionally served with spaghetti. 'Spaghetti alla Puttanesca' translates from Italian as 'Whore's Spaghetti'. It got its name in the 1950s, when brothels in Italy were state-owned. Time was money for these 'civil servants', and shopping daily for fresh supplies was not a high priority. The prostitutes' speciality was a sauce that could be made quickly from store cupboard ingredients. Now this sauce is invaluable to all busy people.

20 ml. olive oil
3 cloves garlic, chopped
3 anchovy fillets, chopped
400-gram tin of Italian plum tomatoes, chopped
120 grams pitted black olives, halved or chopped
60 ml. capers, chopped

Heat the olive oil in a frying pan, and cook the garlic and anchovies until soft. Stir in the chopped tomatoes and juice, black olives and capers. Simmer for 5 minutes. Add the sauce to the pasta of your choice (we have used three-coloured fusilli) and garnish with basil or chopped parsley.

SLOW FOOD – 'THE RIGHT TO TASTE'

The Slow Food Society began in the town of Bra in the Italian region of Piedmont in July 1986 as an expression of revolt against the opening of a McDonald's fast food restaurant in the town. The revolutionaries, led by the society founder Carlo Petrini, lost of course, but a group was instantly founded to protect the enjoyment of the 'two-hour lunch', an Italian institution which appeared to be under threat.

From this humble beginning, the Slow Food movement grew into a worldwide organisation with around 80,000 members in 100 countries by the end of the century. It now has a new manifesto: 'It is a movement which protects the right to taste.' The Slow Food Society has a formal structure for meeting and disseminating information. Each area has a small group of about 100 members who are the grass roots of the society. They are called the *convivia*, and there are over 700 *convivia* worldwide. Each group has its *fudimentary*, or leader, who organises events, initiates 'creative moments of conviviality', organises tastings and raises awareness of relevant local events and products. He or she becomes an 'educator of taste'.

In 1989, the international Slow Food movement was started in Paris on a formal basis. While the head office in Bra is still at the heart of the movement, there are now offices in Switzerland, Germany, America, France and Japan. The same year also saw the beginning of the Slow Food Editore. This is a publishing group which exists to increase consumer awareness of high quality gastronomic products. It also provides some support and protection for artisan methods of production and animals or vegetables under threat. There are currently between 60 and 70 different titles in the Slow Food Editore catalogue, which is available from centres as well as by post from the Internet site. Among their titles is *Osterie d'Italia*, which is the most reliable guide to Italian eating places. They also publish *Vin d'Italie*, which is a bible for imbibers, winegrowers and anyone interested in regional wine.

During the 1990s, another project was started by the Slow Food Society. The Ark Of Taste aims to discover any regional foodstuff which is threatened by standardisation, hygiene laws or large-scale production. Products or methods of production are catalogued and acknowledged as endangered. The Slow Food Presidia then attempts, through economic support and media access from wider groups, to bring pressure to the relevant bodies and offer some kind of protection to the products and producers.

The most important feature of the Slow Food Society is its commitment to local roots in every form of culinary enjoyment. The many thousands of enthusiasts and volunteers in the movement are testament to its importance for the preservation of quality and differentiation of regional tastes in all parts of the world where food is still produced in a natural way.

A Morsel of Cheese

French *haute cuisine* might be dauntingly elaborate to prepare, but on the simple side, what could be more delicious than fresh baked bread and ripe cheese? There were many types of cheese to choose from in the 1990s, and specialist cheesemongers flourished as people sought the taste of genuine, home-produced cheeses in preference to supermarket, prepackaged varieties.

Grilled Goat's Cheese Salad on 'Sgraffito' plate by Habitat.

The right plate for the right purpose – French cheese plates.

GRILLED GOAT'S CHEESE SALAD

Grilled Goat's Cheese is a French dish which 'went global' in the 1990s. Californian cuisine has it served on a bed of fresh salad. Here is our version, served on a Habitat plate.

A generous slice of goat's cheese
Assorted salad leaves, including
  spinach, watercress and rocket
Cherry tomatoes, halved
Toasted almonds
Olive oil

Grill the goat's cheese until just golden and beginning to bubble, and place on a bed of salad leaves. Garnish with cherry tomatoes and sprinkle with toasted almonds. Drizzle with olive oil and serve.

MUJI

MUJI was a completely new concept when it was launched in 1980. It was a store which sold only goods made in Japan that bore a MUJI label. From its outset, it covered a whole lifestyle. Items for kitchens, bedrooms and relaxing areas of the home sat alongside stationery and fashion garments. MUJI even sold bicycles! The common thread was a streamlined, functional look which dropped all excess decoration, colour and pattern. Value for money was important, but the quality of the products was not sacrificed for the sake of cost. A complete lifestyle filled with quality and economic products that could provide a haven from clutter in the turmoil of '80s excesses was very refreshing.

From the beginning, MUJI was committed to ecology and recycling. The company used tree thinnings, recycled paper and board and ecologically sound textiles wherever possible. Projects were sponsored to encourage new uses for old materials, and young designers were used to promote this environmental awareness. Manufacturing processes were kept to a minimum, with materials chosen for their practical use and then polished or textured with a minimum of extra steps taken to create the final product. Empty cases for materials such as lipsticks were made to encourage people not to squander resources.

Polypropylene and aluminium have always featured heavily in MUJI products. These materials fulfil all the criteria for a good MUJI product base; they are cheap, durable and reusable and can be made into a variety of goods without extra finishes being required. Packaging has also always been kept to a minimum at MUJI. Products have been tied or labelled with recyclable materials such as string, corrugated cardboard or brown paper. The logo and materials have always been the same for all products, and the labels have included all relevant ecological information.

Throughout the 1990s, MUJI opened several British stores outside London, but some were unsuccessful and closed after a few years. The MUJI concept has enjoyed worldwide success, however, through its thriving mail-order and online business, taking the principle of 'less is more' into the 21st century.

A stir-fry meal prepared using a MUJI wok, bamboo steamer and olive wood mortar and pestle, shown with a MUJI salt and pepper mill, ceramic pot with lid and sauce bowl.

MUJI 'Goyu' earthenware cups and bowls, with a traditional deep Japanese bowl shape.

SHAKER STYLE

Tim Lamb and Liz Shirley opened a shop selling Shaker furniture and arte-facts in London in June 1989 to cater to the growing interest in simple interiors and natural wood surfaces. The Shaker movement began in the mid-18th century, spreading from Manchester to North America. The Shakers' religious philosophy rejected the values of the world at large, advo-cating a life of simplicity, celibacy and communal living.

Shaker craftsmen believed that they were working within the sight of God, and they took the same care with the finish of the insides and backs of pieces of furniture as they did with the outsides. All work was performed 'to the glory of God'. Although Shakerism as a faith has declined since its incep-tion, the legacy of its craftspeople has remained. Their guiding principles of propriety and purity, and the maxims 'beauty rests in utility' and 'every force evolves a form' have influenced many subsequent design movements and individual artisans.

In the 1860s, the Arts and Crafts movement of William Morris had similar ideals. In the 1930s, the influence could be seen in modernism and the 'less is more' concept of Mies Van der Rohe. The late 1980s and early 1990s again demonstrated a trend toward this 'back to basics' principle, combining quality materials, good craftsmanship and simplicity of design.

Shaker style fruit bowl.

Shaker style stool, bowl and candlesticks.

CALIFORNIAN CUISINE

The cuisine of California has developed through a gradual mixing of the traditions of many different peoples who have settled there. California's history differs from that of America's East Coast, where the food has evolved from a basically Anglo-European tradition that has incorporated the native products of the country. On the West Coast, the influence came through Mexico from the Spanish of the late 18th century, and gradually it blended with native North American traditions. The Spanish brought olives, artichokes, dates, nuts, vines and over 20 varieties of chillies to America. Home produce included corn, beans, pumpkin and squash, as well as wild onions, berries and pine nuts. Fish and game were the main sources of freshly caught protein.

The gold rush of 1848 overwhelmed California. Hundreds of new people settled in the state. San Francisco and Sacramento became boom towns, supplying the mining camps. The canning and preserving industry grew out of a need to supply long-life foods to the settlers. All of these immigrants brought with them their own cooking traditions. From the late 1880s onward, Chinese workers who came to build the railways stayed on and opened restaurants, adding an Oriental touch to the developing multicultural society. These different traditions existed side by side and gradually influenced each other throughout the 20th century.

In the 1950s, the cult of the motor car spawned roadside diners and drive-in restaurants with roller-skating waitresses. Theme restaurants were also encouraged by California's best-known 20th century business, the movie industry. Hollywood and the potential for stardom attracted even more hopeful settlers. California maintained its image as the land of opportunity.

The hippie movement increased interest in vegetarianism and natural, organic foods. By the late 1960s, Californian food began to emerge as a distinctive cuisine with its own idiosyncratic flavours. The minimalism of *nouvelle cuisine* and gourmet dining of the 1970s, combined with fresh, wholesome foods, resulted in a new type of Californian cuisine for the 1990s and beyond. At its best, it has emerged as a cross-cultural blend of fresh, natural produce that is simply prepared, beautifully presented, vibrantly colourful, full-flavoured and delicious. From its melting pot of influences, Californian cuisine has arisen to promote its new-found formula across the globe.

California berry ice cream with fruit coulis.

ABOVE Sliced peppers filled with ricotta cheese.

LEFT Fresh watermelon.

Mexican Cuisine

Mexican cuisine has become very popular in the UK, and many Mexican restaurants have opened all over the country, offering versions of traditional fare such as tortillas, tamales and refried beans. The margarita, a tequila-based cocktail, is the obvious choice of liquid refreshment. It is served with snack versions of tortilla chips and salsa in bars and restaurants worldwide.

Corn and chillies are indispensable ingredients in Mexican cooking. There are hundreds of varieties of chilli grown in Mexico. Coriander is another distinctive flavour in Mexican cuisine, and many types of beans and cheese are used. For the more adventurous palate, there are the traditional mole dishes, for which the crucial ingredient is bitter, dark chocolate.

Legend has it that Turkey Mole was invented in a convent in the Puebla region of central Mexico during the Spanish colonial era. Most nuns were the daughters of aristocrats, and many adventurous mixtures of indigenous and Spanish cuisine were invented in the convents' enormous kitchens. According to legend, the bishop of Puebla invited the Spanish viceroy to dine at the convent of Santa Rosa, which was well-known for its excellent cuisine. The cook, Sr Andrea de la Asuncion, was given the challenge of impressing the viceroy with a meal like no other. She mixed the traditional ingredients of fried garlic, tomatillos and chillies with fresh spices, sesame seeds, ground almonds and peanuts. Then she added the all-important bitter chocolate to the thick sauce, which was then poured over a chestnut-stuffed turkey. The dish was an enormous success, and soon all the convents had their own versions of the new dish. Other sources claim that mole originated with the Aztecs, among whom chocolate was for the consumption of royalty only and forbidden to all women. Whichever story is true, the dish is now widely enjoyed as an integral part of Mexican cooking. It is a dish associated with feast days, of which the Mexican calendar has a great number. One of the best-known in the rest of the world is the festival for the Day of the Dead.

Mexican pottery cross.

THE DAY OF THE DEAD

The Day of the Dead is a tradition which has its roots in the Aztec and other Meso-American civilisations that date back more than 3,000 years. It originally took place during the entire month of August. The Spanish conquistadors tried to eradicate the festival when they arrived in Mexico over 500 years ago, as they considered its rituals sacrilegious. They were unsuccessful, however, so they moved the celebration to coincide with the Christian All Saints' Day and All Souls' Day on 1 and 2 November, and they continued their efforts to convert the indigenous people to Christianity.

Different areas of Mexico have various traditions, but the main Day of the Dead celebrations take place on 31 October and the first two days of November. During this time, families welcome their departed loved ones back through the gateway between earthly life and existence beyond the grave. They believe that this gateway is open only during these specific days in the year.

Families set out shrines in their homes in honour of the dead. These shrines contain favourite foods and drinks of the departed, as well as symbols or tools appropriate to their professions or passions. Paper cutouts depicting skeletons engaged in varied activities are strung as decorative banners. In some areas, the celebrations take place in cemeteries. The graves themselves are decorated with huge bunches of marigolds, candles and food, including the *Pan de Muerto* (Bread of the Dead). All-night vigils, picnics and parties take place at the gravesides. Sugar skulls and other death-related confections are enjoyed by children and adults. People wait for the dead to come back and partake of the things they enjoyed in this life, sharing them with the living. This is not a time of mourning, it is a time of celebration.

GUACAMOLE

2 large, ripe avocados
4 oz. tomatoes, peeled and chopped
½ small onion, chopped very finely
1 small, fresh green chilli, deseeded and chopped finely
1 oz. fresh coriander leaves, chopped
Juice of ½ lime
1 tablespoon of olive oil
Salt

Mash the avocados in a bowl, add the other ingredients and mix thoroughly. Serve garnished with a few pieces of chopped tomato and some coriander leaves.

MARGARITA

This tequila cocktail is a must for fiesta, but do not underestimate its strength!

3 tablespoons tequila
1 tablespoon Cointreau
1 tablespoon lime juice
3 ice cubes

Combine the ingredients in a mixing glass and stir well. Strain into a cocktail glass, the rim of which has been rubbed with lime and dipped in salt.

TOMATO SALSA

1 onion, finely chopped
1 garlic clove, chopped
2 fresh green chillis, deseeded and chopped
1 ½ lb. tomatoes, peeled and chopped
Salt
Pinch of sugar
Fresh coriander, chopped

Put all of the ingredients in a food processor and pulse until roughly blended.

Day of the Dead Feast.

REFRIED BEANS

1 lb. kidney beans, presoaked
2 onions, finely chopped
2 garlic cloves, chopped
1 small green chilli, deseeded
   and chopped
1 bay leaf
2 tablespoons vegetable oil
4 oz. tomatoes, peeled and
   chopped

*Cook the kidney beans in water
with 1 chopped onion, 1 chopped
clove of garlic, the green chilli and
the bay leaf. Bring to a simmer
and cook, covered, over a low heat
for about 20 minutes. Add 1*
*tablespoon of vegetable oil and
continue to cook for up to 2
hours, until the beans are tender.
Heat another tablespoonful of
vegetable oil in a frying pan and
saute 1 chopped onion and
another clove of garlic. Add the
tomatoes. When the beans are
soft, add them a little at a time to
the frying pan, mashing them
into the mixture to form a paste.
Gradually mash in all the beans
and their liquid, adding oil from
time to time until a heavy,
creamy paste is achieved.
This can be served as an
accompaniment to the tortillas.*

Mexican tortillas come in all sizes
and colours. They are made from
white, yellow, blue or red corn, or
alternatively from wheat. Corn tortillas made from *masa* dough are
traditionally flattened in a press,
but wheat tortillas are rolled out.
Tortillas are readily available in
supermarkets in the UK, as are taco
shells. They can be stuffed with
cheese, minced beef, refried beans,
guacamole, salsa – there are many
combinations. For our Mexican
fiesta, the ingredients have been laid
out so that guests may assemble
their own food as they wish.

DESIGNER DINNERS

In this decade of worldwide media coverage, not only designer label clothes were in vogue, but fashion designers themselves were recognised celebrities. Their lifestyles were a popular subject for magazine articles. This no doubt helped in promoting the lines of interior and home wares being launched by many of the top fashion houses. Consumers of the '90s could purchase the entire 'designer lifestyle' look, from evening gowns to coffee spoons. They could even go so far as to match their food presentation to their tableware and napkins.

GIANNI VERSACE was born in Calabria, Italy in 1946. His mother had a dressmaking business, in which he served his apprenticeship. He became a freelance designer in 1972 and moved to Milan. In 1978, with the help of his older brother Santo, an accountant, he launched his first womenswear collection under his own label. He then expanded into menswear and childrenswear. Versace's collections were enormously successful, and throughout the '80s he won countless awards for creativity and innovation in fashion and theatre design. In 1989, he started the VERSUS line, which was aimed at a younger market and cutting-edge fashion pioneers.

In 1993, Versace was awarded the American Fashion Oscar. Later that year, he launched his 'Home Signature' line. This was a range of products for the home, including fabrics, carpets, quilts, cushions and a range of table porcelain made by Rosenthal. The move into household products was something which many major fashion designers explored. They became the gurus of design in all areas of people's lives.

After his tragic death at the hands of a gunman in Miami in 1997, Versace's sister Donatella, who had worked with him for many years, took over the main running of the business. She continues to maintain the high profile and international acclaim of the company today.

MARYSE BOXER was born in Tunisia, but she lived and worked in the UK. She was known for her designs of simple, brightly coloured, sponge-effect ware in unusual shapes, such as scalloped-edged plates and saucers. Heart-shaped plates were also one of her signature products. These were produced in the early '90s by J.E. Heath, a part of the Dudson Group of potteries.

Luxury wares were sold through outlets such as Chez Joseph, the homewares branch of the fashion house Joseph, during the '90s. These included heart-shaped plates made of ceramic and 24-carat gold. Jewelled napkin rings were also part of this Maryse Boxer range.

Many Maryse Boxer designs are now produced by Deruta in Italy, and the range features spots, stripes, checks and borders in wonderfully contemporary colour combinations.

RIGHT Mix and match cups and saucers by Maryse Boxer.

A Versace ceramic coaster.

ABOVE A Maryse Boxer blue plate.
FACING PAGE Mushroom Risotto on a Maryse Boxer plate.

CELEBRITY CHEFS

Celebrity chefs were a major phenomenon of the 1990s. There have been influential TV cooks in every generation, but never in such numbers or with such 'star status' as in the last decade of the 20th century. TV chefs offered all types of cookery advice, but the audience was constantly seeking the latest, most perfect answer. The army of celebrity chefs and the hundreds of hours of broadcasting generated by the TV companies offered a huge choice in styles and methods of food preparation and presentation. Many of them continue to entertain and inform us today.

AYNSLEY HARRIOT first appeared on TV in 1993. His stated aim is to 'make cooking fun'. In 1997, he travelled round the world for his first solo series, 'Aynsley's Barbecue Bible', in which he presented the best open air food from around the globe. Alfresco eating was by then extremely popular in the UK, in spite of the unpredictable climate. Cooking against the clock has been a key feature of Harriot's TV programmes. He had his own series, 'Aynsley's Meals in Minutes', before becoming the presenter of the BBC's 'Ready Steady Cook'.

GARY RHODES has put a contemporary spin on traditional British cooking. He was given the Catey Special Award, the catering industry's equivalent of an Oscar, for helping to revive British cookery. He has also received three Michelin stars. He has presented several TV shows, including 'Rhodes Round Britain'. Rhodes has said that one of his major priorities is to get cooking back onto the curriculum in all UK schools.

RICK STEIN, OBE, is best known for his passion for seafood. He has run his award-winning and internationally acclaimed seafood restaurant in Padstow for over 25 years. Although Stein is a professional chef, most of his recipes rely on simple cooking methods, which he reckons are more akin to the way we all cook.

The Two Fat Ladies, JENNIFER PATERSON and CLARISSA DICKSON-WRIGHT, were brought together by a TV producer for their first TV series of 'Two Fat Ladies' in the mid-1990s. They had met before, but they had never worked together. Dickson-Wright had been a barrister before running her own catering business, and Paterson had, amongst many other things, been a cook for the *Spectator* magazine for 15 years. The motorbike and side car became their trademark, driven by Paterson. Their shows were extremely popular for the 4 ½ years of their partnership, which was brought to an end by the sad death of Paterson in 1999.

HEART-SHAPED MUSHROOM RISOTTO

We spooned this risotto into a heart-shaped mould, then turned it out before serving. This quantity makes 4 hearty servings.

1 oz. dried porcini mushrooms
1 pint vegetable stock
2 oz. butter
2 cloves of garlic, crushed
1 medium onion, finely chopped
2 tablespoons fresh flat leaf
   parsley, chopped
8 oz. mushrooms, sliced
8 oz. Italian Arborio rice
3 fluid oz. dry white vermouth
4 oz. freshly grated Parmesan
   cheese
Salt and freshly ground black
   pepper

Cover the porcini mushrooms with boiling water and soak for about 30 minutes. Drain and chop the porcini, reserving the soaking liquid, which should be combined in a pan with the stock and brought to a simmer. In another heavy-based pan, melt the butter and sauté the onion and garlic. Add the chopped porcini, herbs and sliced mushrooms and toss for a few minutes. Add the rice, stirring to coat the grains. Add half of the vermouth and a cupful of stock. Simmer gently until the liquid is absorbed. Continue to add stock gradually, allowing it to be absorbed and stirring constantly, for about 35 minutes or until the rice is tender. Season with pepper and salt. Stir in the rest of the vermouth and the Parmesan before serving.

NIGELLA LAWSON is the glamorous goddess of the kitchen, and the *femme fatale* of TV cooking. She has promoted the buying, preparation and eating of food as a sexy, sensual activity. She told us all *How to Eat* in her book of that name, published in 1998. *The Daily Telegraph* named the book 'the most valuable culinary guide published this decade'. Author Jeanette Winterston described Lawson as the 'Thinking Person's Cook', and *Tatler* magazine said that Lawson's book was 'a love letter to all things culinary'. Lawson herself says that she does not believe anyone can really cook well unless they love food, and that her own motivation for cooking comes from her desire to eat delicious food.

SOPHIE GRIGSON is the daughter of the food writer Jane Grigson. She spent her early career in pop video production, but then she returned to her true vocation and wrote several successful cookery books. She has presented several TV shows, and demonstrated in 1999 that good food did not have to mean great expense through her show 'Feasts for a Fiver'.

JAMIE OLIVER started working in the kitchen of his parents' pub restaurant in Cambridge at the age of eight. He completed his training at Westminster Catering College, and then worked for three years at the River Café in London. He first appeared on TV in a documentary about the River Café, and was instantly spotted and offered his own TV show. His young, relaxed, funky style attracted a whole new sector of viewers who normally would never have watched a cookery show. 'The Naked Chef' was first broadcast in 1999, although at no point did Oliver ever appear without clothes. Oliver has been a popular choice for companies seeking celebrity endorsements for their products. Sainsbury's employed him as an advisor, and he has appeared in their TV advertisements. He has also acted as Design Consultant for a range of upmarket cookware and tableware produced by Royal Worcester.

HUGH FEARNLEY WHITTINGSTALL is known for his basic, down-to-earth approach to cooking. He is also a supporter of the organic movement. Whittingstall did not have formal training, but he spent some time at the River Café as a sous-chef, where he was considered too messy and was asked to leave. He has been awarded the Glenfiddich Trophy for his 'contribution to widening the understanding and appreciation of excellent food and drink in Britain'. From 1997 onward, the River Cottage in Dorset was the setting for several TV series hosted by Whittingstall, and his accompanying River Cottage cookbooks have been extremely popular.

Lemon and Lime Cream with IKEA heart napkin.

LEMON AND LIME CREAM

This is a simply prepared but very rich dessert. We have served it with ½ inch of cream on top, garnished with a heart-shaped strawberry for that extra touch of luxury. This quantity makes 4 generous portions.

150 grams caster sugar
600 ml. double cream
Juice of 1 lemon and 1 lime

Put the sugar and cream in a saucepan and bring to the boil, stirring constantly. Simmer for 3 to 4 minutes. Add the lime and lemon juice and stir well. Remove the pan from the heat and allow the mixture to cool for about 15 minutes. Pour into your choice of stemmed glass dessert dishes or wine glasses, allowing enough space at the top for the cream. Chill in the fridge for a minimum of 3 hours. This dessert can be made up to 24 hours in advance and kept in the fridge until required. Serve with ½ inch of cream poured on top and garnish with the fruit of your choice.

ALESSI

In 1921, Giovanni Alessi founded the Alessi Company in the village of Omegna, just outside the Italian Alpine town of Crusinallo. Alessi began by making lathe-turned brass and nickel silver coffeepots and serving dishes for the hotel trade. At the same time, metal kitchenware was being made by another branch of the Alessi family in a nearby workshop. Alphonso Bialetti made an octagonal, aluminium-cast coffeepot in 1930 that is still in production today – the 'Bialetti Moka Express', now considered a design classic. In 1932 Carlo Alessi, the eldest son of Giovanni Alessi, joined the company as Principal Designer. He became General Manager in 1945, the same year that he designed the 'Bombe' coffee service. He remained in this position throughout the postwar period, when the company expanded to become a large-scale industrial business with sales reaching over 70 countries.

In 1970 Alberto Alessi, the grandson of Giovanni, suggested that the skills of the two branches of the Alessi family be joined. The new company combined the best of mass production with design and craftsmanship in metal. The mass production catering lines were continued, but Alessi took on the challenge of creating international designs, resulting in the invention of some of the most important domestic items of the 20th century.

The Alessi Company decided to employ some of the most important designers of the time to create limited editions of affordable goods for mass production. The first Alessi *maestro* was Ettore Sottsass, who designed a condiment set in 1972. In 1977, Richard Sapper designed the first stainless steel Alessi coffeepot. In 1984, Aldo Rossi and Michael Graves began a long-term relationship with Alessi, and in 1986 they were joined by Philippe Stark, whose first project was the 'Juicy Salif' lemon squeezer — now a well-established design classic.

Designers employed by Alessi form a roll-call of late 20th century design-masters. Alberto Alessi controlled the company, which he saw as a 'dream factory' that mediated between the designers and the needs and dreams of the market. He worked on the edge of what was considered acceptable, but always with some element of risk. Some Alessi projects set new rules and became ground-breaking designs that are now highly prized by collectors of postmodernist design.

Alessi also decided to look back at some classic designs from an earlier period and reproduce them. The famous geometric tea and coffee service designed by Marianne Brandt at the Bauhaus in 1924 was the first item to be produced under the Archivi label in 1983. A 1934 tea service designed by Eliel Saarinen followed, as well as a collection of teaware designed by Christopher Dresser in the 19th century. The Archivi Collection stands very well beside the best designs created at the end of the 20th century.

Looking forward into the 21st century, there seems to be no field of industrial design which will be unattainable for Alessi. The attitude and commitment of the company to push the boundaries of design ever further should ensure its future place at the forefront of cutting-edge design.

Alessi bottle opener and tray.

'Diabolo' bottle opener by Alessi.

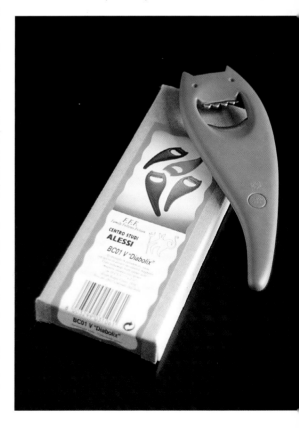

DROOG DESIGN AND ROSENTHAL

The Droog Design Foundation was set up in 1994 by the journalist Renny Ramaker, the editor of the design magazine *Industriel Ontwerpen*, and Gijs Bakker, the head of the Eindhoven Academie for Industrial Design. It was originally founded as a showcase for the work of cutting-edge current and former students from the academy. Later, it promoted Dutch design, a goal which related to the Droog principles of 'original ideas and clear concepts which have been shaped in a wry and no-nonsense manner'.

Rosenthal was founded in 1879 in Selb, Germany by Philip Rosenthal. For over 100 years, it has been recognised as one of the finest porcelain and glass manufacturers in the world. In 1961 the company decided to take one of its parts in a completely new direction. Philip Rosenthal Jr launched the Rosenthal Studio – Linie, which was to recognise that through the centuries the things that people value most and that hold their value always express 'the spirit of their time'. He commissioned the best contemporary international designers to design a range of tableware. Over a period of about 30 years, more than 100 designers were used for this range, and the list forms a 'Who's Who' of modern design: Timo Sarpaneva, Tapio Wirkkala, Lucienne Day and Bjorn Wiinblad were just a few of them.

In 1996 Rosenthal approached Droog Design as 'the spirit of their time' to experiment with ceramic materials. Gijs Bakker himself approached the problem with Dick Van Hoof, one of the Droog team. Bakker finally designed a coffeepot called the 'High Tech Accent', which had a traditional, knitted porcelain cosy over it. Dick Van Hoof fixed on a basic ceramic teapot shape, but allowed the extrusion machine in the factory to dictate the patterns and colours used on the pot. No two were the same.

Rosenthal continues this commitment to new, radical designs being produced every year alongside their traditional requirements for the mass market.

Two designs for Rosenthal by Gijs Bakker in collaboration with Dick Van Hoof. Both are based on a traditional coffeepot shape. The first has a ceramic 'crochet' cover and in the second, the integrated handle is made of plaited organic fibres.

PHILIPPE STARCK AND THE 'JUICY SALIF'

Philippe Starck was born in Paris in 1949. From 1965 to 1967, he was a student at the Nissim Da Camondo School, where he won the La Villette Furniture Award. In 1968, he was commissioned by Quasar to design inflatable furniture, and in 1969 he was appointed as Art Director of the Pierre Cardin Furniture studio. During the 1970s, he worked on various freelance projects, including some notable nightclubs: La Main Bleu and Les Bains Douches. In 1979, he founded Starck Products and in 1982 he was asked to design part of the interior of the Elysees Palace for President Mitterand. This brought him public acclaim as well as many other interior design commissions, including the Royalton Hotel in New York City.

Starck was undoubtedly the leading superstar of European design during the 1980s, provoking questions about the qualities of good design. He designed chairs for home and office use, many of them made in collaboration with leading manufacturers of the time such as Vitra, Driade and Cassina. Often three-legged and made from fine tubular metal, Starck's chairs reminded one of insects. Of the many products he has designed for companies such as Alessi, the 'Juicy Salif' lemon squeezer, created in 1990, is possibly the most famous. All of his Alessi products carried interesting, humorous names, such as the 'Max le Chinois' colander. Starck claimed to be able to design a chair in 15 minutes, and his huge and varied output of design work illustrates that commitment to speed.

Starck has stated that he hopes that there is no such thing as a Starck style. He believes that the particular logic and way of working he employs is more political than designer. He has a point of view and a force of action in his work which is the style of not having a style.

In the 1990s, Starck also started to design a number of public buildings. Some of these were in Japan, but wherever they were located, they all used his own peculiar brand of decoration and quirky imagery. The Asahi Beer Hall and the NanNan Building in Tokyo, as well as private homes such as the Formentera house in the Balearics and the wooden Starck House, are all excellent examples of his architectural work.

The everyday, human but forbidden aspect of food has fascinated Starck and he feels that society is at a crossroads. 'Grand foods' which have been a status symbol within our society for a century are now becoming available to the masses. This is partly good, but requires serious thought about its benefits for the future. Starck feels that it is important to accept without question new foods which owe nothing to the past. A modern world needs to consider and welcome an appropriate new way of living and eating. As a society, we are constantly changing. We should accept the same in our food.

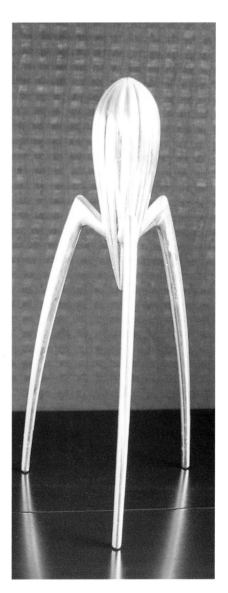

The 'Juicy Salif' lemon squeezer.

Buffet Parties

Buffet parties increased in popularity as a way of entertaining guests, who could choose from a wide variety of different types of dishes, lovingly prepared by the host or hostess from far-reaching global influences or bought from the local deli. Even the large supermarkets increased their ranges of party foods and nibbles from all parts of the globe, and these became a regular feature of 'international' sections of stores up and down the country.

POPEYE PIE

This is a spinach and egg bake fondly known as Popeye Pie, after the cartoon character – eat some and you will have instant strength!

500 grams frozen chopped
 spinach
2 oz. butter, plus extra
 for greasing
1 heaped tablespoon flour
4 fluid oz. milk
2 or 3 oz. grated cheese
Breadcrumbs made from white or
 brown bread
5 large eggs
Salt, pepper, allspice and grated
 nutmeg

Put the spinach in a heavy-based pan with a little salt and allow to thaw slowly. When thawed, add the butter and once it is melted, increase the heat to ensure all excess water has evaporated. Sprinkle in the flour and mix in thoroughly, making sure there are no lumps. Stir in the milk a little at a time. Add the grated cheese. Continue cooking and stirring until the mixture is no longer runny, but not too dry. Leave to cool. Preheat the oven to 180ºC. Butter a ceramic baking dish and press the breadcrumbs evenly over the base. Stir the eggs into the spinach mixture. Add the nutmeg, allspice, salt and pepper to taste and pour over the breadcrumbs. Bake in the oven for 35 to 45 minutes, until the surface is firm to the touch. Allow to cool and cut into squares.

THAI FISH CAKES

Lightly process 1 lb. of skinned and filleted white fish.

Make a curry paste by processing:

*1 stalk lemon grass, chopped
2 lime leaves, chopped
1 spring onion, chopped
A small bunch of coriander,
 chopped
2 cloves of garlic
2 small red chillies, deseeded
½ teaspoon turmeric*

Combine the fish and the curry paste with:

*2 level tablespoons plain flour
2 level tablespoons cornflour
3 tablespoons fish sauce
2 tablespoons caster sugar
2 oz. green beans, sliced
Sufficient water to form a paste*

Form into small cakes and fry in hot vegetable oil until crisp.

TOP OF PAGE Thai Fish Cakes.

LEFT Popeye Pie.

A celebration buffet party.

Canapés and Champagne

As the century neared its end, producers of champagne and sparkling wine were inundated with advance orders in anticipation of demand for millennium celebrations. Radio features advised the public to get their orders in early to avoid disappointment. Fizz was the only drink to have to welcome in the new millennium with a bang. Canapés were the natural accompaniment. These miniature morsels took time and patience to prepare, but were consumed in a second.

Egg mayonnaise, mushroom paté, olive tapenade and even haggis with cranberry garnish are some of the ingredients we have used to make canapés for particular occasions. Cream cheese is an excellent base filling, as it can be mixed with herbs or spices and decorated with all sorts of finely cut vegetable garnishes, including peppers, carrots, cherry tomatoes, mushrooms or any other colourful vegetables. Smoked salmon pieces, caviar, crunchy bacon bits, chopped anchovies, capers and stuffed olives are all excellent additions. Canapé preparation offers an opportunity to play with food and be creative.

SHORTCRUST PASTRY CASES

This is a very quick and easy method of preparing shortcrust pastry, which can then be rolled out and moulded into mini-sized tart tins, which are available in an enormous variety of shapes. Our canapés are featured here in barquette moulds, shaped like little boats, and also in mini tartlet cases. This recipe makes approximately 4 dozen mini tartlets or 20 barquettes.

250 grams plain flour
120 grams chilled butter, cubed
A small pinch of salt
Iced water

Place the flour and butter in a food processor with the pinch of salt and process to the consistency of fine breadcrumbs. Add about 1 tablespoon of iced water and, using the pulse button to avoid overmixing, process until the pastry begins to form a ball. The pastry should be rested and chilled in the fridge for about 30 minutes, after which it will be ready to roll out and cut to the shape of your moulds, or be divided into balls and pushed into your mini muffin tins. The pastry cases could be glazed with a little milk at this stage if desired. The cases should be baked blind at 200ºC for about 10 to 15 minutes, using crumpled greaseproof paper in each case to prevent air bubbles. Remove the paper and cook for a further 5 minutes, until golden. Allow the cases to cool completely in their tins.

SPINACH ROULADE

50 grams of butter
2 cloves of garlic, crushed
15 grams of fresh coriander,
 chopped
50 grams of plain flour
300 ml. milk
50 grams of fresh spinach, finely
 chopped
4 egg yolks, beaten
4 egg whites, separated
Parmesan cheese, grated
Oil for greasing
Salt and freshly ground black
 pepper

200 grams of cream cheese
Chives, finely chopped
1 jar of tomato salsa

Preheat the oven to 190ºC. Lightly oil a Swiss roll tin and line it with lightly oiled baking parchment. Melt the butter in a large pan.

Cook the crushed garlic and the fresh coriander for one minute. Add the flour and cook for 3 more minutes, stirring constantly. Gradually stir in the milk and bring to the boil, stirring constantly, until the sauce is thick and smooth. Remove from the heat and add the chopped spinach. Allow the mixture to cool slightly before adding the egg yolks. Season to taste with salt and freshly milled pepper. You could also add a pinch of nutmeg.

Whisk the egg whites until they are stiff, but not dry, and fold them carefully into the sauce. Pour the mixture into the tin, making sure to fill right to the corners. Bake for about 15 minutes, until risen and golden, with the surface firm to the touch. Sprinkle grated Parmesan cheese over a sheet of parchment paper

and turn out the roulade onto it. Remove the lining paper, cover with a clean, damp cloth and leave to cool before rolling.

Mash the cream cheese to a soft, spreadable consistency, adding some chives or mixed herbs. Spread this mixture onto the base, leaving a 2-cm space at one end, and top it with the tomato salsa. Carefully roll up the roulade, starting from the end with no filling on it, and using the paper to help. Wrap tightly in the paper and chill in the fridge until ready to use. When preparing this for a buffet party, you could roll it from a long end. This is more fiddly to do, but it results in a narrower roll which can be sliced into about 16 buffet-sized portions.

ABOVE Spinach Roulade.
RIGHT Carrot and tomato Sunburst Salad.

SUNBURST SALAD

This is a very colourful salad which looks great served on a green glass dish! The main ingredients are:

Grated carrots
Red and yellow tomatoes, cut
 into wedges
Limes, thinly sliced or cut into
 wedges

Arrange these on the dish and dress with lime juice, olive oil, sea salt and freshly ground black pepper.

HEALTHY EATING

The 1990s saw a proliferation of books on healthy eating, each one promising to be the ultimate guide to solving all health problems by giving readers advice on how to achieve a balanced diet and an improved lifestyle. This type of 'positive nutrition' addressed issues such as detoxing, weight control, pain control, prevention of disease and mood improvement, promising new vitality and a sense of well-being to those who followed the advice and changed their eating habits.

Much emphasis was placed on fresh produce. The government urged everyone to eat at least five portions of fruits and vegetables per day as part of a regular diet. Drinking fresh juices was an appealing way to follow this advice, and a centrifugal juicing machine that could extract juice from most fruits and vegetables with the minimum of effort (except in cleaning) became another must-have gadget for the home. The taste of the freshly-made juice was definitely worth the effort of cleaning the machine!

TOP: LEFT Glass bowl by Blowzone.
RIGHT Kenwood juicer and fresh fruit.

FRESH JUICE

Once you have a juicer, there is no end to the combinations of fruits and vegetables that you can try. Some concoctions will taste better than others, but it is all down to personal taste. Often, the simplest combinations are the most successful. This is a good, basic starter.

Carrot, Apple and Ginger Juice
*4 carrots, topped and tailed and
    cut to whatever size your juicer
    can accommodate
2 apples, cut into quarters
2 oz. peeled, fresh ginger, cut into
    small chunks*

Simply throw all of the ingredients into the juicer, and wait for the juice to appear. A peeled orange is an optional addition, although citrus fruits are often better juiced in the traditional way, with their juice being added to the finished mixture.

The Future of Foods

Technology has been manipulating food for more than 50 years, but in the late 1980s, genetic manipulation suddenly became an even more important issue. By the 1990s, there were eggs to protect against heart disease, artificial fats to lower cholesterol, as well as grains that were disease-free, to name a few. New combinations of genes from plants and animals are continually experimented with. There have always been protests against tampering with natural foodstuffs, but at the end of the 20th century, any form of publicised genetic interference caused a backlash of protest by more than 50% of the British population.

Already, our supermarket shelves are filled with every conceivable type of processed food. As our supermarkets get bigger, they display less truly fresh food, and more canned, dried and frozen food. Sometimes it is easier to buy ingredients imported from Asia than to buy locally produced foods, and it is often cheaper; tiger prawns are more readily available now than Dublin Bay prawns. Out-of-season food has become normal and expected. We often buy exotic foods which have been picked before they are ripe, and which usually have little taste compared to the same foods as they are eaten in their own parts of the world.

In 1996, public confidence in food safety reached an all-time low when BSE, or 'Mad Cow Disease', was admitted by the British government to have killed humans. BSE was caused by modifications to the natural diet of cattle. Disgusted, most people in the country stopped eating red meat, and it was a long time before public confidence could be restored.

In the future, there will still be a battle over food production. Opinion is divided. Many people believe that genetic modification is essential in a battle to eliminate disease in common plant forms. There is also a strong countermovement for natural and organic foodstuffs and farmers markets. Encouragement for supermarkets to stock organic foods is now significant. It's anyone's guess where society will stand on these issues at the end of the next century.

Dining styles throughout the century.

TABLEWARE AT THE END OF THE 20TH CENTURY

At the end of the 20th century, some of the worst predictions of the middle part of the century had fortunately not been fulfilled. Dining at table had not been completely abandoned for a plastic tray in front of a TV screen, with paper plates and throwaway cutlery (or at least not every night of the week). We still cared about the way we ate, but there had been some basic changes to suit our 21st-century lifestyle.

The end of the 20th century brought a lack of formality to most homes and restaurants. Cups and saucers became scarce, and mugs replaced cups in most informal situations. The patterns were infinite and not necessarily in sets. Personal choice made the 'set of six' an outdated concept for many people. Wine consumption in the last decade of the century doubled, but there were many more single-person households, and the need for matching glasses was not so great as it had been. Coffeepots had almost disappeared, apart from the glass coffee cafetiere which was present in almost every British home. Teapots remained as a preference in many homes, despite the inevitable teabags.

Cookware became established as oven- or stovetop-to-table ware, and for every form of tableware and glassware, dishwasher-proofing was essential. Bowls replaced rimmed soup plates and became vital ingredients in every tableware range. Dinner plates have been simplified from many different sizes, which reflected the particular meals, to a single, uniform, medium size, which reflects the mood of the 21st century.

The decline in the number of retail stores in the High Street selling quality tableware products sharply declined towards the end of the 20th century, and was set to decline even further. Inevitably, more customers will turn to mail-order or the Internet to give them a wider choice in purchases for the home or gifts. E-commerce will undoubtedly become an integral part of marketing in tableware, as this new century moves forward.

CONCLUSION

The story of dining during the 20th century is an echo of the century itself. The social and economic changes, and technical advances, which shaped the era also influenced fashion and taste in all areas of life. The century, which was born out of the mechanised industry of the Victorians, ran through two world wars and ended in the micro-technological world that we have today.

The dining table before the Great War was formally set in a different way for every meal, and required appropriate items of crockery, glassware and cutlery for every course. As the century progressed, this formality gradually relaxed and the table became much more casual and fashion-orientated. By the end of the century, crockery and glassware created a mood rather than following a tradition. A similar relaxation of the traditional French *haute cuisine* of Escoffier, which dominated food at the beginning of the century, allowed a more informal approach to cooking, both in the home and in restaurants. By the middle of the century, *haute cuisine* had been replaced by various forms of *nouvelle cuisine*, which relied more on creative use of worldwide ingredients than on complex cooking techniques and reduction sauces.

Lifestyle changes caused by the two world wars, a breakdown of class barriers and a redistribution of wealth, as well as the unparalleled technological advances of the 20th century, have transformed the society the Victorians knew. These social changes have allowed us to look at what and how we eat in a very different way. But are the changes really so great? We still eat from plates not dissimilar to those of the Victorians, and we still mainly drink from glass. We still have formal and informal meals, and although it is possible, we have almost never given in to popping a pill instead of eating a meal.

Food issues are publicised in the media as never before. New statistics and opinions on what is healthy or harmful are broadcast on a weekly basis. We receive constantly varying advice on what to eat to make our bodies healthy and free from illness. There is now more organic produce available, but there are also more fast-food restaurants and 'takeaways' on our High Streets, and more processed foods on our supermarket shelves than ever.

Eating and drinking is fundamental to life, and whatever style you choose, the most important thing is to always make dining, no matter how simple or elaborate, an enjoyable and memorable experience.

Bon Appetit

BIBLIOGRAPHY

Alessi, Alberto. *Alessi – The Dream Factory*, Academy Cologne, Konemann, 1998. ISBN 3-829013-77-9.

Alison, Sonia. *European Cooking*, William Collins and Co., Glasgow and London, 1977. ISBN 0-004351-80-0.

Atterbury, Paul. *Cornish Ware*, Richard Dennis, Somerset, England, 1996. ISBN 0-903685-48-5.

Arthur, Liz. *Robert Stewart, Design 1946-95*, A & C Black Ltd., London 2003. ISBN 0-7136-6410-X.

Atterbury, Paul. *Miller's Twentieth Century Ceramics*, Mitchell Beazley, London, 1999. ISBN 1-84000-034-1.

Atterbury, Paul (ed.). *Poole Pottery by Leslie Hayward*, Richard Dennis, Somerset, England, 1998. ISBN 0-903685-62-0.

Batkin, Maureen. *Wedgwood Ceramics 1846-1959*, Richard Dennis, London, 1982. ISBN 0-903685-11-6.

Beeton, Isabella. *The Book of Household Management*, Ward Lock & Co. Ltd., London, 1899.

Benson, E.F. *Mapp and Lucia*, Hutchinson & Co. Ltd., 1927.

Benson, Nigel. *Glass of the '50s and '60s*, Millers, London, 2002. ISBN 1-84000-538-6.

Bernson, Jens. *Design – The Problem Comes First*, The Danish Design Council, 1982. ISBN 8-787385-08-2.

Be-Ro Home Recipes, Thomas Bell and Co.

Berolzheimer, Ruth. *250 Tempting Desserts from the Culinary Arts Institute*, Consolidated Book Publishers Inc., Chicago, 1941.

Blake, Fanny. *Essential Charles Rennie Mackintosh*, Paragon, 2001. ISBN 0-75255-351-8.

Blanc, Raymond. *Recipes From Le Manoir aux Quat' Saisons*, MacDonald & Co., 1988. ISBN 0-356-19154-0.

Boulestin, Marcel. *What Shall We Have Today*, Windmill Press, Kingswood, Surrey, 1931.

Boxhall, Jan. *Good Housekeeping, Every Home Should Have One*, Ebury Press, London, 1997. ISBN 0-09-185280-3.

Buchman Euald, Ellen. *Recipes for a Small Planet*, Ballantyne Books, New York, 1973. ISBN 0-345-27430-X.

Calloway, Stephen (ed.). *Liberty Of London, Masters of Style & Decoration*, Thames & Hudson Ltd., London, 1992. ISBN 0-8212-1974-X.

Casey, Andrew. *20th Century Ceramic Designers in Britain*, Antique Collectors Club, 2001. ISBN 1-85149-352-2.

Catterall, Claire (ed.). *Food – Design and Culture*, Lawrence King in Association with Glasgow, 1999. ISBN 1-856691-63-2.

Chamberlain, Richard. *Austerity To Affluence: British Art & Design 1945-62*, Merrell Holberton, London, 1997. ISBN 1-858940-46-X.

Chaney, Lisa. *Elizabeth David: A Biography*, Macmillan, London, 1998. ISBN 0-333-65930-9.

Conran, Terence. *The House Book*, Mitchell Beazley, London, 1974. ISBN 0-85533-041-4.

Conran, Terence. *The Kitchen Book*, Mitchell Beazley, London, 1977. ISBN 0-85533-1208.

The Cookery Year, Readers Digest Association Ltd., London, 1973.

Cottington Taylor, D.D. *Good Housekeeping ABC of Cookery*, Good Housekeeping Institute, 1929.

David, Elizabeth. *Elizabeth David's French Country Cooking*, Penguin Books Ltd, England, 1951.

Dixon, Monica and Waller, Emilie. *Shopping and Cooking: Tuesday Morning Talks*, BBC Publications, London, 1935.

Dodsworth, Roger. *British Glass Between The Wars*, Dudley Leisure Services, Jolly and Barber Ltd, Rugby, Warwickshire,1987. ISBN 0-900911-22-0.

Doi, Masaru. *Cook Japanese*, Kodansha International Ltd., Tokyo, 1964. ISBN M-0063423-GS.

Escoffier, Auguste. *2000 Favourite French Recipes*, Treasure Press, London, 1991. ISBN 1-85051-694-4.

Fayet, Roger. *70s Versus 80s*, Arnoldsche Art Publications, 2001. ISBN 3-897901-71-4.

Forty, Adrian. *Objects of Desire*, Thames & Hudson, London, 1986. ISBN 0-500-27412-6.

Frayling, Christopher. *David Mellor, Master Metalworker*, Sheffield Galleries & Museums Trust, 1998.

Hayhurst, Jeanette and Leibe, Frankie. *Glass of the '20s and '30s*, Millers, London, 1999. ISBN 1-84000-070-8.

Hillier, Bevis. *The Style of the Century*, The Herbert Press, London, 1983. ISBN 1-871569-93-1.

Home Chat, April 1936, Fleetway House, London, 1936.

Hopwood, Irene and Gordon. *Denby Pottery 1809-1907*, Richard Dennis, Somerset, England, 1997. ISBN 0-90685-52-3.

Horsham, Michael. *Shaker Style*, Chancellor Press, London, 2000. ISBN 0-75370-353-X.

Jack, Florence B. *Good Housekeeping Cookery Book*, Good Housekeeping Magazine Co Ltd., 1925.

Jack, Florence B. *Good Housekeeping Invalid Cookery Book*, The Good Housekeeping Magazine Ltd., 1926.

Jackson, Lesley. *The New Look: Design in the Fifties*, Thames & Hudson Ltd., London,1991, 1998. ISBN 0-500-27644-7.

Jackson, Lesley. *20th Century Factory Glass*, Mitchell Beazley, London, 2000. ISBN 1-85732-267-3.

Jackson, Lesley (ed.). *Whitefriars Glass: The Art of James Powell*, Richard Dennis, 1996. ISBN 0-903685-40-X.

Jackson, Lesley. 'X-Ray Visions', *Crafts Magazine* No. 172, Sept. / Oct. 2001.

Jaffrey, Madhur. *Indian Cookery*, BBC Publications, London, 1982.

Jenkins, Steven. *Ceramics of the '50s and '60s*, Millers, London, 2001. ISBN 1-84000-372-3.

Jenkins, Steven. *Midwinter Pottery*, Richard Dennis, 1997. ISBN 0-903685-55-8.

The Journal of the Glass Association, Vol. 3, 1990. ISBN 0-9510736-2-1.

The Journal of the Glass Association, Vol. 5, 1997. ISBN 0-9510736-4-8.

Kinchin, Perilla. *Taking Tea with Mackintosh*, Pomegranate Communications, Inc., California, 1998. ISBN 0-7649-0692-5.

Leath, Peter. *The Designs of Kathie Winkle*, Richard Dennis, 1999. ISBN 0-903685-67-.

Lytton Toye, Doris. *Vogue's Contemporary Cookery*, Conde–Nast Publications, London, 1947.

Masson, Lucia. *La Belle France: A Gourmet's Guide to the French Provinces*, Societe Francaise des Presses Suisse, 1964.

Mattingly, Lilian. *Complete Cookery*, Pearson Ltd, London.

Morgan, Conway Lloyd. *Starck*, Univers Publishing, New York, 1999. ISBN 0-789302-27-6.

Notley, Raymond. *Popular Glass of the 19th & 20th Centuries*, Millers, London, 2000. ISBN 1-84000-188-7.

Opie, Jennifer. *Scandinavian Ceramics and Glass*, Victoria and Albert Museum. ISBN 1-85177-071-2.

Patten, Marguerite. *Marguerite Patten's Century of British Cooking*, Grub Street, London, 1999. ISBN 1-902304-14-4.

Patten, Marguerite. *Marguerite Patten's 1000 Favourite Recipes*, Treasure Press, London, 1983. ISBN 1-85051-090-3.

Powers, Alan. 'The South Bank Show', *Crafts Magazine* No. 172, Sept. / Oct. 2001.

Quintana, Patricia. *The Taste of Mexico*, Stewart, Tabori & Chang, New York,1986. ISBN 0-941434-89-3.

Robertson, Laurel with Flinders, Carol and Godfrey, Bronwen. *Laurel's Kitchen*, Bantam Books, California, 1976. ISBN 0-553-12278-9.

Rombauer, Irma S. *The Joy of Cooking*, J.M.Dent and Sons, London, 1931.

Ryan, Deborah S. *The Ideal Home Through the 20th Century*, Hazar Publishing, London, 1997. ISBN 1-874371-81-4.

'Scandinavian Design', *Casa Vogue*, October 1977.

Smith, Delia. *Delia's How To Cook Book One*, BBC Worldwide Ltd., London, 1998. ISBN 0-563-38430-1.

Spieler, Marlena. *The Flavour of California*, Thorson's / HarperCollins, London, 1992. ISBN 0-7225-3099-4.

Sweet, Fay. *Alessi – Art and Poetry*, Thames and Hudson, London, 1998. ISBN 0-500018-57-X.

Tea-time Favourites – Cooked the New World Way, Radiation Publications Dept., London.

Toklas, Alice B. *The Alice B. Toklas Cook Book*, Penguin Books, London,1954.

Walker, Susannah. *Queensberry Hunt, Creativity and Industry*, Fourth Estate Ltd., London, 1992. ISBN 1-857-020-111.

Webb, Mrs Arthur. *Economical Cookery 3, Autumn 1933*, BBC Publications, London, 1933.

Yesterday's Shopping – The Army & Navy Stores Catalogue, 1907. David & Charles Ltd., Devon. ISBN 0-7153-4692-X.

WEBSITES

BBC	www.bbc.co.uk
Delia Smith	www.deliaonline.com
Ken Hom	www.kenhom.com
Slow Food	www.slowfood.com
Versace	www.versace.com

PICTURE CREDITS

All original Wedgwood images by courtesy of the Wedgwood Museum Trust Limited, Barlaston, Staffordshire, England. Our special thanks to Mrs Lynn Miller.

All Robert Stewart material reproduced by kind permission of Dr Sheila Stewart and The Glasgow School of Art Archive, who also provided images of Charles Rennie Mackintosh and Miss Cranston's Tea Rooms. Thanks to Peter Trowles and Sarah Hepworth and to George Rawson in the library.

Historical textile images lent by the Textile Department of The Glasgow School of Art.

All Ministry of Food leaflets are from Crown Copyright Sources. Thanks to Rosanna Salbashian at DEFRA for advice.

BBC cookery leaflets reproduced by kind permission of the British Broadcasting Corporation.

Rowntrees Jelly recipes reproduced by kind permission of Premier Foods.

Army & Navy Stores Catalogue (1907) items are from *Yesterday's Shopping* (David & Charles, 1969) by kind permission of the publisher.

All Good Housekeeping and Housekeeping Institute material reproduced by kind permission of Good Housekeeping / National Magazine Company.

All Clarice Cliff items are from the collection of James Ferguson, as is the George Logan dinner service and the Liberty tea service.

The Burleigh Ware is from the collection of Eleanor Mason.

Bird's Custard advertisements reproduced by kind permission of Premier Foods.

The Charlotte Rhead dinner set is from the collection of Iain Campbell.

Bovril advertisement reproduced by kind permission of Unilever.

Jacob's Biscuits advertisement reproduced by kind permission of The Jacob's Bakery Ltd.

Hovis advertisement reproduced by kind permission of RHM Bread Bakeries Division.

Schweppes advertisement reproduced by kind permission of Cadbury Schweppes.

David Mellor photograph reproduced by kind permission of David Mellor.

Images of IKEA kitchen products reproduced by kind permission of the IKEA UK Press Office.

Images of Muji kitchen products reproduced by kind permission of the Muji Press Office.

Rosenthal 'Suomi' coffeepot images and Droog Design images kindly supplied by Rosenthal China.

All large format photography by David Ferguson, who got us into some very strange positions in the quest to achieve the right lighting effects, but on whom we wreaked revenge by making him eat all the food in the pictures! Additional photographs by Anne Ferguson and Carol Paterson.

INDEX